W9-AAI-659

BUSINESS

ORCHESTRATION

BUSINESS

ORCHESTRATION

Strategic Leadership in the Era of Digital Convergence

Johan Wallin

John Wiley & Sons, Ltd

Copyright © 2006 John Wiley & Sons Ltd, The Atrium, Southern Gate, Chichester, West Sussex PO19 8SQ, England

Telephone (+44) 1243 779777

Email (for orders and customer service enquiries): cs-books@wiley.co.uk
Visit our Home Page on www.wiley.com

All Rights Reserved. No part of this publication may be reproduced, stored in a retrieval system or transmitted in any form or by any means, electronic, mechanical, photocopying, recording, scanning or otherwise, except under the terms of the Copyright, Designs and Patents Act 1988 or under the terms of a licence issued by the Copyright Licensing Agency Ltd, 90 Tottenham Court Road, London W1T 4LP, UK, without the permission in writing of the Publisher. Requests to the Publisher should be addressed to the Permissions Department, John Wiley & Sons Ltd, The Atrium, Southern Gate, Chichester, West Sussex PO19 8SQ, England, or emailed to permreq@wiley.co.uk, or faxed to (+44) 1243 770620.

Designations used by companies to distinguish their products are often claimed as trademarks. All brand names and product names used in this book are trade names, service marks, trademarks or registered trademarks of their respective owners. The Publisher is not associated with any product or vendor mentioned in this book.

This publication is designed to provide accurate and authoritative information in regard to the subject matter covered. It is sold on the understanding that the Publisher is not engaged in rendering professional services. If professional advice or other expert assistance is required, the services of a competent professional should be sought.

Other Wiley Editorial Offices

John Wiley & Sons Inc., 111 River Street, Hoboken, NJ 07030, USA
Jossey-Bass, 989 Market Street, San Francisco, CA 94103-1741, USA
Wiley-VCH Verlag GmbH, Boschstr. 12, D-69469 Weinheim, Germany
John Wiley & Sons Australia Ltd, 42 McDougall Street, Milton, Queensland 4064, Australia
John Wiley & Sons (Asia) Pte Ltd, 2 Clementi Loop #02-01, Jin Xing Distripark, Singapore 129809
John Wiley & Sons Canada Ltd, 6045 Freemont Blvd, Mississauga, Ontario, L5R 4J3, Canada.

Wiley also publishes its books in a variety of electronic formats. Some content that appears in print may not be available in electronic books.

Library of Congress Cataloging-in-Publication Data
Wallin, Johan.
 Business orchestration : strategic leadership in the era of digital convergence / Johan Wallin.
  p. cm.
 Includes bibliographical references and index.
 ISBN-13: 978-0-470-03071-4 (cloth : alk. paper)
 ISBN-10: 0-470-03071-2 (cloth : alk. paper)
 1. Strategic planning. 2. Leadership. I. Title.
 HD30.28.W3375 2006
 658.4′092—dc22

                                                                2006016580

British Library Cataloguing in Publication Data
A catalogue record for this book is available from the British Library

ISBN 13 978-0-470-03071-4 (HB)
ISBN 10 0-470003071-2 (HB)

Typeset in 11.5/15pt Bembo and Univers by SNP Best-set Typesetter Ltd., Hong Kong
Printed and bound in Great Britain by TJ International Ltd, Padstow, Cornwall, UK
This book is printed on acid-free paper responsibly manufactured from sustainable forestry in which at least two trees are planted for each one used for paper production.

CONTENTS

ACKNOWLEDGMENTS   xi

INTRODUCTION   xv

PART I: CONDITIONS FOR PRIME MOVERSHIP

1 VALUE-CREATING CAPABILITIES   7

The Anatomy of Value Creation   12
The Offering: the Case of an Auction House   20
Operational Capabilities   24

2 FOCUS ON LEARNING   31

Digital Convergence and Learning   34
Learning in Communities   39
The Impact of Digital Convergence on Offerings
    and Capabilities   43

Learning Contexts   47
The Nature of Creative Work   53

3 ORCHESTRATING LEADERSHIP   59

Alternative Orchestration Strategies   65
Orchestrating Leaders   71
The Orchestration Arena   79

PART II: LEARNING CONTEXTS

4 INFORMATION ACQUISITION   89

Securing Seamless Information Transmission   95
Recouping Investments by Shifting Focus from
    Consumers to Carriers   101
Leadership Implications – The Value of an
    Orchestration Platform   106

5 PROBLEM SOLVING   111

Leadership Implications – Institutionalizing
    Collective Regional Knowledge Building   120

6 CO-EXPERIENCING   125

Composing, Orchestrating, and Contemplating   134
Leadership Implications – Experience Provision
    as a Tool to Drive Change   136

7 INSIGHT ACCUMULATION   141

The Central Tenets of the Linux Philosophy –
    Sharing Information and Having Fun   145
Leadership Implications – Learning-Based Customer
    Segmentation   150

8 TRANSITIONAL OBJECTS   155

Supporting Learning with Transitional Objects   157
Information Acquisition and Transitional
    Objects   159
Problem Solving and Transitional Objects   161
Co-Experiencing and Transitional Objects   163
Insight Accumulation and Transitional Objects   164
Appropriate Transitional Objects in Different
    Learning Contexts   166

PART III: BUILDING CAPABILITIES

9 CORE RESOURCES   173

Excellence in Execution – Building a Superior
    Supply Chain Strategy   175
The Influence of Digital Convergence on the
    Cell-Phone Market   179
Who Will Own the Customer?   182
Leadership Implications – Industry Mapping   187

10 OFFERING CONCEPTS   191

Leadership Implications – Balancing Efficiency
    and Creativity   202

11 CUSTOMER INTERACTIONS   207

A Historical Preview of Customer Communities   211
Embodied Values as Nurturers of Customer
    Communities   217
Leadership Implications – Co-Aligning the
    Strategy with Major Customers   223

12 VALUE CONSTELLATIONS 227

The Evolving Nature of Communities 238
Ethos – the Glue of a Resource Community 240
Leadership Implications – Building New Value
  Constellations 243

13 THE IOCC FRAMEWORK 247

The IOCC Framework 255

PART IV: THE LEADER AS ORCHESTRATOR

14 THE LEADER AS CONDUCTOR 265

Conducting an Orchestra: Instilling Disciplined
  Creativity 266
Orchestrating Based on Power or Knowledge? 273
The Game Plan 278

15 THE LEADER AS ARCHITECT 281

Architecture Shaping its Environment 288
Operational Architecture 289

16 THE LEADER AS AUCTIONEER 299

Information Architecture 310

17 THE LEADER AS PROMOTER 315

Social Architecture 323
The Orchestration Architecture 324

18 THRIVING, AWARE, AND ENGAGING 331

Characterizing an Orchestrator 344

EPILOGUE 355

The Business Idea 355
The Business Leader as Statesman 357
Orchestration and the World of People 359

NOTES 365

REFERENCES 375

INDEX 385

ACKNOWLEDGMENTS

This book is a practitioner's view on strategy and leadership. It starts from the simplest case, and gradually moves on to illustrate the complexity facing managers and leaders today. The idea to start from a very simple case was suggested to me in 1990 by Professor Philip Kotler, when we discussed different possibilities for researching the topic of product strategy. I want to thank Professor Kotler for his supportive attitude in my early years exploring the field of management through the lens of the practitioner as researcher.

A constant source of new ideas during the journey leading to this book has been Håkan West, ex-vice president of Information Management at Nokia. For a number of years he has challenged me in the process of developing the concept of orchestration in business.

When considering the impact of the social architecture, Cathy Peng, with experiences from three continents – Asia, North

America, and Europe – provided invaluable support. Another important external inspirer has been Alfredo Ambrosetti. His insights about the intelligent society especially helped to sharpen the arguments.

Two other people that have provided encouragement are Johan Horelli, ex-CEO of Kone Elevators, and Aulis Salin, ex-CEO of Sonera. They, as well as Håkan, are members of the Synocus board and have closely been following how the framework has gradually evolved. By constantly challenging me to make my arguments clearer, they have forced me to flesh out my thinking and be more explicit. Their mentorship has been invaluable throughout the entire expedition resulting in this book.

I would also like to thank my colleagues in Synocus Group. Patrik Laxell was the lead coordinator of the 'Managing in the Knowledge Society' study. Henrik Hultin was responsible for the 'Regional Brain Gain' study, and Petri Pohjala was the project manager for the 'Prime Movership in Digital Convergence' research project. The whole team of Synocus professionals has been highly committed to these projects. Even if putting the ideas together was my responsibility, I feel that I am entitled to talk about we throughout the book. This is the result of the collaborative effort of the whole Synocus team.

The material presented here provides the summary of many years of work. This work could easily have filled yet another book. The ultimate responsibility for balancing what has been included and what has been left out is solely mine. But I hope that most of those who have shared some of the experiences during the multitude of learning moments will recognize the ethos and the emergent new understanding resulting from these initiatives. A great thank you to all who have contributed and participated, but have not been mentioned! Finally thanks to my family, Elina, Ghita, and Michael, my eternal source for inspiration and creativity!

I dedicate this book to the tradition of the 'Scandinavian School of Management' and to the memory of its originators Eric Rhenman and Richard Normann.

Helsinki, April 2006
Johan Wallin

INTRODUCTION

With the advent of the computer, it is possible to digitize almost everything. Through digital convergence text, photographs, videos, speech, and experiences are constantly accessible via the Internet. Using this information for continuous learning is the lifeblood of business. How to manage learning within the extended enterprise has thus become a key strategic challenge.

Digital convergence means that a number of 'industries' are facing a situation where existing business systems are profoundly changing. Future success will be based on completely different criteria than those that have made the firm prosper historically. Facing such a 'disruptive' period means that firms have to balance between how they pursue their existing business model and maximize short-term revenue streams, and at the same time prepare for future competition. We are entering the true knowledge society and leaders have to nurture learning and orchestrate for value creation.

This book is the result of two streams of ideas. The first is what in an exposé of 'strategic schools' has been identified as the

Scandinavian 'Cultural School of Management',[1] being occupied with organizational culture and the role of the leader. The originator of this school was Eric Rhenman, who first of all considered himself as an organization theorist.[2]

The other stream relates to capability building, which already in the 1970s was recognized as an integral part of strategy by Richard Normann.[3] In his last book Normann noticed that one strategic option for an organization is to identify capabilities and organize to nurture them. This book addresses how to do this in practice.

For more than 10 years I was fortunate to work with Richard Normann, both in consulting and research. How to build capabilities within organizations became the focus of my own research efforts. Some of the results from this research have been presented in the book *Prime Movers*,[4] which I wrote together with Rafael Ramírez. In that book we concentrated on identifying how different contexts create opportunities for companies to compete either based on their existing capabilities, or by building new ones. If that book provided an outside-in view on the changing competitive landscape, this book is more of an inside-out view on how to manage and lead when the circumstances change. But it respects what we discovered regarding prime movers, i.e. that successful strategy stems from the value-creating potential of the capabilities of the firm. The book consequently starts by discussing the four operational capabilities identified already in *Prime Movers*:

- generative capabilities securing continued development of *core resources*;
- transformative capabilities by which new *offering concepts* are developed;
- relationship capabilities to foster value-creating *customer interactions*; and
- integrative capabilities based on which *value constellations* are formed.

Building capabilities requires that individuals learn new skills. Therefore an emphasis on capabilities automatically implies focus on how to nurture learning and creativity in the extended enterprise. Four different types of learning contexts can be identified.

Learning is *information acquisition* when the learner knows what he or she will learn, and how long it will approximately take. Here the learning individual is an information acquirer.

Learning has another character when the challenge is to solve a genuinely new problem. In *problem solving* the expected outcome is known, but how long it will take to find the solution cannot be specified in advance. Science very much follows this principle, for example mapping the human DNA was such a problem. The learner as a problem solver can be characterized as an explorer.

One striking feature of creative industries is that they often follow highly disciplined procedures in respect of timetables. A fashion company presenting a new collection at an upcoming fair cannot compromise on the timetable. But the fair is not just the termination of the creative project. It is also a shared experience between the designers and the external world, i.e. customers, competitors, the press etc. The outcome of *co-experiencing* as learning is open, whereas the timetable is fixed. In many ways the learner is a co-performer.

The fourth context for learning is the continuous *insight accumulation* an individual has when interacting with the outside world, and reflecting upon new observations and experiences. Such insight accumulation can later on prove to be very valuable in other contexts, forming the bridge from chance to serendipity and further to gradually more conscious strategic actions. Making these connections means that the learner becomes a true inventor.

In management a lot has recently been discussed and written about capabilities. However, what seems to be missing is that capabilities are built only if individuals learn. For individuals to learn they have to be motivated, based on their natural talent and their interest. Motivating individuals to learn in turn asks for leadership to create both intellectual and emotional contexts that commit the individuals to active learning for the benefit of the enterprise. This brings the human being, the individual, back to the center stage when striving for excellence and evaluating strategic performance.

When building new capabilities all value-creating activities are potential contributors in respect of both efficiency and learning. A meeting with a customer can generate a deal but can also provide the seller with valuable new information that can be used for capability building. In the same way suppliers can be both sources of knowledge and cost-efficient subcontractors. Leaders have to increasingly mobilize external resources for collaborative value creation.

When value creation and learning are combined in activities we call them orchestrated activities. Orchestrated activities are then a broader concept than value-creating activities. The role of the leader is to provide the incentives and contexts for valuable orchestrated activities to take place. Depending on the type of learning four orchestrator roles can be identified. The orchestrator types (with the most common learning context in brackets) are:

- *conductor* (information transmission and acquisition);
- *architect* (problem solving);
- *auctioneer* (co-experiencing); and
- *promoter* (insight accumulation).

The concepts introduced here – digital convergence, the knowledge society, value creation, the extended enterprise, learning, capability building, and leadership as orchestration – are all parts of the new context facing managers and leaders. How they relate to each other is depicted in Figure I.1.

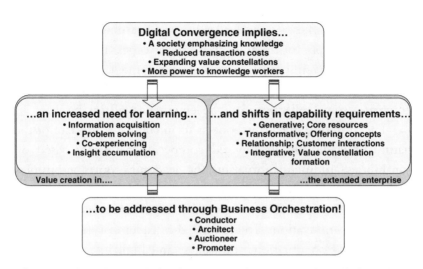

Figure I.1   The need for business orchestration; the whole and its parts

The book proceeds so that the first three chapters introduce the prerequisites for prime movership, the ultimate objective of business orchestration: Value-Creating Capabilities (Chapter 1), Focus on Learning (Chapter 2), and Orchestrating Leadership (Chapter 3). Subsequently each of the following parts looks deeper into these prerequisites.

Part II deals with the four learning contexts. Here the focus is on the individual as a learner, and the four learning contexts – information acquisition, problem solving, co-experiencing, and insight accumulation – are illustrated with practical examples. In addition the notion of transitional objects is introduced as a means to improve the learning process.

Part III analyzes the four components of operational excellence, the results of capability-building: the core resources, the offering concepts, the customer interactions, and the value constellations. The last chapter in this section presents how new capabilities are built through a process of initialization, operationalization, crystallization, and commercialization.

Part IV synthesizes the leadership implications by presenting concrete examples of the four orchestrator types. In the concluding chapter thriving, awareness and engagement are introduced as key characters of a successful orchestrator. Finally, the Epilogue comprises some reflections on the emergence of this book.

The ambition with this book is to introduce an update of the nature of leadership in a world competing primarily based on capabilities. In such a situation the leader becomes a business orchestrator, who has to nurture learning and creativity to be able to build the capabilities needed to simultaneously drive efficiency and innovation. To do this the leader has to guide his actions based on situational awareness and high interaction with the organization and its stakeholders. How to establish the shared awareness, provide the appropriate learning contexts, and build the relevant capabilities during different phases of the evolution of the firm becomes a major challenge. Providing some new insights into this leadership aspect is what the book, *Business Orchestration*, wants to achieve.

PART I

CONDITIONS FOR PRIME MOVERSHIP

*B*aron Pierre de Coubertin, born in 1863, was a French pedagogue who thought that part of how to improve education was to focus on sport, which he considered an important part of the personal development of young people. His plan was to revive the Olympic Games, based on the original ideas from the ancient Olympics in Athens. De Coubertin organized an international congress in June 1894 at the Sorbonne in Paris, and there he proposed to reinstate the Olympic Games. The first modern Olympics took place in Athens in 1896.

When recreating the Olympic Games and forming the International Olympic Committee to handle the administration Baron de Coubertin hoped to foster international communication and peace. He had a grandiose idea with a strong cultural basis. His achievement was to pave the way for purposeful emergence to happen.[1]

De Coubertin was one of the greatest orchestrators of modern times, creating a movement, which now more than 100 years later is still live and vibrant. And he did it not for personal gain, but because he considered himself as an idealist, whose mission was to make education more successful. De Coubertin once said:

> The most important thing in the Olympic Games is not winning but taking part. The essential thing in life is not conquering but fighting well.

De Coubertin wanted to improve the knowledge and learning aspects of the society. Now 100 years later, thanks to new converging information and communication technologies, we have the knowledge society. This society has emerged because of market forces, not because of any single individual initiating it. Market capitalism has permanently changed the rules of competition. The difference compared to the Olympic Games is that for businesses, participation in the competition of this new society is not voluntary. Everybody has to participate, be they countries, industries, corporations, or individuals. But market capitalism is also more brutal in respect of winning. For people not using their full potential, the outcome of this new competition can be disastrous.

The tsunami catastrophe in South-East Asia in December 2004 was in many ways an eye-opener regarding the possibilities of technology. The most depressing finding is that many lives could have been saved if available technologies and systems had been in place to warn the people. But because such warning systems cost money they had not been built, as the nations affected could not afford them. Another more encouraging finding was that the communication taking place over the Internet provided the most reliable knowledge about what really happened during the first hours of the catastrophe.[2] A website formed by a self-organized group of scuba divers, acting as a spontaneous nerve center on the spot, emerged as the intellectual prime movers in the immediate aftermath of the catastrophe. They were much more effective than traditional organizations, such as ministries and embassies, in respect of finding out the effects of the tsunami in this situation of true ambiguity. In the same way the aftermath of Hurricane Katrina in New Orleans saw a multitude of websites emerging as the information-sharing platforms between family members or as support tools for victims.

Companies such as Tetra Pak and Nokia have been successful prime movers because their innovations contributed to permanent changes in our daily lives. Richard Normann suggested a new word for this, eco-genesis. Prime movers genuinely change the world around them. When prime movers change the business landscape and redefine the rules of the game they mostly have to mobilize other actors to collaborate in order to be successful. How this is taking place is described by Normann as 'the birth of a context for co-dwelling'.[3]

The learning from the tsunami scuba divers provides indications of how the 'micro-organizing' of such a context for co-dwelling emerges and shows how learning, capability building, and leadership interact in unconventional circumstances. What it demonstrated is that a new organizational behavior comes to the fore when the control mechanisms of the traditional industrial society are put out of work. The implication is thrilling: there exists a better way of doing things, a new way, which is waiting, and pops up once we are not able to keep it suppressed. Most of the time we succeed in 'keeping things in order,' but more and more often we meet situations where we are astonished by how things that shouldn't happen still happen, and the outcome surprises us, positively. The argument of this book is that this new way in which people interact, make decisions, and take actions is precisely the key tenet of the knowledge society. It is also argued that enabling such processes to emerge and form is becoming a main challenge for leaders to keep their organizations competitive. Establishing awareness and enabling purposeful emergence become compulsory.

In ancient Greece the Olympics created a culture of 'the ideal athlete'. A national ethos and character was shaped, and the doctrine of the ideal character was applied to all contests. Through athleticism the model of human perfection was defined. The perfect athlete was distinguished by physical beauty, strength of character, and inner fortitude.

The hero of ancient Greece was an individual. In the same way today's knowledge-based competition often sees the results depending on the collective contribution of a multitude of individuals. And while the Olympic Games are discontinuous, taking place every fourth year, the knowledge competition is running all the time, every day, 24 hours a day.

But there is one thing that these two movements share. According to de Coubertin Olympism is inseparable from culture. This book will support this view. When competition is based on knowledge, culture plays a significant part, and leadership is about how to instigate the right culture for success to follow. This leadership is ultimately about establishing trust, nurturing creativity, building capabilities, and then allowing perfection to occur. We will introduce the notion of a thriving character to illustrate this, and will revert to this at the end of the book.

At the core of the knowledge society is individual learning. Improved access to information and people through modern information and communication technology is reconfiguring how learning takes place in networks and organizations. Unfortunately these technologies are not yet fully utilized across the whole world to improve the quality of life of all global citizens, as the tsunami case brutally showed.

If learning individuals and their creativity form the foundation of the knowledge society, capabilities in turn are the building blocks that provide commercial success. Building capabilities in networks by combining own and addressable resources is the way the orchestrating leader exploits value-creating potentials in the market.

Leadership is about synthesizing all this. What does this mean in different types of organizations, be they commercial firms, public organizations or communities evolving around emergent issues? The answer is that a new form of leadership is emerging. This leadership style requires the ability to perform in the present, to follow the response from the market to recognize new opportunities, and to inspire and encourage the value-creating knowledge professionals. To succeed the leader has to direct and orchestrate a number of simultaneous activities. The paradox here is that less is more. The better the foundation for value creation to 'happen,' the less effort is needed by the leader for the process to progress and flourish.

This first part of the book introduces some relevant concepts for understanding the implications of knowledge-based competition and digital convergence. Through the means of a fictional story about the emergence of an entrepreneur Chapter 1 introduces such notions as value creation, offerings, business models, values, and capabilities. Chapter 2 in turn shifts the perspective to the outside world and the impact of digital convergence. In this chapter the new context for competition and value creation is portrayed, and the main reasons for increased focus on learning are identified. Chapter 3 opens up the black box of orchestration as a new perspective on leadership.

The overriding belief of this book is that we are entering a new interesting era in management and leadership. This era highlights the art dimension of leadership. It is an era that will recognize the importance of the individual as the ultimate source of knowledge and creativity, but also understands that only through the collective contribution of complementary knowledge and creative skills will superb results emerge both in respect of efficiency and effectiveness. Creativity cannot be forced. But neither can we wait for creativity to just happen. So the challenge is to pursue the apparent oxymoron of disciplined creativity. This is what the art of orchestration is about.

CHAPTER 1

VALUE-CREATING CAPABILITIES

How are strategies created? How do capabilities emerge? These are profound strategic questions that are seldom addressed in the management literature, but are ones that managers have to grapple with on a daily basis. Therefore we will start the reasoning about the new context of management and leadership by presenting a fictional story about a modern Robinson Crusoe becoming an entrepreneur.

In the following story we will see that there are two fundamentally different ways to create a strategy. One is the industrial approach where the instinctive behavior is control and empire building. Another, but perhaps less frequently adopted philosophy, is one of mobilizing external resources and orchestrating an evolving ecosystem. Choosing between these two alternatives will be at hand at a very early stage, even during the evolution of the simplest business, as the case below will show. And very complex decisions arise from quite basic conditions. In the following the development path of Robinson Crusoe will be portrayed . . .

Robinson is a survivor from a shipwreck, and lives on an island with only one other inhabitant. He can survive with three ingredients of daily food:

- one portion of water
- one portion of potatoes (five potatoes)
- one portion of oranges (two oranges)

Robinson can fulfill his need for nutrition in the following way:

- To fetch the water he needs to work 1/2 a day (water cannot be stored on the island).
- To find five potatoes he needs to work 3/8 of a day (potatoes can be stored, but not longer than seven days).
- To find two oranges he needs to work 1/8 of a day.

By working the whole day Robinson can thus find the nutrition he needs to stay alive.

After a while Robinson finds out that there is also another survivor on the island, Stevens, who had come to the island earlier.

Stevens has one advantage compared to Robinson: he can find potatoes easier on his land than Robinson can, but on the other hand he cannot find oranges that easily. Stevens gets in touch with Robinson and gives Robinson the following proposal: He would like to exchange oranges and potatoes with Robinson. The conditions would be as follows:

- Stevens would not buy less than two oranges at a time.
- For two oranges he would give Robinson five potatoes.
- For three oranges he would give Robinson five and a half potatoes.
- For four oranges he would give Robinson six potatoes.

If Robinson decides not to trade with Stevens he would have to continue to work all day to get the food he needs. If he wishes to trade, Robinson has several options. If he only wants to work enough to get his daily food he can cut his working time by 25%. He can also build up some stock of potatoes if he cuts his working time by less than 25% and collects additional oranges to trade against potatoes. At this stage an orchestration opportunity has emerged, Stevens contacted Robinson from a traditional, industrial perspective. He wanted to develop a barter arrangement to improve efficiency. However, as we will see, the knowledge perspective provides an additional layer that provides the platform for more opportunities. Whereas Stevens's worldview was restricted to the industrial domain, Robinson saw possibilities not yet identified by Stevens. Robinson thus becomes an orchestrator.

Robinson's choice will depend on how he values his spare time. It might be that he is not interested in the extra return he could get by producing some extra oranges for Stevens. Another question is whether he could use the spare time in order to produce something else, which will give him additional satisfaction with his situation. Answering these questions means for Robinson that he has to have some form of overriding principles, or values, to guide how to prioritize in situations of choice. The values are then about what type of state of existence Robinson considers worth attaining in his life.

Values are generalized, relatively enduring and consistent priorities of how an actor wants to live.[1]

The trading agreement suggested by Stevens revealed that Stevens had higher production costs of oranges than Robinson, but lower production costs of potatoes. As long as the trading possibility exists for Robinson one can say that there is a stable market situation. The rational decision for Robinson is to start to trade with Stevens, and this way both will improve their efficiency. This then implies that Robinson will have available spare time.

As Robinson gets additional spare time he decides to use it to develop a new offering. Both he and Stevens are carrying water from the same spring. The amount of work needed for this is the same for them both, half a day. When discussing with Stevens, Robinson finds out that Stevens would be prepared to pay him five potatoes if Robinson would supply him with the daily portion of water.

Robinson invents a jar that can be carried. He can now bring two portions of water from the spring, if he is using this jar. The time needed to bring the two portions is three-quarters of a day. Robinson now has two sellable offerings in his mix: oranges and water. Both offerings include a substantial quantity of service activities, and the water offering is mainly a transport service. From Robinson's point of view the main question is how the offerings affect his spare time, and what can be traded against the offerings.

An **offering** *is a limited set of focused human activity intended to generate positive customer value and exchange value for the provider of the offering.*[2]

The strategy of a commercial actor is to get the best result out of his resource base. In the case of Robinson this means the use of his own time. By developing a new offering he has created a situation which further emphasizes the importance of his values, i.e. how he compares spare time with further entrepreneurial development. Robinson decides to develop his business opportunities.

One problem Robinson now meets is that his production capacity is bigger than what his customer can consume. By working seven days Robinson has produced his own food, and at the same time he has increased his stock of potatoes to seven portions, whereby he has to start to eat the oldest ones in order for them not to rot. This means that he does not have to work more than 62% of a day the next week (bringing water and oranges for himself). In a period of two weeks he thus cannot use more than 81% of his production capacity. For Robinson this is unsatisfactory. He therefore decides to use the spare time for innovation.

Robinson has recognized that not very far away from the island there is another island with inhabitants. In his spare time Robinson starts to build a raft. Using the raft he is able to visit this island daily. On the island there are several inhabitants. They are very fond of both oranges and potatoes. For Robinson there are new acquaintances on the island: bananas, grapefruits, and coffee. This creates a quite complicated situation for Robinson: he can offer the inhabitants on The Other Island oranges and potatoes, but he can also bring back some grapefruits, bananas, and coffee to Stevens, and trade these against potatoes. At the same time Robinson has to consider that his time now may suddenly become a constraint for the further development of his business.

One way out of the problem is to start to cooperate with Stevens. He knows that Stevens has a lot of capacity to produce potatoes. Stevens has previously not been very interested in working too much, but he has got very fond of coffee, and is prepared to do some extra work to get more coffee. At the same time, however, Robinson is afraid of giving Stevens too much information about his own business secrets. Perhaps Stevens will start to build a raft himself, and trade his potatoes directly with the inhabitants on the neighbor island.

The situation Robinson is now facing is to more profoundly define his business model.

*The **business model** defines the value-creation priorities of an actor in respect to the utilization of both internal and external resources. It defines how the actor relates with stakeholders, such as actual and potential customers, employees, unions, suppliers, competitors, and other interest groups. It takes account of situations where the actor's activities may (a) affect the business environment and its own business in ways that could create conflicting interests, or impose risks on the actor; or (b) develop new, previously unpredicted ways of creating value. The business model is in itself subject to continual review as a response to actual and possible changes in perceived business conditions.*[3]

Once Robinson has made up his mind regarding his aspirations he can make the detailed plans for his activities, or processes, and how he will further develop his business model.

*The **aspirations** define how strongly an actor is prepared to act in order to succeed according to his or her values.*

Robinson will suddenly find out that in his relatively restricted environment he already has a quite complicated task in choosing what offerings to focus on and what processes to develop. When we add to this the uncertainty regarding how long his market will be free from invaders from other islands, we see that Robinson from very simple beginnings suddenly will be meeting some very critical decisions with profound implications for the future . . .

THE ANATOMY OF VALUE CREATION

The Robinson case illustrates that different people have different priorities. Some like oranges, others coffee. Some want to relax and not take on more duties than necessary, whereas others are driven by an entrepreneurial spirit. Certain individuals are highly occupied with how they can further improve the world around them, like Robinson.

The values and aspirations of individuals are the building blocks for value creation. Without values we could not make choices in situations of ambiguity. And without aspirations we would not direct our energy towards more than the ultimate minimum. Robinson was driven by both his values and aspirations to do more than his neighbor Stevens.

Zetterberg has identified six cardinal values: the pursuit of wealth, order, truth, the sacred, virtue, and beauty. Already Max Weber had identified *Lebensordnungen* (life-orders) and *Wertsphären* (value-spheres). They were the economic, political, intellectual, religious, familial, and erotic life-orders and spheres of life-activity. Zetterberg left out what he calls the microsociological familial and erotic value spheres and added the ethical realm.

When considering the business context one can argue that four of Zetterberg's values are relevant: pursuit of wealth, search for knowledge, civic virtue, and beauty. Order in the original Zetterberg sense would in the business context correspond to level of risk, ultimately expressed as the need to survive. The sacred could be seen broader as a sense of belonging to something, not necessary a religious community. This sense of belonging would then also include the familial sphere suggested by Weber to be one of the cardinal values.

The six cardinal values here adopted would then be: pursuit of wealth, search for knowledge, civic virtue, beauty, survival, and belonging. Robinson has evolved from struggling for his survival to pursue other values as well. It seems that he has an interest in pursuing wealth creation, and that this value for him is of relatively greater importance than is the case of Stevens. Quality of life, or the value of beauty, seems to be more appreciated by Stevens.

There is a cultural bias towards the interpretation of values. They are part of the culture and affect how offerings are used in a society. So for Robinson the first interactions with the inhabitants on the other island should also reveal whether they emphasize different values than those in favor by himself or Stevens.

Value creation is about human activity. The way value creation options opened up for Robinson highlights the interaction between planning and acting, thinking and doing. As the example shows sometimes doing precedes thinking and an external incident may trigger a chain of events that may have profound consequences for an actor, like the appearance of Stevens enabling Robinson not to just work all the time to stay alive. Offerings were defined as a limited set of human activity. The notion of activity was of special interest of the Russian psychologist Lev Vygotsky,[4] who by the time of his death in 1934 at the age of 37 had laid the foundations for a psychology of culture and consciousness. According to Vygotsky activity is the smallest unit of analysis which preserves both the link between mind and society and the coherence of different actions and movements. The concept draws attention to relationships between motives and the contexts of actions. The settings for different activities are not determined by objective, physical features but are provided by those who engage in them. Activities are triggered by some stimuli, but once undertaken the activity in itself starts to change the environment, which also may result in unpredicted implications. So can tools developed to make it easier to do a predefined thing later turn out to have the potential of triggering new events, events that would not otherwise have been possible.

Human activity is principally a continuous process of discovery. Any discovery is a creative achievement, which involves a degree of personal investment; it can only be achieved by active participation. This implies that learning occurs as people do more than they yet know how to do. As they move forward they will retrospectively understand what they actually learnt. The activities shared by different actors transform the relationships between individuals and communities. The shared activities are thus part of a complex web of mutual interactions. However, activities will not take place without initiators. Activities are triggered by somebody who sees opportunities better than others, an expert. There are different forms of expertise. Becoming an expert is a creative process as people 'do more than they yet know how to do'. Descriptions of what should be happening are likely to lag behind emerging improvisations.

The origins of expertise lie in different cultures and histories. The tasks that the expert engages in are situated and context based. Experts respond to particular contingencies, using the material, social, and institutional resources available. Expertise is closely related to ambition. Blackler defines expertise as effective activity. Robinson in our example can be considered an expert. He could envision the possibility to expand his scope of activities in order to pursue his own aspirations of wealth creation. To achieve these goals he has had to have a strong involvement, take initiatives, and as the case of motivating Stevens showed, also be flexible. Such skills are needed if the aspirations are high. So aspirations require expertise and skills to become more than empty words.

The tradition of activity studies is organizational. However, activities provide an interesting conceptual framework for analyzing value creation also as a collaborative effort involving a multitude of actors. This will be further highlighted in the next section, which takes a more detailed view on the value creation initiated by Robinson. In Chapter 3 we will bring the discussion one step further and look into how such activities are orchestrated.

The activities carried out by Robinson provided the basis for value creation. We can define value creation as follows:

Value creation is the process of co-producing offerings (i.e. products and services) in a mutually beneficial seller/buyer relationship. This relationship may include other actors such as subcontractors and the buyer's

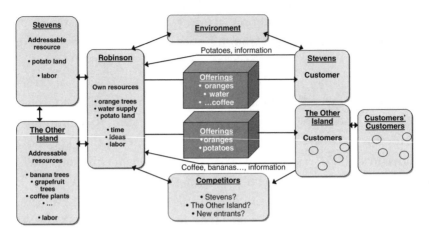

Figure 1.1 The value constellation around Robinson

customers. In this relationship, the parties behave in a symbiotic manner leading to activities that generate positive values for them. The actors brought together to interact in this process of co-producing value form a **value constellation**.[5]

Even if Robinson did not have many actors with whom to interact, the value constellation around him illustrates how value is co-produced. As Figure 1.1 shows, Robinson considers Stevens both as a customer and as an addressable resource, and a potential competitor. In the same way the inhabitants on the other island are also resources (providing coffee). Without coffee Robinson could not motivate Stevens to use some more time to produce additional potatoes that Robinson can trade against other products from the other island.

The notion of value constellation addresses the market for goods and services (the demand) and the resource market (the supply) simultaneously. Value constellations emphasize the symbiotic relationship between actors. More traditional product/market thinking underlines the competitive perspective. In the product/market thinking the focus is on defining the best output strategy of the respective actor. The offering is the output.

Product/market thinking usually separates the resource allocation process to provide the offering from the customer interaction process to sell and deliver the offering. As the Robinson example shows these two processes are not necessarily separable. How well Robinson can motivate Stevens to work depends on what he can trade with the inhabitants on The Other Island. And to pay these inhabitants Robinson needs the potatoes produced by Stevens.

In value constellations actors engage in selling and buying. The starting point of any trading arrangement is the value a customer pays for a particular offering. In the case of Stevens he was considering oranges as valuable. He could package his own resources into something tradable, potatoes, and was thus able to obtain oranges from Robinson.

To understand the value of an offering to a customer, the customer value, we need to know how the good is perceived at the moment of the purchase and what happens to it after the purchase. In the case of Stevens the reason why he was interested in oranges could be called net satisfaction contribution. (The notion of net satisfaction contribution means that if the offering has elements that affect the satisfaction in a negative way (e.g. psychological 'costs') these costs are deducted from 'gross satisfaction contribution' to get net satisfaction contribution. Perhaps Stevens did not like to peel the oranges, but he was very fond of the taste.)

The nutritional and culinary pleasures attached to the oranges are thus forming the basis for how valuable Stevens considers the offering. However, to achieve the advantages related to oranges Stevens will have to make some sacrifices as well.

Firstly he has to compensate Robinson for the oranges. As he can use potatoes as a trading currency, this means that the work he has to do to find the potatoes is the price for the oranges. This can be called the *initial cost*. But other costs will incur as well.

Stevens may have to pick up the oranges from Robinson. This means some additional work, and could be called *interface costs*.

Once he has the oranges in his possession he will have to prepare the oranges to be able to eat them. This can be called *integration costs*.

Finally, as he has his meal prepared he still has to get rid of the peel of the oranges, again asking for some additional work. This we can call *life-cycle costs*.

All these benefits and costs relate to the physical good, the oranges that Stevens will get. However, when he considers his dealings with Robinson he can potentially get some additional benefits, which depend on the nature of the relationship, not on the offering as such. For instance, during one of his dealings he learned about the possibility to get water from Robinson. This could be called a *learning advantage*.

The relationship with Robinson also may contain some risks: What if Robinson will only provide him with low quality oranges, or if taking a paranoid view, if he tries to poison Stevens? This element is *the relative risk position* related to the offering and the supplier providing the offering. These elements together form the total customer value. The customer value is thus the net satisfaction contribution (NSC) less the costs for the customers to include the offering into his or her own value-creating process including the life-cycle costs, adjusted for possible risk and learning impact.

Co-productive value creation for customers contains two distinct perspectives: the 'single event' transaction and the 'process' relationship over time (which basically consists of a sequence of transactions). Focusing on individual transactions implies that each transaction should cover its own costs plus generate a margin. In the relationship logic, customer relationships are seen as extending over time, and are often conceived of in terms of a 'life cycle'. The relationship logic doesn't solely focus on the profitability of individual transactions. It also considers the profitability of all the transactions involving one customer – in other words, all of the transactions that take place during the life of the relationship between the supplier and the customer. In such relationships, some up-front seed investments might be needed to generate later revenues. As the case of Stevens and Robinson showed, Stevens could learn things from Robinson that later turned into new value-creating transactions (e.g. the possibility to obtain water from Robinson and pay with potatoes). Current costs, therefore, are not simply expended outlays but are, in part, an investment in lower future costs. In this respect the learning benefits from a customer relationship may prove to be of high value.

Likewise, from the supplier's point of view, current costs to build customer relationships can be regarded as investments in higher future returns. For example, key account management thinking recognizes that relationships evolve over time, with each specific transaction affected by the history of the relationship, and the relationship modified by each specific exchange. Individual transactions are not only affected by market considerations (price and product specifications), but also by relational or process factors, which require different account management strategies to be adopted as the relationship evolves. In this respect Robinson was systematically trying to better understand how Stevens could be an important part of his addressable resource base in addition to being his most important customer.

In a relationship-driven economy, the relative importance of value elements other than the selling/purchasing price is increasing. This applies to the supplier as well. The supplier's exchange value can therefore be defined in a similar way to the customer value. The exchange value is the selling price less the resource costs for the supplier to provide the offering adjusted for possible risk and learning impact and also considering possible goodwill or reference value of the offering and its impact on the future competitive position of the supplier.

How value is perceived depends greatly on the observer. Different customers see products differently. In other words value or the perceived value is not objective but subjective. The value of an offering is contingent, more than subjective. It does not reside 'in' an individual, independent of his actions, or 'in' a good independent of the interactions to which it is subjected.[6]

An offering is therefore not something that exists, independently, in itself. An offering is the output produced by one (or several) actor(s) creating value – the 'producer' or 'supplier' – that becomes an input to another actor (or actors) creating value – the 'customer'. The offering both results from, and contributes to, a bundle of activities that enable the buyer to perform activities in a different way than if the offering had not been acquired. Firms collaborate and compete to make competitive offerings available.[7]

Capabilities in turn consist of the routines by which a firm, or a network, will be able to constantly perform those activities that are needed for the offering to be designed and provided. A capability can be defined as follows:[8]

*A **capability** is the ability of an organization to perform a coordinated set of tasks, utilizing organizational resources, for the purpose of achieving a particular end result.*

Having introduced the basic components of value creation and capability building through the case of Robinson we will further deepen the understanding of the offering as the means of value creation by the example of an auction house.

THE OFFERING: THE CASE OF AN AUCTION HOUSE

The auction business consists of three tasks: (i) solicit goods from a multitude of suppliers; (ii) put them together into attractive auction offerings; and (iii) attract auction buyers to attend the auctions.

Supplier solicitation consists of several activities. Continuous communication with the suppliers is needed. Insurance packages to secure the suppliers from logistics risks have to be developed. Different forms of supplier contact forums have to be established, and here communication using a web portal is an effective means to keep the suppliers updated.

An attractive auction event is based on four pillars: the physical design of the premises; the use of information technology; the expertise and service-mindedness of the personnel; and the availability of third-party services.

The physical layout of the premises has to enable a smooth and efficient working environment for buyers. The auction room, the invoicing, shipping and telecommunication rooms, and the restaurant have to be located centrally within a short distance from each other. The auction center can also host third-party services such as bank offices and travel agents. The availability for restrooms is another advantage. For the biggest buyers there could be the alternative of renting permanent offices within the building. The warehouse has to be designed to make sure that the products are stored and handled in the best possible way.

The information system forms the digital nerve center of any successful auction business. Using the possibilities offered by sophisticated database technology, one can today design and build integrated auction systems. By using satellite technology it is even possible to enable remote bidding from all over the world with video coverage and high-quality sound transmission.

The personnel have to meet the demanding expectations of the international buyers. Great emphasis has therefore to be put on the training of the frontline personnel. Developing a genuine service attitude is paramount. If the personnel are able to respond positively to situations of emergence, this will add to the perceived quality of the auctions. If the customer clearly can see that the service organization understands him and is prepared to listen to him and discuss with him, then he will respect the auction house as a partner. Quickly addressing and solving emergent problems is the best guarantor of customer satisfaction. Ultimately an auction company is a service company. Demanding auction buyers ask for good service in a multitude of ways:

- efficient auctioning (fast, reliable auctioneers);
- flexible invoicing (in alternative currencies);
- easy pre-auction viewing (well-educated and informed support staff);
- high-class restaurant service (accommodating different tastes and cultures).

An auction center has to work in close collaboration with airlines, travel agencies, and financial services providers. Shuttle buses connecting the auction center with a number of hotels will further enhance the buyer experience. Correspondingly the auction offering can be described as a package consisting of three dimensions. The three axes of the offering package correspond to the physical, service, and relationship content of the offering.

The three-dimensional offering *consists of hardware, software, and peopleware corresponding to the physical, service, and relationship content of the offering.*

The three-dimensional offering of the auction house is illustrated in Figure 1.2. As the offering only has meaning from the viewpoint of the customer, different customers will appreciate different elements of the offering.

The most important physical elements of the auction house offering are the lots offered for auction. However, the premises are also part of the physical content of the offering.

An auction is a real-time service, and the variety of service elements relating to the offering includes hotel services, transport, shipping, catering, banking, information services, and of course the running of the auction. This represents the service content of the offering.

Service Content

1   Logistics services
1.1 Invoicing and shipping
1.2 Delivery accuracy
1.3 Warehousing
1.4 Flexibility in urgency

2   Financial services
2.1 Multi-currency invoicing
2.2 Alternative payment methods
2.3 On-site bank

3   Information services
3.1 Wireless connections
3.2 Global news services
3.3 Sales statistics

4   Restaurant services
4.1 Ethnic food
4.2 Special diets
4.3 Fully licensed
4.4 Continuously open

5   Third-party services
5.1 Forwarding agents
5.2 Travel agents
5.3 Airlines
5.4 Hotels

Relationship Content

1   Characteristics of key personnel
1.1 Access to salespeople
1.2 Competence of auctioneers
1.3 Company know-how
1.4 Pro-activity of personnel
1.5 Market knowledge
1.6 International network

2   Collaboration processes
2.1 Easiness of interaction
2.2 Long-term cooperation
2.3 Mutual solicitation possibilities
2.4 Capability to react quickly to new
      emergent customer needs
2.5 Trust

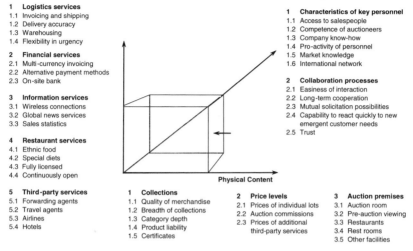

Physical Content

1 Collections	**2 Price levels**	**3 Auction premises**
1.1 Quality of merchandise	2.1 Prices of individual lots	3.1 Auction room
1.2 Breadth of collections	2.2 Auction commissions	3.2 Pre-auction viewing
1.3 Category depth	2.3 Prices of additional	3.3 Restaurants
1.4 Product liability	third-party services	3.4 Rest rooms
1.5 Certificates		3.5 Other facilities

Figure 1.2   The three-dimensional offering: auction house case

The service element of the offering is something we get without necessarily reflecting on who is the individual providing the service. Not all services are of this character. Sometimes we look not only for the service activity, but also for the individual relationship. In an auction business the credit approval process is to a large extent something which is handled in this spirit. Established customers expect to discuss their credit limits with certain individuals with whom they feel confident and secure. This part of the offering can be called the people or the relationship dimension. The distinction between the service and the relationship dimension is that the former focuses on the actual service activity, whereas the latter is more occupied with the maintenance of a longer term personal relationship. This relationship then entails the carrying out of the service activity in a confident and trusted atmosphere.

The value-creating potential along each axis of the offering depends on the value-creating process of the customer. What is important is to recognize which are the service elements that are only hygienic parts, or potential sources of dissatisfaction but not of increased satisfaction, and which parts are those that really provide exceptional satisfaction. For different customers this perception can vary considerably.

OPERATIONAL CAPABILITIES

Value creation stems from a combination of three ideas:[9]

- Discovering a new way of creating value for customers.
- Bringing together a combination of capabilities creating this value.
- Creating uniqueness in this in order to appropriate part of the value created.

To establish a successful auction it is necessary to mobilize a multitude of actors. This network of actors has to collaborate to enable the offering to be provided. So the way of creating value is quite different from the way Robinson as a self-sufficient inhabitant on the island got his first idea of an offering. Robinson was initially fully occupied by securing his daily living. Then Stevens appeared, and a market was established. Robinson and Stevens had some comparative advantages compared to each other. By negotiating a barter arrangement both of them were better off specializing. Each had possession over a scarce resource, which was tradable. The supply was represented by the access to the physical resource. The demand in turn was represented in the form of a single customer: the two men traded with each other. Managing this was quite straightforward. All the elements were known: the supply and demand, the price function, and the limitations on how far the business could be exploited (the limitation of how long potatoes could be stored). So, from the perspective of Robinson, the managerial task was one of control. He should work as much as possible to exploit the trading opportunities, but he could not work more than he could eat. This resulted in a utilization rate of 81% of Robinson's production capacity.

He used his free capacity to build the raft. This was an entre-preneurial activity. He could not know if there would be any further business opportunities on The Other Island. So in the short term, when he built the raft, this activity was a risky invest-ment for the future. He acquired a strategic option that could turn out to be of value. And so it did. He suddenly became aware of new tasty food alternatives, bananas, grapefruit, and coffee. But now his business model was not adequate any more. He had to figure out on which conditions he would trade different mer-chandise. Should he pay for bananas, grapefruit, and coffee pri-marily with potatoes, which could be produced by Stevens? Or should he pay with oranges that he could produce himself? This meant that he had not just to consider his own resources and the customers. He had to genuinely figure out a new offering, or perhaps several offerings. Should he even bring someone from The Other Island to his own island to collect oranges? The chal-lenge was how he could create uniqueness in this offering formula in order to appropriate part of the value created. So transforming the demand into something that would create value for all the involved parties was the primary task. On top of that Robinson now had the opportunity to get a larger part for himself, if he could mobilize the addressable resources appropriately. So besides that he needed to design the offerings he also needed to organize the value constellation. The resource side was not only depending on what he was doing, but also he had to rely on the contribu-tion of both Stevens and the inhabitants of The Other Island to make his new business model successful. The managerial task was now more demanding and he had to coordinate a quite intricate set of activities.

The capabilities required by Robinson during the initial situation, when he was dealing only with Stevens, are depicted

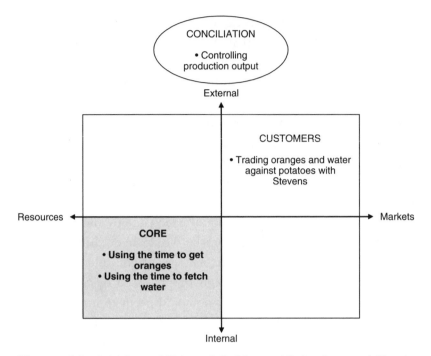

Figure 1.3 Initial capabilities of Robinson (distinctive capability in bold)

in Figure 1.3. We here introduce the notion of operational capabilities and leadership capabilities. Operational capabilities relate to how the actor is matching supply and demand, separating the internal and external perspectives on the value-creating process. The leadership capabilities relate to how the matching of supply and demand is governed. The leadership capability initially is about how the value-creating process is framed, how Robinson conciliates his own aspirations with the needs and interests of Stevens.

The core based upon which Robinson's business was formed was his proprietary resources, the access to the orange trees, and how he used his own time. This combination can be called the distinctive capability. A distinctive capability provides the actor with a unique business model and corresponding business success.

The logic of Figure 1.3 is that there are four types of operational capabilities. These capabilities are based on two dimensions, and are related to markets (demand) or resources (supply), and have internal or external focus. The core represents the internal resources that provide the basis for the business, e.g. products, assets, and processes. The customer quadrant represents the way the enterprise interacts with the customers. On top of the operational capabilities is the leadership capability that keeps the operational capabilities together, conciliation.

The early business activities of Robinson asked for the capabilities of an industrial actor. The core was based on access to proprietary resources, the orange trees, and production capacity, i.e. Robinson's own available time. As long as this setting prevailed one could say that Robinson operated in an *industrial mode*.

Once Robinson had his raft ready and could visit The Other Island the context of the value-creating process radically changed. Now he was confronting a much more complex situation. Assuming that Robinson's aspirations still are unchanged, he now has to 'internalize' the demand function, as can be seen from Figure 1.4. He has to understand what different customers want. Based on this he has to transform these customer expectations into offering formulas or concepts. But the offerings will require the mobilization of resources out of his direct control. The same actors that provide the resources, Stevens and the inhabitants of The Other Island, are also the customers to be served. When designing the offerings Robinson will have to simultaneously consider the implications this has on the value constellation.

In Figure 1.4 we have added two more operational capabilities. A concept is the way an enterprise has 'internalized customer needs' and developed ways to provide value to customers. Constellations in turn relate to how the enterprise is able to address external resources for the purpose of complementing own internal resources to create value.

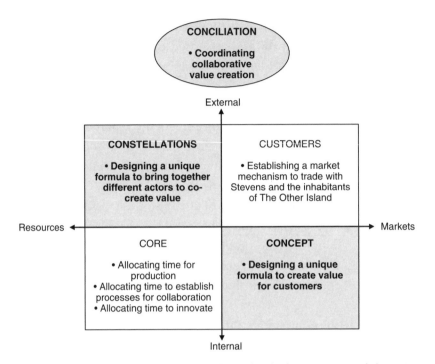

Figure 1.4   The impact of The Other Island (distinctive capabilities in bold)

Managerially Robinson has to coordinate collaborative value creation, to conciliate this he needs good negotiation and persuasion skills to pursue all participants to agree on the shared agenda. He needs to balance different actors and viewpoints and he cannot enforce the end result. If he is successful the actors will not only comply with whatever suggestions he will come up with. They will also proactively suggest improvements based on their own experiences and insights. Successful framing of the value constellation through his offering design solution will enable Robinson to emerge as the leader within the value constellation. If his values still underline wealth accumulation he could have a good opportunity to appropriate a considerable share of the added value this arrangement will give rise to.

Strictly speaking Robinson develops personal skills and not capabilities. Capabilities are by the definition previously introduced an organizational property. However, for the sake of illustrating the dynamics relating to capability building the Robinson case is used to break down these dynamics into their basic constituents. The scalability of personal skills into organizational capabilities is fully possible. If Robinson and Stevens successfully expand their businesses and form companies, employing new entrants coming to the island, they could form two companies, Robinson Inc. and Stevens Inc. Then the ability to perform the similar duties would reside within organizations. What originally were individual skills would have become organizational capabilities.

To further illustrate how to operationalize capabilities we will revert to the way an auction house functions. Here management has to develop a comprehensive offering to attract international buyers. The auction house cannot independently provide the resources needed for the offering. The lots have to be solicited from suppliers all over the world. The auction offering has to support the motivation of both suppliers and buyers. Successful auctions are the best way to attract both of them. The capabilities needed by an auction house are depicted in Figure 1.5.

The examples provided here have shown that the word 'offering' instead of 'product' enables a better understanding of the dynamics of collaborative value creation. The notion of offering addresses the issue of value co-production, recognizing that both customers and suppliers can learn through the interaction manifested in the offering. It also highlights the opportunity for one actor to take the leading role to bring a constellation of actors together to pursue collective value creation. Such an actor will here be called an *orchestrator*, and the capabilities to carry out such an orchestrating role will be called *orchestration capabilities*. Chapter 3 will develop a more in-depth definition of orchestration in business.

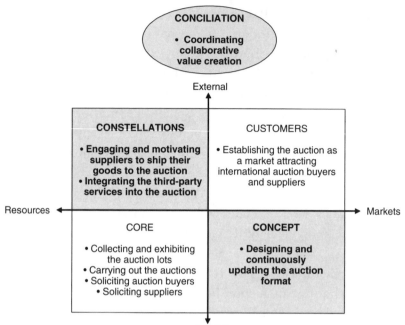

Figure 1.5   The capabilities of an auction house (distinctive capabilities in bold)

The next chapter will further discuss the implication of orchestration as a way to create value. The argument is that digital convergence and enhanced possibilities to use information technology to flexibly reconfigure resources and capabilities open up more possibilities for successful orchestration.

CHAPTER 2

FOCUS ON LEARNING

At the 1968 Olympic Games in Mexico City the sport of high-jumping event was won by Dick Fosbury, an American who revolutionized the sport by introducing the 'Fosbury Flop'.

For decades, the method that virtually all high jumpers used was the straddle method of jumping. Using this method, the jumper kicks one foot up and rolls over the bar face down. Fosbury, a high-school student from Oregon, learned the method of high jumping taught to him by his coaches and modeled after the usual straddle method. His jumps, though, were mediocre at best. He just couldn't seem to grasp the straddle method of high jumping. Fosbury preferred to use more of a scissors method, popularized by children leaping fences. Eventually, he refined this technique and started to jump backwards from the point of take-off. Fosbury turned just as he leapt, flinging his body backward over the bar with his back arched, following with his legs and landing on his shoulders. His jump gained international attention and was called the Fosbury Flop.

The Fosbury Flop revolutionized high jumping, and it clearly originated from the insights of one single individual. When the idea was introduced, it met with resistance. People whose dominating ideas were supported by the old worldview were too single-minded to even question their existing methods and approaches. So, for example, Fosbury made tremendous progress in high school, but his coach tried to get him to change to the straddle method. He finally accepted Fosbury's method of jumping after he had worked with Fosbury for a while.

But even after Fosbury had won his gold medal, most of the existing elite high jumpers stuck to the straddle technique. The problem was that they had invested so much time in their technique and movements that they couldn't give it up, so they were stuck with what they knew. It took almost a full decade before the flop began to dominate the sport.

Gradually also research in biomechanics showed that from a physical perspective the method introduced by Fosbury was actually superior to the old straddle method.

A high jump can be broken down into three phases: run-up, takeoff, and bar clearance. After takeoff, the center of gravity follows a path called a parabola. The parabola should reach the maximum possible peak height. As the center of gravity travels along the parabola, the body should rotate around the center of gravity in a way that will allow the successful clearance of a bar set as high as possible.

In a Fosbury Flop, the rotation consists of a 'twist' (a rotation around the longitudinal axis of the body) which turns the back of the athlete toward the bar, and a 'somersault' (a rotation around a transverse axis) which makes the shoulders go down and the knees go up. The combination of these two motions produces a twisting somersault rotation, which leads to a face-up layout position at the peak of the jump. Combined with an arched configuration of the body, this position allows the athlete to clear a bar set at a height that is near the maximum height reached by the center of gravity.[1]

What is interesting with the flop style is that junior athletes that learn the style by just doing it aren't necessarily aware of the intricate physiological requirements of what they are doing.

The athlete has to coordinate − 'orchestrate' − the simultaneous movements of many muscles in a time-critical way to perfect the jump. This behavior has to be learned, and then practiced over and over again in order to result in a world-class athletic performance. When learned at a young age this takes place by just imitating, for an experienced athlete it is almost impossible to first unlearn the old habit, and then learn the new one.

The Fosbury Flop example thus illustrates the challenge in getting a new idea to gain ground. People cannot simply be told to accept a new way of doing something, even if there are clear results visible. One's previous experiences will form strong fences against accepting something new. People need to gradually experience for themselves how adopting a new process will be beneficial. The actual revolution in high jumping came about from the kids who saw it on TV, and had nothing to lose. These children said, 'Gosh, that looks fun − let's do that.' The new generation of high jumpers emerged from these grade-school kids who didn't have coaches who would say, 'No, you stick with the straddle.'

The Fosbury Flop case has two lessons for the business world. Firstly, a new idea radically changing the value-creating logic has a huge potential meaning that the one coming up with this idea is going for gold. Secondly, once the use of this idea is widespread, competition increases. Then those who have the best talent combined with meticulous training are going to win. Consequently there are two ways to succeed in the competition, either by inventing radical new ways to compete, or by perfecting the ability to perform according to the existing practice. Most companies have to pursue both these paths, in an optimal combination. They have to be both creative and efficient at the same time.

So Fosbury used knowledge to change the rules of physical competition. But this knowledge didn't remain proprietary. This also illustrates the shift when moving to the knowledge society. In the industrial society, a company could protect itself by proprietary access to physical resources, in the way that Robinson could exploit his access to oranges. In this respect, the company was more safeguarded from competition. Today technology has provided people with the possibility to learn and experience more per unit of time than ever before. This means that the competition is more transparent, and the need to be simultaneously creative and efficient has become more important.

DIGITAL CONVERGENCE AND LEARNING

Digital convergence can be defined as the union of audio, video, and data communication and its processing into a single source, received on a single device, delivered by a single connection.[2] An early company attributed to have recognizing the convergence of the communications industry and computer industry is NEC. Already in the early 1970s, its chairman Kobayashi started to build a strategy, which later was identified as C&C, Computers and Communication. Bill Gates, in turn, during his 1994 Comdex keynote speech, portrayed the future of the computer industry as a new age of 'digital convergence,' in which traditional information sources – books, catalogs, consumer services, and even works of art – would exist in digital form and be accessible by users from televisions, hand-held devices, or PCs.[4] Gates' vision was expressed as follows:

> This is broader than technology – it will affect how we communicate, organize and (engage in) commerce . . . This industry will

be at the center of all of it. We'll be shaping the information highway.

In spite of such a long existence as a concept, digital convergence didn't take off easily. Professor David Yoffie of Harvard argued early on that technology and deregulation alone would not lead to digital convergence.[5] Computing and communication costs had been declining for decades, without the promise of digital convergence materializing. For digital convergence to be realized greater managerial creativity would be needed according to Yoffie. What became the trigger for digital convergence was the broadband Internet.

In the era of digital convergence, communication and interaction inside networks are of paramount importance. To innovate in a systemic fashion firms form webs of alliances, in order to come up with new appealing offerings to intrigue consumers. Emerging technologies are in need of standards that at least approximate universality. But at the same time there is an increasing tendency toward an open approach to standards, in which other companies are allowed to license the hardware and software of the emerging technology. The more systemic an innovation is intended to be, the more such an open attitude seems to be required.

Digital convergence changes the industrial structure from vertical to horizontal, and systemic innovation will be undertaken by alliance networks. Although such networks are vulnerable to opportunism, these seem to be capable of producing systemic innovations, because mutual relations are stabilized by substantive and procedural commitment.[6] As any conceivable 'system' tends to cover a much broader spectrum, systemic innovation by one firm seems ever more improbable. A firm that intends to innovate in a systemic fashion has no option but to 'network,' horizontally, and to try to cover the system parts outside its own domain.

These networks combined with new technologies provide individuals with many more options for learning and entertainment. We have hundreds of satellite channels, and access to billions of Internet pages. This possibility to learn more effectively also means that we get bored faster. As we have got used to one thing we suddenly become aware of new things, and our interest shifts. The human being is a curious creature. Ultimately our curiosity drives technology development. We expect technology to increase our possibilities to learn and experience more, faster and better – to live and thrive in a constant hunger for new experiences and deeper insights. And of course, we want it all, and at lowest possible price.

Digital convergence also opens up possibilities for less developed countries. The same Internet is available on a global basis. Entrepreneurial individuals situated anywhere have much better opportunities to explore and exploit opportunities today than what was the case 10 years ago. This means that new entrants emerge to exploit capitalists' relentless chase for improved efficiency and lower costs. This encourages the exploitation of comparative advantages. But also new creative solutions can find their markets more effectively. A large number of Israeli software firms have become world-class without having to establish large international organizations, and a number of start-ups in the Nordic region immediately started to operate on a global scale thanks to the improved communication possibilities provided by the Internet. The voiceover Internet company, Skype, is here a good example.

This development has increased transparency. We know how global competition affects us. In the same way that every high jumper all over the world is aware of the existing rankings of the best jumpers, we know the pecking order of leading companies, universities, and even countries regarding how well they perform. Immediately after a new idea has sprung up, everybody is aware and everybody wants it. With the help of the Internet, the customer is better informed, but is also more price-conscious and will not accept established players charging considerably more than, for example, a less well-known company from Korea or China. The notion of the 'China price' was introduced in the United States to mean that once the other elements of a deal were agreed upon, the buyer as the last point wanted the price to be lowered by 30%, referring to price quotes from a Chinese supplier.

In this chapter we will argue that it is highly probable that the pace of change will remain high in the nearest future, and therefore the need to learn and adapt will stay on top of the enterprise agenda. Digital convergence has established three fundamental conditions that provide the basis for a new form of competition; different from the one we got used to in the industrialized context. These conditions are *pervasive computing*, the *extended enterprise*, and the rise of *virtual communities*. These new phenomena provide the foundation for individual learning to continue to be one of the main drivers for future societal development.

The computer is now facing us all over the place. The car has more computing power than the space ship that put Armstrong on the moon in 1969. Using the computer in a cell phone you can now check in at airports by showing an SMS message and identification. We have intelligent clothing, and GPS (global positioning system) enables us to identify our present location with an accuracy of a couple of feet. This trend of pervasive computing is affecting our daily life to an extensive degree. It provides us with both more functionality of products at reduced prices and new functionalities, like, for example, the digital camera phone. Such devices, the embodiments of digital convergence, have become possible because of open, modular standards for global provision of integrated services – extensions of the Internet architecture. Innovative new services are brought to the global market quickly. Coalitions of companies to create, deliver, and support a solution offering are formed rapidly and flexibly.

The second condition provided through digital convergence is the extended enterprise. This requirement is forced upon companies due to the need to exploit global comparative advantages. As the Robinson and Stevens example showed, it is not efficient when everybody does the same thing. In the global economy this has meant that less developed countries with lower labor costs are now getting an increasing amount of work from countries with higher costs. Companies are forced to address the most suitable resources to bring a product or a service to the market, at the lowest possible cost. In many cases it is not appropriate to form subsidiaries in the low cost locations, but instead companies form collaboration agreements with firms already present there. These suppliers then are treated almost as subsidiaries, as keeping promises to customers entails that the supplier carries out his part of the deal. The extended enterprise is effective and flexible. An architecture based on combining open, standards-based services is easily enhanced when needed. On-demand IT services allow distributed organizations to swiftly develop required services for their customers anywhere in the world without investing in underlying infrastructure.

Another driver towards the extended enterprise is the notion of core competence.[7] This concept, launched by professors Prahalad and Hamel at the beginning of 1990s, made corporate leaders recognize that their firms possess certain valuable knowledge that has been built up over decades, and is very difficult to copy by other firms. The ultimate task of any corporate leader is to focus on how to use this knowledge in the best possible way. The implication of this is, of course, that not all knowledge the firm has provides a core competence. If one company is doing only office cleaning for other companies, it is highly probable that this company becomes quite good at cleaning offices. So probably it will be more efficient not to have an in-house office-cleaning department, but to make a contract with the office-cleaning company and let it take care of this job.

This phenomenon has been called subcontracting or out-sourcing, or when jobs go to another continent, offshoring. These business structures can be referred to as extended enterprises. Why we here prefer to talk about the extended enterprise is that in spite of the fact that the task is contracted to a third party, the function is still an integral part of the value-creation process of the outsourcing organization.

But digital convergence doesn't just provide efficiency im-provements. Technology also supports and brings back some human behavior that naturally existed in the pre-industrialized era, but lost priority during the industrialization phase. One can argue that industrialization meant the individualization of the society. But the human being is a social creature; we do not want to just be on our own, at least not all of the time. This has caused the rise of different forms of communities, the third significant con-tribution by digital convergence. The open source movement is one well-known example. Linus Torvalds, as the initiator of the Linux development, has here become a role model. Also customer communities emerge. Often these are formed by individuals pur-suing their self-interests in their private lives, but doing this in a social context. So we can talk about technology-supported social-ization, originating from individual self-interest.

LEARNING IN COMMUNITIES

The open source initiative is an example of a professional com-munity. Open source does not motivate individuals through financial incentives, but it has still created an enormous amount of value over the last couple of decades. Therefore economic theorists are puzzled. Why do knowledge workers provide their contribution free of charge?

If we look upon the open source community as an arena to co-produce value, there has to be some gains for everybody participating. The member of the open source community is both a supplier and a customer. When he is a supplier, he clearly provides his contribution to the customer, i.e. the network, in the form of his programming efforts. However, he has to gain something; otherwise no activity would take place. So what he gains we can describe as the services the community provides to him. Linus Torvalds described what he perceived as valuable during his early days in the open source community as follows:

> One of the things that made Linux good and motivational was the feedback I was getting. It meant that Linux mattered and was a sign of my being in a social group. And I was the leader of the social group. There's no question that was important, more important than even telling my Mom and Dad what I was doing. I was more concerned about the people who were using Linux. But this was my life: I ate. I slept. Maybe I went to university. I coded. I read a lot of email. I was kind of aware of friends getting laid more, but that was okay. Quite frankly, most of my friends were losers, too.[8]

So for Linus Torvalds technology provided a means to get virtual access to other people. Virtual communities thus can represent a source of enjoyment, even to the degree that the addictive nature of the Internet can lead to situations where individuals become so immersed by the virtual world that they can no longer function normally in the real world.

This means that virtual communities, either professional or consumer, can provide value for individuals in respect of two very basic needs: safety and social interaction. For professionals, open source engagement can also provide value in respect of self-esteem and self-actualization. Great contributions in the open source community will be recognized by peers. If this in itself is not a major cause for active participation, the personal feeling of having achieved something is another potential source of satisfaction.

The most important currency in today's society is knowledge. Thus a potentially great contribution of an economic transaction is new knowledge, i.e. learning. This means that part of the value of a transaction is not registered in the monetary system. As the case of Robinson and Stevens showed, our time is divided between working and striving to reach individual fulfillment. On their island they had to work to stay alive. Professional workers don't work long hours because they have to stay alive. So the question is what do we really want to do with our lives? In the knowledge society we want to learn new things, so engaging in activities providing us with new knowledge is something of value. Exactly what we want to learn may vary, but the important thing is that virtual communities provide opportunities to learn. And one possible currency by which we can pay is our own time, for example the time we are prepared to use to contribute to open source development activities.

So the way we use time at our disposal, once we have secured our daily food and shelter, can be directed towards activities increasing our knowledge base and providing a positive social context. The industrial society emphasized extrinsic values. Efficiency and excellence were high on the list of priorities. Goods and services, matching the uniform perceptions of what was considered as 'representing goodness', drove the markets. Technology was designed to improve our daily lives in a rational sense. In the knowledge society things are less absolute. What is actually fun and how to measure beauty are some of the more intriguing questions facing today's developers and marketers. More generally, the knowledge society has increased pluralism and reduced predictability. This of course confirms the observation that knowledge and learning are key currencies of this society.

Professional and customer communities share many characteristics. They consist of individuals pursuing self-interests. But these interests are not purely economical. The community members also have a common interest in some areas that complement economic value creation such as knowledge creation, a sense of belonging, civic virtue, or aesthetics. The activities of these communities in an open, collaborative world create platforms for interaction that also can be exploited by individuals who do not really share these communal traits. For example, in eBay, such individuals can use the platform for trading goods and services. From the community perspective they still contribute in two ways. Firstly, their buying provides transaction revenues for the community. Secondly, their transactions further enrich the fact base about the market for goods and services.

Such fact base enriching activities for a third party mean that open source and watching television share many traits as value-creating activities. If we watch a program on television we may do this to learn something new, so an important component of the value is learning. It may also be that the program enables us to share some thoughts about it with our colleagues at work the following day. In this respect it also provides some value from the social interaction perspective. If the program has an interactive element, we may get invited to express our opinion by sending a text message by our mobile phone. (Often we have to pay to give the service provider this additional benefit!) This way of perceiving television watching is according to the industrial view. We buy a service, and we pay for it. So here we consider it as perfectly legitimate to expect that we allocate part of our leisure time, free of charge, to consume this service, and pay for this. What we don't usually reflect on is that the broadcaster is selling the use of our time to advertisers, who pay for the access to us as objects for their sales promotion activities when we watch the program.

There are some interesting comparisons if we consider Internet-based activities as an alternative to spending time in front of the television. Using the Internet we can regulate the interaction based on our own interest. If we are highly interactive we will probably be rewarded, one way or another. The social interaction is also considerably higher compared to television watching.

American youths spend almost four hours a day on average watching television. This implies a considerable growth potential of Internet-based socially engaging services and activities, shown for example by the fact that the average eBay customer stays one and a half hours on the site, once logged in.

The television became the social centerpiece of the industrial era, uniting the family to watch predefined content driven by media and advertisers. The knowledge society is providing the individual with more choices and increased potential for self-actualization. The good thing is that as an individual I can today flexibly surf between both worlds. If I am interested in sports I can follow the football league on my favorite channel. Once the match is over I can spend some time engaged in a chat within my open source community.

THE IMPACT OF DIGITAL CONVERGENCE ON OFFERINGS AND CAPABILITIES

Pervasive computing, the extended enterprise, and virtual communities have bearings on how offerings are co-produced. Pervasive computing affects the physical product content. Products include more intelligence, and enable the customer to configure the product as needed, and provide interaction in a much more flexible way than before. The difference between analog and digital technologies is one example. The traditional analog videocassette represented sequential processing, and provided a step-by-step, predesigned process. Using digital technology, the mode of thinking is different. Digital design offers flexibility, and is also more adoptable to users with different expectations.

The extended enterprise in turn has promoted a new service logic where capabilities are flexibly assembled on demand, and then separated when the value-creating mission is completed. A new trend in retailing is the creation of one-time collections, which by design provide mass exclusivity. The campaign by clothing retailer H&M together with world-known designer Karl Lagerfeld during autumn 2004 is a case in point. The collection was more or less sold out in a week. H&M never intended to develop a permanent Karl Lagerfeld line of fashion: the objective was to create a very visible experience, which would attract the attention of both the public and media. The success of the Lagerfeld collection was well tracked by H&M, and the learning benefited later campaigns.

The community trend emphasizes the role of the customer as a co-creator of value. Companies such as Amazon use feedback from the customers to further add value to the offerings, and different incentives are provided to encourage the customers to engage in such information sharing. To ensure commitment the service providers must emotionally engage the customer. They do this in part by making sure that the values they represent resonate with the values of those individuals with whom they want to interact.

Digital convergence has a profound impact on how value is created and requires a new set of capabilities. To use Robinson as an example, we could first view his opportunities from an industrial perspective. In this view, Robinson should be occupied with how he could maximize his resource bundles. He would try to form contracts in order to exploit the information advantages he momentarily possesses by getting access to either the natural resources or the labor at discounted prices. The industrial perspective easily fosters a zero-sum game mindset, where the competition between actors is emphasized.

Another perspective is to see learning as key input and output factors of value-creating activities. For instance, the learning of an Amazon reader is an output of her own activity but an input to the purchasing process of the next customer. Collectively using the creativity and knowledge of all the customers in the community creates plus-sum benefits that serve all participants. For such a behavior to emerge there has to be a definition of a formula for how the different parties would interact in the collaborative effort. This formula becomes the mechanism for shared pain and gain. To be able to convince everybody about the benefits of such a way to cooperate, a certain amount of trust has to be established among the individuals. This is not only a question about how well the formula for shared pain and gain technically is defined. What the individuals will evaluate is whether they trust the other individuals and the one(s) acting as a node in the network. A central factor affecting the level of trust is whether the communicated aspirations are corresponding to observed actions. The values expressed have to be observable from past behavior.

In the industrial age managerial focus was on control. In the knowledge age the values and aspirations are the foundations for successful value constellations. Network mobilization and actor motivation cannot just be controlled by the central node in the network. The coordinating function is instead more a question of conciliation, how to resolve differences and mediate between conflicting interests among the members of the value constellation.

The values will form the character of the organization, and the aspirations set the course. The course setting requires continuous scanning of emerging issues, and to evaluate whether to put them on the agenda and delete some other topics. If this responsibility does not always reside with a single actor, the alternative is some form of self-organizing process, whereby the resulting capability is based on collective action.

In the knowledge society the capabilities for governance of value creation of an extended enterprise of an open network can be called the orchestration capabilities. These capabilities result in three specific outputs: the course for the enterprise; the conciliation of the operational activities; and the character or culture of the whole enterprise.

The capabilities to orchestrate a value constellation built on community nurturing are depicted in Figure 2.1. Leadership capabilities have a different emphasis in the knowledge society

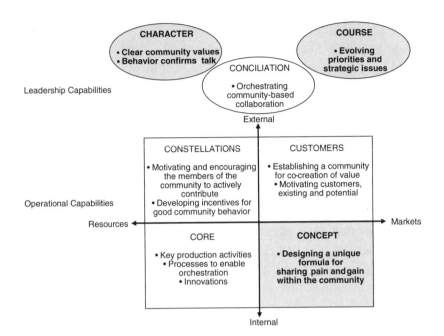

Figure 2.1 Capabilities for community nurturing (distinctive capabilities in bold)

compared to the industrial society. The role of control dominates in the industrial setting. The ideal state of a knowledge-based business is that a transparent automated value appropriation mechanism provides the control mechanism and also generates fees for the nodal actor (be it an individual, a firm, or a collective). Everybody accepts that the value added by the orchestrator exceeds the charge upon the community, and as long as this is the case the community can grow and thrive.

Another difference between industrial value creation and knowledge-based orchestration is that in the former the basis for the business model is to be found in the core, the resources and processes based on which the industrial success is built. When success is based on knowledge the concept becomes the center-piece of the business model. In this way Baron de Coubertin defined the principles for the modern Olympic Games, Linus

Torvalds the rules for kernel development in Linux, Google the formula for how pages and advertisers are ranked, and eBay the code of conduct for the virtual auctions. Common to all these successfully orchestrated movements is that they have a strong cultural attachment, and that this cultural side is actively endorsed by the leading actors. The cultural aspects then also strongly influence the character and the course of the movement. Subsequently Figure 2.1 introduces two capabilities not previously discussed. 'Course' relates to how the enterprise is figuring out how to handle possible changes in its business model, and 'Character' relates to the culture and values of the enterprise. The operational capabilities will be dealt with in Part III of the book, and the leadership capabilities will be covered in Part IV.

LEARNING CONTEXTS

One of the first people to highlight the need for more focus on learning within organizations was Arie de Geus. He worked for Royal Dutch Shell for 38 years and among other things had been responsible for the scenario planning unit. He was fascinated with how bad managers were at recognizing major shifts in the surrounding business context. He therefore suggested that the long-term success of a company is dependent on the ability of its senior managers to absorb what is going on in the business environment and to act on that information with appropriate business moves. In other words, success is dependent on learning. The main problem related to learning in organizations that de Geus and his colleagues at Shell had discovered was that the speed of learning was slow – too slow for a world in which the ability to learn faster than competitors may be the only sustainable competitive advantage.[9]

De Geus' experience was that it typically took 12 to 18 months from the moment a signal is received until it is acted upon in a large organization. The issue was not whether a company could learn, but whether it could learn fast and early. The critical question therefore becomes, 'Can we accelerate institutional learning?' De Geus found three reasons why management teams did not easily get into a creative mode:

- Firstly, most people can deal with only three or four variables at a time and do so through only one or two time iterations.
- Secondly, people have difficulty in recognizing the nature of complex systems (like markets or companies) where cause and effect are separated in time and place.
- Thirdly, people often have difficulties in sorting out relevant information from the less important one, thus easily getting drowned in information overflow.

For organizations to speed up learning the top management teams have to change their mental models and engage in thinking that gets beyond the traditional operational decision-making agenda. But there are different types of learning contexts that require different forms of leadership and management. We need to learn to become more efficient and reduce costs, but also to create totally new ways of providing value to the customers. But we also need to learn how to be able to follow a community, and to provide the contexts where community members are able to voice their wishes and interact among themselves to maintain the community atmosphere. This implies that learning is a very broad concept. We continuously learn new things, by communicating and socializing with other individuals, by reading the newspaper, by watching television, by just observing the outside world and reflecting – our previous learning may be reconfigured, and we can make new insights and learn new things. Brain researchers are now convinced that we even learn while we are sleeping.

To a large degree, learning in organizations takes place in different groups. This means that one of the first tasks when defining different learning contexts is to distinguish between information transmission and the social construction of knowledge. Both of these processes provide the learner with new insights and knowledge. Information transmission is the transfer of knowledge from one individual to another. Here it is assumed that the way the transformed information appears as understanding for the learner is more or less identical to the way it is understood by the transmitter of information.

Learning as a social construction of knowledge refers to the collaborative, community-based, conversational work aspects in building understanding. From this perspective, learning is at its heart a social process. The word 'construction' refers to the importance of active, engaged building of new knowledge from prior knowledge and new experience. When thinking of learning as a social process, it is also important to realize that learning is situated. Situated learning is context specific and applicable for a particular situation at a certain point in time.[10]

A situated, social, constructivist view differs from the more conventional transmission perspective on learning. Traditional learning communicates disembodied ideas via lecture or text. The constructivist perspective emphasizes contextualization. Transmission assumes that knowledge is passed from the knowledge holder to the learner without significant distortion of transformation. The constructionist perspective recognizes that learners play an important role in constructing what they hear or read, and, by building on prior knowledge, they may distort even the purest input. Further, the transmission perspective tends to ignore social aspects of learning or limits those aspects to extrinsic motivation. In contrast, constructivism views learning as inherently social, in both process and outcomes.

The constructivist view of learning emphasizes that humans learn not only by receiving and copying impressions and information from the outside world, but also by constructing and reconstructing own mental conceptions of the world. But this takes place in a social context. Thus in order to learn deeply, one has to become an active partner in the learning process.

Learning in a business context has proven to be a tricky issue to operationalize. Practice has shown that people have different learning styles. Certain individuals, indeed, are more gifted and better at rapidly adapting to new situations. Therefore, there will not be any attempt here to delve into the concept of how individuals learn differently. Instead, the focus will be on what the learning context is, how leaders can make sure that the learning context is properly understood, and that the chosen way to manage this learning is appropriate.

Organizational learning can take place either as individual learning or 'knowledge infusion'. An organization learns in only two ways: (a) by the learning of its members; or (b) by ingesting new members who have knowledge the organization didn't previously have.[11] Research has shown that much of the knowledge base on which organizational capabilities are built is 'tacit'[12] and 'sticky'[13] to its nature. Thus it is difficult to obtain such knowledge by recruiting new members to the organization. Congruent with this, organizational learning needs the right preconditions for individual learning. The type of organizational learning needed is to a great extent dependent on the type of capability one wants to develop.

Building a state-of-the-art procurement capability within a global organization requires efficient information transmission across the organization. Due to a variety of coding principles and differences in purchasing routines it is a great challenge to establish a common platform for global procurement. In such a situation, just providing transparent information across the organization and making sure this fact base is continuously updated provides the foundation for more efficient *information acquisition* by the procurement professionals.

In services, customer satisfaction depends upon how well a supplier can solve problems that arise in the use of products or services. A study of photocopier repair technicians showed that they were much more productive if instead of information transmission (through, for example, training and repair manuals), they formed an occupational community where they could easily contact each other and informally exchange experiences and tell each other 'war stories'. The information transmission process focused on problems with the machines, whereas the discussions within the community were much more relating to how to deal with the customers and how to handle potential problems between the customers and their machines. With the use of mobile phones technicians could even access the expertise of their colleagues in real time, and further improve their individual learning capacity.[14] This shows how effective *problem solving* can be based on self-organized collaborative action. The collective effort provided value to the customer as well as increased the total sum of knowledge across the individuals within the organization due to internal information spillovers that occurred when the technicians were solving customer problems.

Clearly, not all learning is related to solving existing problems. Learning is also needed for the future, and requires building skills and attitudes that allow handling of new situations in an effective and organized way that is based on generic skills related to change and renewal.

Changes are the backbone of the fashion industry: here learning and creativity have less to do with solving predefined problems than with creating mind-boggling experiences. The previously mentioned Karl Lagerfeld campaign by H&M is a good illustration of this, and will be discussed more in depth in Chapter 6.

The fashion industry is also a prime example of a business almost totally based on creating experiences. Another industry starting to resemble the fashion industry is consumer electronics, where fashion models of mobile phones, game consoles, audio equipment etc. are introduced with increasingly shorter cycles. In these industries the customer is perceived as a *co-experiencing* learner, with whom the supplier wants to interact to bring the experience to the next level. So, for example, Adidas has introduced an open website, where customers participate in the design process of next generation sneakers.

All three situations – global procurement, customer problem solving, and customer experience generation – involve organizational learning. On top of such learning there is the need to constantly prepare for unpredicted situations, such as the one faced by mobile phones manufacturers in late 2003, when demand for clam shell phones suddenly surged. As market tastes rapidly change and competition intensifies there is a need to increase the overall understanding and *accumulate insights* of underlying phenomena and market patterns in order to be able to rapidly act when new circumstances prevail.

As illustrated in Figure 2.2 we can now identify four different types of learning that take place in organizations, all of which are relevant, but which have different roles to play depending on the industry, the competitive context, and the phase of development of the firm.

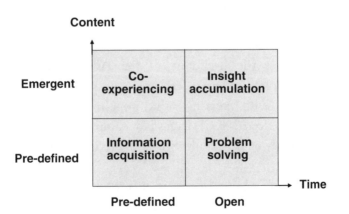

Figure 2.2 Learning contexts in organizations

Irrespective of which specific learning context is at hand, the increased amount of creative work has a substantial impact on how organizations function and what leaders have to do in order to make their organizations successful. The notion of knowledge worker was introduced almost 50 years ago by Peter Drucker,[15] but not until now, with the support of new technology, do we see the real breakthrough of knowledge or creative work.

THE NATURE OF CREATIVE WORK

By taking a broad definition of creativity to involve the production, conceptualization, or development of novel and useful ideas, processes, or procedures by an individual or by a group of individuals working together, creativity exists along a continuum, with creative activities ranging from minor adaptations to major breakthroughs. Given this, some level of creativity is required across a wide spectrum of jobs.

However, the level of creativity required and the importance of creative activities differ depending on the job in question. The social perspective on creativity should therefore not be primarily focused on outcomes, but instead more emphasis should be put on the work processes related to creativity in different contexts. This means that one needs to differentiate between 'big C Creativity,' which is the eminent creativity of celebrated geniuses, and 'little c creativity,' or the problem-solving ability that is more widely distributed among people. When including the 'little c creativity' the role of creativity is much larger in society than the one suggested by the fairly narrow definition of 'creative industries'.[16]

To make this distinction clear, Professor Richard Florida has defined the creative class as those who create marketable new forms or who work primarily at creative problem solving.[17] They include artists and designers; scientists and engineers; and creative professionals, managers, and technicians in many fields. They make up a third of the US workforce, up from less than 20% as recently as 1980. Their ranks will swell further as the 'creative content' of many formerly rote jobs continues to rise – at least in smart workplaces.

Florida introduces the notion of 'creative worker,' which he considers as synonymous to 'knowledge worker' coined by Drucker in the 1950s. Florida very much supports the interpretation by Drucker that knowledge workers – or creative workers – do not respond to financial incentives, orders, or negative sanctions the way blue-collar workers were once expected to. The key to managing these workers, Drucker wrote, is to treat them as 'de facto volunteers' – people whose commitment is highly contingent and whose motivation comes largely from within. Florida's observations suggest that different intrinsic factors are important to creative workers. As people want to exercise creativity and have impact, challenge and responsibility are highly important motivation factors. They appreciate the sheer joy of the intellectual game – to work on 'exciting technology' – but they also want to know that their work makes a difference. Creative workers are willing to work long and hard. But what puts them off is an effort to no avail: the project is dropped, pecked to death, or strangled in red tape. They also need flexibility. Creative work has its own peculiar daily rhythms, with periods of intense concentration followed by the need to relax and recharge, or to 'incubate' an idea. That's why many creative workers like a long midday break to recharge for what is essentially a second workday.

According to the original definition by Drucker, 'knowledge workers' manipulate, analyze and synthesize information, frequently projecting future business scenarios utilizing 'what if' models. Knowledge workers require a good deal of formal education and the ability to acquire and to apply theoretical and analytical knowledge. They require a different approach to work and a different mindset, and above all they require a habit of continuous learning.

The critical factors in the productivity of knowledge work are such things as attitudes, adequate information, workflow, job relationships, and the design of jobs and teams. Above all productivity in knowledge work is dependent on putting into the job the person with the right performance strengths for the assignment. An important notion is that knowledge workers are not 'labor'; they are 'resources' – and resources have to be managed for optimum yield rather than for minimum cost.

It has also been recognized that organizations have to give attention to the information needs of 'knowledge workers'. These highly skilled, expensive, overworked professionals are increasingly critical to corporate success. Their information needs are at the cutting edge of the business. One type of information support is through highly specialized systems, which can be designated as 'power tools' – examples include CAD workstations for engineers, CASE tools for systems designers, or terminals for financial dealers. Other types of support are more general computing and communication facilities and access to information from diverse sources, using, for example, internal or external databases, the Internet.

Knowledge workers are persons whose training and experience have taught them which questions must be asked and answered in order to determine the next step towards a corporate goal. For example, marketers who compare their own company's products with those of competitors examine their relative positions in the marketplace, compare this information with trends in demand, and draw conclusions which form the basis for new performance targets and strategies to achieve those targets.

Creative work requires a proactive stance, as management cannot always present the subordinates with exact goals in respect of the outcome of the creative process. Problems can be described on a continuum of open versus closed. An open problem is, e.g.

how to improve the sales efficiency of the organization. A more closed problem is how to make software able to facilitate activity-based costing. The more open the problem is the more it requires that the problem is formulated by the individual. Before formulation can begin, the problem must be identified. Creatively solving open problems thus involves both scanning the environment to find a problem and then defining the problem in such a way that it can be solved.[18]

Dealing with open problems involves more scanning and defining activities than solving more traditional closed problems. The more ambiguous the situation, the greater the possibility that it cannot be identified or solved by a single individual, but will require a collaborative process involving several people. In such a case a network may prove much more effective than a traditional organizational hierarchy. Network theorists like László Barbási[19] and Duncan Watts[20] have shown that while hierarchies are suited to provide control in well-defined contexts, so-called 'multiscale' networks without 'critical' nodes are better at producing innovative solutions for ambiguous problems. Watts calls such networks 'ultrarobust'. These networks basically collectively display an organization capability the individuals never knew they had, but that was triggered by the shared ambiguity and problem-solving challenge the members of the network faced.

In light of the above the following definition of creative work is suggested:

Creative work is human activity aimed at combining information and experience in order to separately or simultaneously:

- present a solution to an identified problem;
- provide an experience; or generate new insights that may be valuable to the creative individual.

The definition of creative work presented here considers work to be creative based on what the individual undertaking the activity thinks, not by what the external world evaluating the outcome of the activity thinks. The definition not only encompasses the cognitive type of creative work (problem solving), the creative arts (experience provision), but also the increasingly important 'little c creativity' (insight generation for the creative individual). The definition also emphasizes the open nature of creative work. There may be several benefits coming from one single creative activity. The optimum case is that the creative individual solves a problem in a way that is an innovative experience for herself, and perhaps her colleagues, and at the same time the experience provides her with some new, valuable insights.

The challenge facing the executive looking for a winning formula is thus sourcing and coordinating at least three elements of the competitive setting:

- The knowledge pool: the creative individuals and their learning potential.
- The existing capabilities and the foreseeable capability development options in respect of both organization-specific and addressable capabilities.
- The possibilities to establish and manage a portfolio of orchestrated learning activities aiming at leveraging on existing strongholds and building new ones.

What different orchestrating contexts the above-mentioned challenges create is the topic of next chapter.

CHAPTER 3

ORCHESTRATING LEADERSHIP

The requirements for learning argued for in the previous chapter are in themselves nothing new. Competition has always forced organizations to adapt and learn, and to develop new capabilities to stay successful. However, what is new today is that learning to an increasing degree results from the interactions the firm has with its environment, in the context of the extended enterprise. And as the resources existing outside the firm are not fully controllable, the orchestrating company in the middle, and its leaders, have to apply another leadership style compared to a situation where all the resources reside within the company. Sometimes these types of situations emerge based on careful planning, in other cases firms are confronted with these challenges abruptly, as was the case with Toyota in February 1997. The following case study describes how Toyota recovered from a potentially disastrous fire.

Toyota: Recovering from a Breakdown in the Production System[1]

At 4:18 a.m. Saturday, February 1, 1997 a fire erupted at Aisin Seiki's Kariya plant number 1. By 8:52 a.m. the lines dedicated to proportioning valves (P-valves) and two other brake-related parts were almost completely destroyed, along with special-purpose machinery and drills that could take months to reorder. The sudden destruction of the P-valves lines was hurting Toyota badly, because Toyota sourced nearly all of its P-valves to Aisin, which manufactured them exclusively in this plant.

Because of the just-in-time inventory system, Toyota had only one day's worth of P-valves in immediate stock. On Monday, February 3, Toyota announced the shutdown of 20 of its 30 assembly lines and two days later practically all of Toyota's and most of the related firm's plants were closed. Toyota was facing one of the worst crises of its history with large repercussions affecting the entire Japanese car industry.

However, as a result of intense collaboration between firms in the Toyota-tiered network of suppliers, and also involving firms outside the Toyota group, disaster was averted and assembly plants were reopened after only two days of complete shutdown. Within days, firms with generally no previous experience with P-valves were manufacturing and delivering the crucial parts to Aisin, where they were assembled and inspected before being sent to Toyota's and other client's assembly plants.

The recovery was an example of truly orchestrated problem solving: more than 200 companies reorganized themselves and each other to develop at least six entirely different production processes, each using different tools, different engineering approaches, and different organizational arrangements. Virtually every aspect of the recovery effort had to be designed and executed on the fly, with engineers and managers sharing their successes and failures alike across departmental boundaries, and even between firms that in normal times would be direct competitors. But this would not have been possible without strong support from the crisis management provided by the provisional command center established at Aisin Seiki. At least 300 Toyota personnel from production control, maintenance, production engineering, purchasing, quality control, and material handling could be seen at Aisin at any time during the first three weeks after the fire. Another 40 people were sent to Aisin from other car manufacturers as well.

The flow of personnel within and among firms, the various meetings organized to disseminate solutions to technical bottlenecks, and other coordination measures exerted by Aisin's 'emergency response unit' and by Toyota's production control department, all contributed to a striking outcome that was more than just the sum of individual efforts. This emergency response unit was set up at 5:30 a.m. on Saturday, February 1, to centralize and coordinate efforts to deal with the imminent crisis in an orderly and organized manner. It dealt with issues relating to production, material handling, liaison with customers, and general affairs. The unit's first meeting was held at noon the same day, and meetings were subsequently held 27 times until February 21. The coordination task was considerable as the recovery process involved over 200 firms of which 62 took direct responsibility for P-valve manufacturing.

The incentives for everybody to collaborate to find a solution were very strong. Initially there were no explicit principles for how the economic compensation would work out, but people basically assumed that compensation for their efforts would be forthcoming and fair.

Those external firms who 'voluntarily' offered their help were in many ways forced to cooperate with Aisin and Toyota.

Failure to do so might have jeopardized future business relations with Toyota group firms. In addition, because of JIT, most suppliers were losing millions of yen every day that Toyota plants remained shut.

On February 4, three days after the fire, the first 'alternative' volume P-valves were rolling off the temporary lines hastily set up by an Aisin supplier, Koritsu Sangyo, marking the beginning of the recovery process. Two days later Toyota's Tahara plant was reopened. By Monday February 10, all Toyota group assembly plants were back to normal, with production volumes of 13 000 to 14 000 vehicles per day, and another week later production levels were back to pre-fire 15 500 vehicles per day.

Duncan Watts has also analyzed the network effects in use during the recovery process.[2] His conclusion is that this kind of coordination could only partially be designed in a conscious way, and it was not newly developed in this drastically short time frame. The surprising fact was that it was already there, lying dormant in the network of informal relations that had been built up between the firms through years of cooperation and information sharing over routine problem-solving tasks. No one could have predicted precisely how this network would come in handy for this particular problem, but nobody needed to – by giving individual workers fast access to information and resources as they discovered their need for them, the network did its job anyway. The important thing is that the emergency response unit provided the shared situational awareness needed for the appropriate self-organization to take place. The role of such an orchestrating function easily gets too little attention. In the tiered network Toyota was the undisputed leader, but first-tier suppliers in turn orchestrated similar self-organized initiatives for coordination and knowledge sharing within their own supplier bases.

> Based on shared awareness, there was an astonishing collective ability of firms and individuals alike to react quickly and flexibly. The capabilities existing within the network could be identified and deployed thanks to shared experiences and the trust among the individuals, developed through previous socializing and collaborating on unrelated and routine problems. Another important explanatory factor was the informal relationships and the personal process knowledge and understanding that these relationships had engendered.

Other examples of how individuals among themselves develop new capabilities, once the external incentives and the relevant information and resources are available, have also been found in the military field.

CNN showing American soldiers fighting against the Taliban in Afghanistan, riding horses, and using laser-designators, GPS receivers and satellite communication systems to call in precision air strikes, captured the transformation of the army from the industrial society to the knowledge society. This new way to combine traditional warfare with information technology has been called network-centric warfare (NCW). Such an approach is seen to be reshaping the US military doctrine, operations, and acquisition plans.[3]

Orchestration has also become a popular term in information technology itself. So did AT&T, for example, in 1990 introduce a networked computing solution that aimed to increase efficiency and productivity of workgroups by coordinating and automating the flow of work, communication, and information. It was called 'Rhapsody Business Orchestration Solution'.[4] This perspective on orchestration as systems integration – a way to 'orchestrate people, information and processes to solve business problems and achieve business objectives, from defining customer needs, to developing products, to distributing products, to servicing them' – became used more often throughout the 1990s. The notion of 'project manager' was replaced with the notion of 'systems integrator,' as the emphasis shifted from coordination of internal resources to include an increasing amount of external resources to be integrated into the final delivery. It also highlighted the importance of choosing the right systems integrator, the right choice in this regard was seen to be a key success factor for demanding IT projects. Systems integration was thus viewed as a way to tie together technologies to solve business problems. The notion of 'supply chain management' strengthened the shift in focus from an internal to an external perspective.

One description of an orchestrated network used the notion of the strategic center to refer to the orchestrator. Successful companies like Ikea began to orchestrate roles and relationships among a constellation of actors and mobilize the creation of value in new forms and by new players.[5] In this sense orchestration could be seen as the continuous design and redesign of complex business systems. Advances in information and communication technology have later been the main drivers behind the transition towards this new perspective on the firm and its interfaces with the outside world.

It has also been suggested that companies engage in concept research that focuses on optimization and re-optimization of the entire range of variables across commercial relationships to address the question, 'How would we organize affairs among us if we were part of one and the same organization, rather than two or more commercial organizations coming together to carry out a transaction?' It then becomes possible to think in terms of business partners — instead of in terms of suppliers and customers — involved in the co-production of one overall result.[6]

The notion of orchestration has also been used by cognition researchers. Learning involves the engagement of meta-cognitive faculties such as planning, monitoring, evaluating, anticipating, and the regulation and orchestration of cognitive processes (i.e. awareness, attention, and memory).[7] Strategic management of innovative activities can be treated as purposive attempts to orchestrate knowledge development and its application in the firm. The metaphor of the orchestra implies assembling and coordinating the performance of human and instrumental resources.[8]

Combining the above viewpoints the following definition of orchestration can be put forward:

Orchestration is the capability to mobilize and integrate resources for the purpose of providing an offering to a customer and simultaneously create value for the customer, the orchestrator, and the network members involved. The orchestrator considers the constraints, based on which conversations are nurtured, to define and execute the purposeful resource allocation to create, produce, and provide the customer with the offering.

It is worth mentioning that according to our definition of customer and exchange value in Chapter 2 an offering can exist, and provide value without monetary transactions taking place. In this respect, activities undertaken within the open source community can also be perceived as offerings. The mobilization of these activities can correspondingly be categorized as acts of orchestration.

ALTERNATIVE ORCHESTRATION STRATEGIES

In the knowledge society the distinction between customers and suppliers is not as clear-cut as the traditional terminology suggests. In spite of that we will maintain the notion of customers as 'downstream business partners,' and suppliers as 'upstream business partners'. The same actor within a value constellation can perform both an upstream (e.g. subcontractor) and a downstream (e.g. dealer) role, if this company is a multi-business conglomerate. Common to all actors within the value constellation is that they are available as addressable resources in the value-creating process.

A firm matching customer potential with resources in the form of offerings has to evaluate whether it focuses on existing or new customer potential, and whether it predominantly wants to mobilize existing or develop new capabilities for the purpose of creating value. The orchestration effort of the nodal firm is therefore based on an explicit or implicit assumption regarding which operational capability to strengthen. Using the operational capabilities introduced in Chapter 1 we can consequently identify four different orchestration perspectives:

- core solidification (strengthening the core resources of the firm);
- concept crystallization (cooperating in offering design);
- customer collaboration (engaging customers in value co-creation);
- constellation cultivation (reinforcing the value constellation).

The first form, core consolidation, provides the customer with predefined offerings, for which the orchestrator contracts a substantial part of the resource input to subordinates. Such arrangements can, for example, be found in the apparel industry:

> A less sanguine approach to network organizations might be to consider them as hierarchically ordered. In such settings, core firms downsize, retaining their core competencies and the high value-added production components. Highly dependent subcontractors that service the low value-added aspects of production become subordinate to such core firms. Subcontractors in the network are small firms that engage in excessive competition because of their subordinate and dependent position in that hierarchy, because barriers to entry are low and because deregulated labor markets often encourage a wage depressing approach to flexibility. Conversely, other small firms in the network, which

are powerful by virtue of their preferential location in the value chain, have disincentives to acquire specialist contractor firms and vertically integrate because their costs in doing so might exceed their profit gains.[9]

Another option for the orchestrator is to more actively engage in the crystallization of concepts on behalf of its customers. For example, the Italian design firm Alessi acts on behalf of (and in close collaboration with) its customers with an emergent approach to the design, development, and provision of new offerings. Alessi, when serving large retailers, fulfills the offering designer role in relation to the retailer, when the ambition is to find a new best-selling consumer accessory. An offering designer also nurtures its own network of designer, manufacturing, and other partners and uses this to proactively suggest offering designs to its customers. In the same way leading fashion design companies, such as Nike, can be perceived as offering designers.

Another alternative is to aim at continuously expanding and/or strengthening the customer community surrounding the orchestrator. Such an orchestrator looks for possibilities to engage the customers in shared value creation and reap economic gains through fees based on the transaction volumes passing through the orchestrator. Such a strategy could be called customer collaboration. Here Amazon is an example.

The apparel industry has also seen the emergence of firms that do not provide any production function themselves. An often-used illustration of this type is Li & Fung, the Hong Kong-based broker between Asian manufacturers and overseas merchants for transactions in apparel. This form of orchestration can be called constellation cultivation. Such an orchestrator acts as a broker and bundles the necessary resources to provide the customer with the offering. This is the way Li & Fung operates. Another well-known company applying a similar orchestration strategy is Ikea, the leading global furniture and home decoration company, which we will return to in Chapter 16.

Recent writings about orchestration have focused on firms that have selected orchestration as the strategy. What has been missing is the identification of the above-mentioned different roles of the orchestrator. Li & Fung is primarily a constellation cultivator, which is a completely different strategy than the one of Nike being a concept crystallizer or Microsoft a core consolidator. The introduction of the Internet has enabled the emergence of firms focusing on customer collaboration, of which Amazon.com is an example. All these companies have developed strong orchestration capabilities, and, based on these capabilities, have developed a strategy that could be called an 'orchestration strategy'. But the more granular capabilities behind the orchestration capability are quite different when we compare Li & Fung, Microsoft, Nike, and Amazon.com. Therefore this book is interested in the more granular and fine-grained process-forming orchestration capabilities, which then can be used to pursue different orchestration strategies. In the following some of the underlying learning differences behind respective orchestration strategy will be presented.

Constellation cultivation is to a high degree about information brokerage. The role of the orchestrator is to effectively and efficiently configure resources for the purpose of value creation. The prime example of this type of firm is Li & Fung, a $5 billion global consumer products trader acting as a supply chain manager for US and European retailers sourcing high-volume, time-sensitive consumer goods, primarily in Asia. Li & Fung offers comprehensive logistics services and has an extensive network of suppliers in China. It concentrates on soft goods (mainly clothing), but also sources hard goods such as handicrafts, home furnishings, shoes, sporting goods, and toys. Cargo destined for North America accounts for a majority of the company's sales.[10]

Li & Fung manages supply chains for international companies. It does not own any production facilities but instead specializes in offering its customers a one-stop service, ranging from the development of products through sourcing raw materials and managing production all the way to the consolidation of shipping. This asset-light approach is particularly critical in Asia, where currency fluctuations can dramatically alter the value of assets. Li & Fung puts together resources in the form of 'assortment packaging'. Managing dispersed production and supervising manufacturing programs are the major services that Li & Fung provides to discount chains. To provide its assortments Li & Fung has to constantly transmit information back and forth between its customers and the chosen suppliers.

If Li & Fung primarily configures resources based on the requirements of discount chains, Nike in turn is an orchestrator that develops such requirements in the first place. Nike is a company known for the ability to continuously come up with new successful offerings, being a concept crystallizer. Nike is good at sensing and applying the latest trends to create successful fashion. Nike is not selling directly to its end customers, but has developed an impeccable track record for being able to follow, strengthen, and create trends that provide growth opportunities and brand extension. Here the learning effort is much more one of deepening the understanding of a particular application area.

When Amazon.com was launched in 1995 it was heralded for its feel-friendly culture that drew talented young people to apply to work there. Founder and CEO Jeff Bezos insisted on hiring the brightest, most intelligent, and versatile people he could find. He wanted people who could share his vision and were willing to work to achieve it. He tried to establish a sense of community due to sharing both hard work and fun with his employees.

Amazon.com has a business model that combines both cost efficiency and creativity. Cost leadership is pursued by differentiating primarily on the basis of price. Due to this strategy, Amazon.com always makes sure that it offers the same quality products as other companies at a competitive price. The creative part is seen in their way of orchestrating customers as co-producers of value, by actively writing book reviews and making recommendations.

For Amazon.com the way customers are engaged in making book reviews provides a means to create a customer community. Customers become part of the Amazon.com community by contributing reviews. These reviews are carefully vetted by Amazon.com staff to make sure that they are relevant and tastefully done. The result is that customers feel that they can trust one another's recommendations and reactions. In all, Amazon.com tries to leverage social and community opinion making on its site.

The final way of orchestrating for value is by actively using networks to consolidate the core resources of the firm. Here the ecosystem of Microsoft is perhaps the most visible example of a very successful orchestration strategy. It has been estimated that there are more than 30 000 companies that actively participate in the beta testing of Microsoft's new software products. Microsoft has skillfully managed separate developer communities around different products. For example, the Visual Studio Industry Partner program was established in 1999, and in five years it grew to include more than 200 members including companies such as Borland, Compuware, Intel, IBM, Mercury, Oracle, SAP, and Tibco. The developer communities provide work worth hundreds of millions of dollars a year by beta testing and debugging errors in the Microsoft software. Increasingly other technology companies like Oracle and Nokia are actively nurturing their own developer communities to reap similar benefits.

The four orchestration strategies – core consolidation, constellation cultivation, concept cultivation, and customer collaboration – require different types of orchestration skills, and different leadership personalities. The traditional way of perceiving network orchestration is to see it as a performance carried out by a determined nodal actor, a developer community supervisor like Microsoft, a resource aggregator like Li & Fung, an offering designer like Nike, or a community nurturer such as Amazon. But there is also another model appearing, one relying more on just providing the platform for a higher degree of self-organization to take place and resource aggregation to happen without a lot of guidance from the center. The way Linux evolved is one example, and the approach taken by eBay another. But in all these cases the orchestrating principles still apply, the collaborating actors have some shared goals, have accepted some rules for how to collaborate, and are learning continuously during the process of accomplishing the shared mission.

Constellation cultivation without strong central guidance has to be directed somewhat differently than the other forms of orchestration. In such a case creating a shared ethos and motivating the participants based more on values than on the actual offering seems to be the main role of the orchestrator. In this respect Li & Fung is strongly bringing the voice of the customer as the gluing force for its value constellations. For eBay the network is simultaneously both the resource and the customer community. eBay really only provides the facilitation for the self-organized value-creating behavior. To keep the network members accepting that they do all the real value-creating work, and in addition pay a fee to eBay, the role of eBay as an orchestrator is therefore to constantly strengthen the loyalty of the most active community members, as they are the ones driving the community forward. In the same way the Linux community is brought forward by its most active members.

ORCHESTRATING LEADERS

Orchestration capabilities provide the preconditions for operational capabilities to be built and leveraged. But which are the operational capabilities to build? The orchestrating leader has to develop situational awareness to enforce the proper alignment of the capability-building activities with the constantly changing competitive context. This awareness has to be shared and promoted throughout the network. The insights of the leader and the other significant actors have to be actively communicated and debated with the rest of the organization. Awareness is thus a collective property, and the higher level of shared awareness the greater the probability for superior performance.

This need for shared awareness has become one of the key development areas of the US Army. Consequently it has embraced a new doctrine, where situational awareness and network centric thinking are offering totally new views of how collaborative action can substantially increase the efficiency of combat forces. One situation where such shared awareness about the political constraints for a military operation was absolutely crucial was the Kosovo campaign in 1999. General Wesley Clark, Supreme Allied Commander Europe, had to manage the NATO alliance operations, involving the careful orchestration of 19 national policies and 19 legal perspectives, many of which hinged on the nature of targets selected and the risk of collateral casualties. If the secretary of state, Madeleine Albright, was to address an appeal from one foreign minister or another to change the course of the campaign, she needed to understand the campaign. The awareness thus had to be shared on many levels in the command chain.[11]

John Stenbit, US assistant defense secretary for command, control, communications, and intelligence, has argued that network-centric warfare is predicated upon the ability to leverage shared awareness to enable such on-the-fly innovation as the horse-riding space fighters in Afghanistan. They illustrate how tactical forces can innovate in real-world combat to have an immediate impact on advancing issues that might otherwise take years to take hold, if imposed top-down on reluctant organizations.

Four tenets form the foundation of network-centric operations:[12]

- A robust networked force that enhances information sharing.
- Enhanced quality of information and situational awareness that stems from information sharing and collaboration.
- These elements – particularly at the tactical level – enable 'self-synchronization,' leading to sustainability and speed of command.
- Combining all these dramatically increases operational effectiveness. This 'cognitive advantage' allows a networked force to execute the so-called 'OODA loop' faster than an enemy (OODA refers to observing, orienting, deciding, and acting[13]).

These tenets can also be applied outside the military domain, and seem to be generic preconditions for collective creativity to emerge. So the question is not just about 'combat effectiveness' but also about 'capability-building effectiveness'.

The need to continuously build new organizational capabilities forces leaders to relentlessly nurture learning within the firm. But few firms have the luxury to carry out the learning offline. Instead they have to make learning part of the ongoing value-creating business activities. This means that there is a need to orchestrate the interaction with the customers, suppliers, and other constituents to provide valuable learning for all parties continuously.

Learning takes place in diverse forms. Various learning contexts ask for different approaches. When Merrill Lynch decided to make its transformation and become a leading Internet company, the challenge was to transmit its own knowledge to the customer in a user-friendly and efficient way. The customer suddenly could access the existing knowledge repository of Merrill instantly, and at low cost. This will be discussed in more detail in the next chapter.

Another type of learning occurs when solving genuinely new problems. Many companies look to transform themselves into problem solvers. For example, IBM has communicated such a strategy, and we will look into that in Chapter 5. In these cases the customer expects support when exploring uncharted waters. Orchestrating external knowledge into the problem-solving teams is a prerequisite for success.

Not all learning takes place according to strictly predefined scripts, we learn a lot spontaneously as workers, shoppers, or practitioners of various activities. Companies like Apple and Nokia have realized this and have started to stage events for their customers to get involved in co-experiencing such events.

Apple's retail stores are designed to be stores around the customer's life experiences, and Nokia in turn tries to reach out to music fans allowing their Nokia Theatre to bring the worlds of entertainment and mobility closer together. Here the learning is complementary to the shared experience the event provides. The customer is now not just a learner, but also a co-performer on stage. The orchestrator facilitates a live performance where improvisation plays a central role. This is the focus of Chapter 6.

The orchestrator can also engage suppliers and customers in a dialogue. As author James Surowiecki has suggested, the orchestrator taps into the 'wisdom of crowds'. Companies such as eBay, Amazon.com, and Yahoo activate their members to participate in something which could be called future-inventing communities. The orchestrator is here composing on the fly as the emergent process unfolds. A deeper look into this will be taken in Chapter 7.

Orchestrating for learning often doesn't go without challenges. For Merrill Lynch the challenge was how to flexibly and intuitively make its vast knowledge repository available for the customers. This implied a billion-dollar investment in a new information platform, which however caused both delays and internal friction.

When IBM entered the path towards becoming a problem solver it recognized the need to expand its pool of expertise. For example, in the healthcare sector it teamed up with the Mayo Clinic to strengthen the resource base.

Harley-Davidson is a pioneer in staging experiences for its customers, but when Peter Fonda and Dennis Hopper introduced the chopper in the 1969 movie *Easy Rider* it took the company several years to figure out how to turn this into an advantage. Today a large part of the Harley-Davidson motorcycles bought are immediately sent off to a custom detailer, who completely customizes the bike. The unique Harley thus becomes a co-created artifact, where the customer takes the final responsibility for the end product.

To foster communities the orchestrator continuously has to stimulate the dialogue. eBay, eager at keeping its community vibrant and active, decided to pay multi-billion dollars for the two-year old Internet telephone service startup Skype to further enhance the conversations within the eBay community.

All four learning contexts – information transmission, problem solving, co-experiencing, and insight accumulation – have different characteristics. Each also asks for its own orchestration approach. In the following the leadership implications of each of the learning contexts will be introduced. Part IV of the book looks into this in more detail.

The orchestrator as conductor

Esa-Pekka Salonen, the music director of the Los Angeles Philharmonic orchestra, seems to be able to modify his performance to match the audience, the skills of the players, and his own continuing exploration of rhythm, melody, and harmony. This can take place in the context of performing a single piece of music, but also in the much broader sense of revitalizing the interest for music in the Los Angeles area. He has rejected the idea that a conductor can see a symphony orchestra as a kind of blueprint of the Berlin or Vienna Philharmonic just moved into another part of the world. Instead a symphony orchestra has to function in the context of its cultural environment. When the Disney family donated $100 million to build a world-class performance venue, the first thing that went up was a six-level parking garage. That's LA. The car park was completed first, and then people started thinking about what to put on it.

The role of a successful conductor is to apply the orchestration skills both internally when conducting and externally when shaping the context wherein the orchestra can perform. Working around the core, the conductor systematically builds up the performing capacity of the orchestra. The learning is about perfecting the performance. But then there is the complementing task of renewing the program. Here the work is much more about involving the external world. What are the expectations of the audience? The sponsors? Are there interesting guest artists that could be available? In this role the challenge is to come up with new ideas and present a new repertoire that will thrill the audience and make the musicians enthusiastic. Chapter 14 will further discuss the conductor metaphor of leadership.

The orchestrator as architect

The architect is a problem solver working very closely with the external constituents to be able to sense and transform the expectations into a physical artifact. Frank Gehry, the architect most known for the Guggenheim museum in Bilbao, Spain, had close collaboration with both Esa-Pekka Salonen and Diane Disney Miller, the daughter of Walt Disney, when designing the new home of the Los Angeles Philharmonic.

The design of the building started with Mr. Gehry's own ink-on-paper scribbles. He then directed his squad of sorcerer's apprentices in Santa Monica to build scores of models that interpreted and expanded on his sketches. When Mr. Gehry declared himself satisfied, other experts were called in to translate the final models and digital images into two-dimensional plans and working drawings – as well as complex electronic instructions that could be fed to the makers and assemblers of millions of parts. In this work he also engaged a number of external experts that could contribute to the final result, as, for example, Japanese acoustician Yasuhisa Toyota, whose responsibility was to make the hall an acoustic masterpiece.

Gehry's ultimate ambition was to make the building an important icon. It should be an exciting structure that says 'things are happening here'. More about the leader as architect in Chapter 15.

The orchestrator as auctioneer

If a conductor has to exercise control in a very subtle way the almost opposite applies to a good auctioneer. Physically the setting is very much the same: a large hall where one single person is perceived to have full control of the room. But behind this visual similarity we will find two almost contradictory logics of orchestration. The conductor stands with his back towards the audience and his attention is totally devoted to his playing musicians. The auctioneer in turn has to watch the audience to identify the slightest indication of interest in a potential buyer. The auctioneer controls the room, enjoys a lively rapport with the audience, varies the pace and, most important, keeps the audience awake. The very best auctioneers can marry the art of theater with their expertise to drive prices to levels unthinkable beforehand, while the very worst can lose control and forfeit the confidence of the room.

Conductors and auctioneers alike will succeed if they can create a particular spirit among those under their control, the musicians or the auction buyers. But the way they do it differs. The conductor aims for a harmonized performance. The auctioneer in turn will create a momentum that almost hypnotizes the audience and establishes confidence in a market that didn't exist or price levels not yet seen. Whereas the success of the conductor is how well he could mobilize the artists to perform against a predefined target, the auctioneer will be exceptional if he can push the limits of the market far beyond the expected levels. As the conductor looks for coherence, the auctioneer wants to find irregularities and rapidly exploit them to become new de facto standards.

Christopher Burge, honorary chairman of Christie's America, has stated that what makes the auction such good theater is the unpredictability, the mercurial mood of the room. A great auctioneer sustains the thrill and instinctively knows when to alter his pace and when to conjure that one last bid – even when the bidder himself thought he had finished. Chapter 16 will present other auctioneers and their perspectives on what makes a good auction.

The orchestrator as promoter

As Linux grew, its founder Linus Torvalds felt a growing sense of responsibility. He was a poster boy, holder of the Linux trademark and maintainer of the Linux kernel. Millions of people relied on Linux. Community interests versus commercial interests had to be balanced all the time. Torvalds had to hold his ground within the community as someone who could be trusted from both a technology and an ethical standpoint. His responsibility was that the largest collaborative project in the history of humanity was managed effectively. Somebody coined the phrase 'benevolent dictator' to describe how he ran the whole thing.

. In the Linux community a programmer cannot contribute without knowing the context. A transparent architecture providing situational awareness is thus a must for the Linux community to work. This architecture provides guidance and support in a flexible way. Orchestrating for learning is carefully architected, and purposefully executed.

Linus Torvalds can be seen as a promoter, an initiator of a movement that has gained global attention and generated admiration and respect. Torvalds became a leader by default, but in 2004 he was recognized as one of the 25 most influential individuals in the world by *Business Week*. How to lead without really leading is further reflected upon in Chapter 17.

THE ORCHESTRATION ARENA

The leader as an orchestrator can be compared to a professional golfer. The golfer also has to master diverse skills, and there are interesting similarities between the four orchestrating contexts and the challenges facing a golfer.

The foundation of playing golf is the tee shot, the opening shot of the game, where you can put your ball on the tee, and perform against what you have practiced again and again, learnt through accumulated knowledge and playing according to a pre-set plan.

However well a golfer practices, he will occasionally miss the fairway, or green, with the tee shot. This means he will have a trouble shot, perhaps from a bunker or from heavy rough. In this case the problem-solving skills are important.

If the tee shot has been successful on a short hole, then the ball has landed on the green, and the shot to be executed is a putt. The putt is comparable to customer interaction, as the mechanical performance of the putt is only half of the result. It is as important to read the green and take the breaks and grain of the grass into consideration. Like Tom Watson said, the business of putting is 10% mechanics and 90% feel.

The fourth category of a golf shot is the fairway shot. Here the versatility is the largest. The fairway shot can be played quite similarly to the tee shot. But if the fairway shot is to be made from close to the green, it starts to resemble the putt in its nature. So the execution very much depends on the context. The insights accumulated for how to play the shot are decisive for whether execution will be successful or not.

In golf you have to master all four categories of strokes. Similarly, in business you have to be able to orchestrate in different contexts. But in business as in golf, most people have some natural strength. John Daly is a formidable driver from the tee, and Tom Watson is one of the best putters and short game specialists throughout the times. But what golf lately has seen is that the best recipe for success is to be good throughout the whole repertoire of shots, like Tiger Woods.

Leaders taking an orchestration approach are faced with the challenge to play against the competition and master the constantly changing competitive landscape. The leader can think of him- or herself as a professional golfer that is playing a new golf course every day. The cumulative score is what counts. New decisions have to be made shot by shot, hole after hole. Every shot counts. The winner is the one consistently performing, leveraging upon strengths, and adapting and learning as the game proceeds.

Achieving constant high performance is based on a lot of practice and learning. How to learn for different purposes and in different contexts is the focus of the second part of the book.

PART II

LEARNING CONTEXTS

The first part of the book introduced the three major building blocks for leadership in the knowledge society: the different orchestration contexts, the importance of learning, and the four operational capabilities, based on which the actual value creation of a firm takes place.

This second part looks into the intricacies of creativity and learning, and raises the question whether some of those truths that became undisputed basic propositions during the industrial age now have to be rethought. One such unchallenged tenet relates to the distinction between strategy and operations, design and implementation. How to steward the development of the organizational capabilities in a changing world is the most critical responsibility a leader has. Two schools of thought have thus far dominated the strategy literature, both of them somewhat static in their nature.

The first one took its origin from the external world and was pioneered by Michael E. Porter,[1] and has primarily become known as the industrial organization view.[2] According to this approach, the most important task of leadership is to choose the right competitive setting, and within this setting to choose an appropriate strategy: cost leadership, differentiation, or a niche strategy.

The second perspective has been called the resource-based view of the firm. The best known proponents of this perspective are professors Birger Wernerfelt[3] and Jay Barney.[4] Their view is that the firm is the result of its own accumulation of resources, and thus how to leverage upon this unique set of resources is the main responsibility of leadership.

The challenge with both these perspectives is that to become reliable normative practices in management they implicitly require a certain degree of predictability of the future business environment. In the case of the industrial organization view, the key challenge is to know which competitive setting to concentrate on. Similarly, in the resource-based view, organizations always have more available resource development alternatives than they can afford to pursue. Which resource bundles to bring forward has to be based on some, implicit or explicit, estimate of the future value of the different resource bundles.

It is relevant to state that both the industrial organization view and the resource-based view are appropriate frameworks for strategic decision making in certain contexts. If the competitive landscape is changing due to, for example, deregulation, then an industrial perspective is a useful and relevant approach. A major utility in Europe facing the deregulation of the energy market will be served by thinking about industrial analysis and strategic positioning.

In the same way, companies like Ikea, which have developed a unique set of resources and capabilities, will benefit from considering how the resource base can be protected, and how to develop these resources to keep them valuable, rare, and inimitable. Ikea has established its industrial position as the leading global player in home interior and furnishing. The challenge is, of course, how to leverage and build upon the past success.

An increasing amount of organizations are facing the dilemma the US Army had in the 1990s, when the breakdown of the Soviet Union meant that the main reason for existence disappeared. This, in effect, is happening for many firms seeing their industry move from the industrial society to the knowledge society. They must access the value of their existing resources, and must also determine how sustainable they will be when the competitive context changes. During such highly turbulent periods it is difficult to rely on either industrial analysis or resource development projections. So what to do?

De Geus stated that when organizations are facing discontinuity and truly have to learn, they depend on the ability of the senior managers to absorb what is going on in the business environment and to act on that information with appropriate business moves. Another observation by de Geus was that radically changing external conditions requires a learning process. This process is likely to go through a number of iterations, during which the management team's original mental model or dominating ideas will change considerably. De Geus continued that the only competitive advantage the company of the future will have is its managers' ability to learn faster than their competitors. The companies that succeed will be those that continually nudge their managers towards revising their views of the world.[5]

This statement poses an interesting opening for thinking about how to manage in the knowledge society. If matching the future market potential (the industrial context) with our own capabilities (the firm resources) is the key challenge, this matching process is ultimately a learning process. Can we then be better guided by not trying to concentrate on either the industrial context or the resource base, but instead try to better understand the logic of the matching process? The proposition of this book is that this perspective could truly be an option to consider, and this second part of the book will take a look into that specific area. Is it plausible that organizations facing genuine uncertainty should focus on how they best can adapt by using their natural learning style and creativity to guide them through periods of genuine uncertainty?

Originally research on creativity was very much focused on creative individuals.[6] Creative processes are indeed dependent not only on having creative individuals, but also on having the social context favorable to handle the creative task at hand. Professor Teresa Amabile of Harvard Business School suggests that all humans with normal capacities are able to produce at least moderately creative work in some domain, some of the time − and that the social environment (the work environment) can influence both the level and the frequency of creative behavior. She has defined creativity as follows:

Creativity is the production of novel ideas that are useful and appropriate to the situation.[7]

Research has indicated that highly creative individuals say the most important characteristics that set them apart are curiosity and drive. These traits can be described as 'the yin and the yang' of creative work. Curiosity is open and playful, while drive is serious, competitive, and achievement-oriented. Both are required for creativity to become actualized. Creativity is usually also associated with originality. But in business, originality isn't enough. To be creative, an idea must also be appropriate − useful and actionable. It must somehow influence the way business gets done − by improving a product, for instance, or by opening up a new way to approach a process. We need disciplined creativity.

There also seems to be strong support for a view that creativity in business to a large extent is based on expertise. Such expertise can be viewed as the set of cognitive pathways that may be followed for solving a given problem or doing a given task – the expert's 'network of possible wanderings'. The expertise component includes memory for factual knowledge, technical proficiency, and special talents in the target work domain.

A challenge from an organizational point of view is the impact of rewards and time pressure on creativity. Professor Amabile and her colleagues propose that when creativity is under the gun, it usually ends up getting killed. Although time pressure may drive people to work more and get more done, and may even make them feel more creative, it may cause them to think less creatively. But they admit that such a short answer is not the whole story and present examples such as the *Apollo 13*'s flight to the moon as an example where creativity seemed to be sparked by extreme time pressure.[8]

Employees with high scores in creativity tests produce highly creative outcomes only when they are surrounded by a context that facilitates their creativity. Such a context is one that provides complex jobs under supportive, yet non-controlling, supervisors. These conditions seem to allow employees with generally creative personalities the freedom to focus simultaneously on multiple dimensions of their work, by providing them opportunities to voice concerns and receive plenty of positive, constructive feedback and to work without too many external controls or constraints. These employees can thereby take advantage of their creative potential. In contrast, when employees with generally creative personalities work under conditions that lack one of these contextual features, their creativity is reduced. Simple jobs and controlling, nonsupportive supervisors seem to inhibit the expression of their attraction to complexity, tolerance of ambiguity, intuition, and self-confidence.

Recognizing that creativity doesn't come in one standardized form means that the leader in the knowledge society has to be sensitive and attuned to what is the appropriate learning approach to embrace in different situations. The four different learning contexts within organizations introduced in Chapter 3 can each have their appropriate usage. However, using these different learning contexts as a basis one could also suggest that it is plausible that organizations have a learning ethos, i.e. a learning style, which is the byproduct of its evolution towards what it has become. This would then suggest that when the organization has to cope with a new challenge, intuitively the collective behavior will follow an established learning pattern, which has been ingrained into the organization historically. Whether this is positive or negative depends on the situation.

The four learning contexts – information transmission, problem solving, experience provision, and insight accumulation – are all further discussed in this part of the book.

Chapter 4 shows how two organizations, Merrill Lynch and Nokia, facing the Internet whirl of the 1990s acted in the face of this new situation. For Merrill Lynch the Internet was a serious threat against its existing business model. Experts predicted that it would not be able to compete against smaller and more nimble competitors. Nokia in turn was the darling of the stock market. It was expected that the Internet would provide even more possibilities. Jorma Ollila was on the front cover of *Wired* magazine in September 1999 and his vision was expressed as 'Put the Net in Your Pocket'. How the two companies succeeded with their Internet strategies was quite surprising. Retrospectively, the right strategy for each of these companies was to build around their existing strengths and apply an information transmission learning strategy.

Different scenarios are depicted in Chapter 5. Here the organizations do not cling to their strongholds as Merrill Lynch and Nokia did. Instead they decide to exploit the opportunity to service customers looking for creative solutions to their problems. To exemplify this we will examine the case of ownership shift in Nautor, the producer of Swan yachts, and IBM's new strategy of focusing on solutions. In the knowledge society companies also have to be able to solve their customers' problems on top of providing the product. How to instigate a problem-solving mentality into the organization and the surrounding network is the subject of Chapter 5.

Common for learning strategies for both information transmission and problem solving is that what to learn is in some way recognized at the outset of the learning journey. Surprisingly, often the most beneficial outcome of a learning experience is when it produces something which was not originally expected but, when retrospectively considered, is highly valuable. In Chapter 6 this learning approach will be investigated in more detail. Such learning cannot in the same way be guided by any pre-set objective. Still it can become a very important complementary part of the overall learning strategy of the organization. If the industrial society was first and foremost about rationality, facts, and functionality, the knowledge society is more shaped by opinions, feelings, emotions, and experiences.[9] This suggests that customers and suppliers should be seen as members in a co-experiencing value constellation. This puts new requirements on management. The Karl Lagerfeld 2004 fall collection for H&M is a case in point and the way Apple revolutionized the music industry with the iPod another.

In Chapter 7 we will discuss how to facilitate emergent learning in networks and motivate individuals even when the end state cannot be explicated. Here the involved individuals' accumulation of insights form the intellectual fuel, based on which the community can move forward. The open source community around the Linux operating system is used as an illustration of a collective learning process. Linux has emerged without both strong direction in respect of its content and pre-defined timelines against which it would have been directed. Another illustration of the same phenomenon is the leadership philosophy adopted by Bill Bratton when fighting crime in New York City.

In the final chapter of Part II transitional objects will be introduced as a means to speed up learning. The different requirements on transitional objects for the four learning contexts will be laid out in some detail.

CHAPTER 4

INFORMATION ACQUISITION

This chapter will view the knowledge society through the lens of established players. With examples it will show how information technology often is not sufficient to permanently change competitive positions. However, technology can become a means to strengthen competitiveness when it is mobilized to enhance existing strong capabilities. Then an established player can cement its position and make it even more difficult for the competition to find inroads to the market once conquered.

Often, efforts related to the use of information technology to support learning concentrate on information transmission. The use of computers and common databases can provide support for learning, especially the acquisition of explicit knowledge created by somebody else. In addition, it is also important to have a complementary human-centered process to get the full benefits of the investment in digitized information repositories. Most of the solutions relating to how one can use computer systems, databases, and applications to support learning emphasize individual learning. A key advantage of such solutions is that they can take into consideration different individual learning patterns. However, the slower than originally expected expansion of e-learning seems to reveal that the way information acquisition can be effectively facilitated through purely human–machine interaction is facing some barriers. In the following, two cases will be used to illustrate the challenges related to this.

Merrill Lynch: Slashing Prices by 90% – and Winning!

On June 1, 1999, Merrill Lynch stunned the brokerage industry – not to mention its own investors – by announcing that it would let its retail customers choose how to buy or sell stock. One of the options was to make the trade on Merrill's website and pay $29.95. The price for a typical $10 000 transaction, when the order had been placed with a Merrill Lynch financial consultant paying standard commission, had been $250. Within two days of the announcement, Merrill shares had tumbled 16%, erasing $5 billion in market value.

Merrill Lynch had virtually invented the full-service, full-commission brokerage business. It had historically been a market maker by creating a new retail brokerage business model that had proved extremely successful. Now it faced the threat of new competition, invaders that aimed at making Merrill Lynch's business model obsolete. Suddenly it had to change from being a market maker to a follower.

Before the announcement the press had hailed Charles Schwab as the most successful financial services company in responding to the impact of the Internet.[1] It was predicted that it would be very difficult for Merrill to go after online trading, because it would attack their own main business of handling customers through brokers.

Originally Merrill Lynch vice chairman John Steffens had dismissed Internet trading as a 'terrible threat to Americans' financial lives'. But as Schwab's market capitalization passed that of Merrill Lynch on December 28, 1998, Steffens had already started to prepare Merrill for the greatest strategic change, since his 1984 white paper on the concept of asset gathering, or attracting a customer's assets to one institution. This concept had paved the way for Merrill to become the market leader in financial brokerage.[2]

Merrill's top management realized that the Internet had permanently changed the competition in its retail business. Retail clients could now buy and sell securities at almost the same price as the brokers, and they were not tied to the broker to get to the market. The moment of truth came at a 1999 March meeting of Merrill's executive committee.

Merrill decided to not just follow the trend, but to make a total commitment to embrace the Internet technology as a means to regain its position as a leading actor in the financial services industry. It started to build an institutional portal that was an array of websites designed for use by corporate clients. It offered its institutional clients the possibility to track their holdings and buy and sell a wide variety of stocks, bonds, futures, and options with the click of a mouse. The system was an electronic replica of Merrill's global capital markets businesses. The ambition was that all the things Merrill's own professionals could do, could and should be done electronically by the clients themselves.

Building an institutional portal was a bold strategy. It could have cannibalized Merrill's existing business; but the move also provided the possibility that Merrill would get the first-mover advantage in the important institutional market. The strategy was everything that Merrill had not been on the retail side of its business, where its decision to enter the

Internet was two years behind its most important competitors – Schwab being the most notable one.

On December 1, 1999, the online retail trading service, Merrill Lynch Direct, was launched. This was a head-to-head competitive move against Charles Schwab, allowing people to trade electronically across the Internet at $29.95 per transaction. The launch was accompanied by a press release stating that Merrill Lynch Direct combined content, intelligence, and innovation to create the smartest place for the self-directed client to invest online. Merrill Lynch Direct was positioned to complement, and not to replace, the value of professional advice and guidance provided by the Merrill Lynch Financial Consultants. The intent was to make it easy for clients to link Merrill Lynch Direct with multiple Merrill Lynch accounts.

The stakes were staggering. At risk was everything from the legacies and careers of Merrill's executives to the firm's ability to stay out of the arms of suitors such as Chase Manhattan Bank. At the heart of the battle was Merrill's fight to remain king of the financial hill.

The biggest challenge was to change the company culture, the Merrill ethos. It had to expunge its image as a Luddite[3] firm. And it had to change from a high-cost bureaucracy to a tech-savvy, change-friendly, flat organization operating on considerably lower margins. But at the same time the respect for research should be maintained.

The reason why Merrill had not moved earlier was that it had become too occupied with its own legacy. Its own internal regime had become a core rigidity.[4] Merrill, like other Wall Street firms, required all of its employees to have their brokerage accounts exclusively with Merrill. The reason was that it was easier to track insider trading if employees could only trade with their employer. The downside was that for all Merrill staff they didn't really personally know what was going on in the Internet world.

But the Internet also had its upside. Good brokers could still continue to earn their keep by offering good stock ideas or helping pick mutual funds or doing financial planning. Yet many were overpaid order-takers who were not really adding value. This was now revealed by the Internet. In this respect it increased transparency and sharpened focus.

The new Merrill Lynch strategy worked brilliantly. By combining strong advertising and aggressively using its financial strengths Merrill Lynch was able to recover its sales initiative by this new strategy and regained its position as the undisputed number one in its market segment. It also used the change to streamline its operations, and in spite of considerable growth, in 2003 the number of brokers had been reduced to 14 000 from 17 000 in 1999.

When the Internet bubble burst and the market turned bearish Schwab floundered. As customers stopped trading, Schwab's commission revenue evaporated – and it gradually became clear that the company was in a very tough place. It was being squeezed from both ends of the brokerage market, from the full-service firms like Merrill Lynch on one end and the deep online discounters like Ameritrade on the other. In July 2004 its once hailed CEO David Pottruck had to go, as the stock had declined to less than $10 compared to $60 at its peak during spring 2000. By the end of May 2004 the market capitalization of Charles Schwab was $13.4 billion compared to Merrill Lynch's $54.6 billion.

What the battle between Schwab and Merrill Lynch showed was that the existing capabilities of Merrill Lynch, based on its history dating back to 1914, represented high leveragability. This asset could be realigned with the new demands of the market. Merrill Lynch's strength was its long-term relationships with the customers handled by its commissioned brokers, the financial consultants. Once the Internet frenzy had calmed down the financial services market started to reappreciate the value of real-world relationships in addition to efficient and flexible virtual services. By building on its strengths Merrill Lynch was able not only to fight back, but also to reposition itself as a leader in its field. By effectively using its commissioned broker network and external resources to build its technology platform it could consolidate around its strong core, world-class research delivered personally to the customers.

What new technology enabled Merrill Lynch to do was to provide its brokers with much more information in order to further improve the quality of advice to the customers. For the most demanding retail customers, this was extremely important. The mapping technology supporting the broker's workstation presented data with size, value (through colors), and hierarchy and allowed users to click on and call up specific data sets from the map. The software allowed users to build dynamic, interactive, three-dimensional treetops from hierarchical company financial reports, share them with users via the Internet, and integrate them into existing applications.

The burst of the Internet bubble revealed that the number of users, or traditional 'market share' was not an appropriate measure of the strength of a business. E-Trade, the darling of the early Internet hype, could present impressive growth figures in respect of how many customers it had signed up. But its $17 500 average customer balance paled next to Schwab's $106 000 and Merrill Lynch's $180 000. For E-Trade it proved utterly difficult to increase the balance of its existing customers, because many of them did as a matter of fact not have that much to spend anyway. And to break into the customer base of Schwab and Merrill Lynch was easier said than done, because their customers were used to complementing the virtual services with support from their personal advisers. Instead, Merrill decided to move even further upscale. The strategy was to focus on $1 million plus accounts. This represented a move from more of a broker business to an adviser business. And at the same time costs were slashed vigorously. Between 2000 and 2001 Merrill cut 20% of its employees, and in 2004 it announced that its annual revenue per broker was $712 000 compared to, for example, Morgan Stanley standing at $451 000.[5]

SECURING SEAMLESS INFORMATION TRANSMISSION

Merrill Lynch identified the wealthy consumers as its primary targets. In this segment its financial consultants were also of most value. The focal point of Merrill Lynch's strategy became the broker's workstation. Byron Vielehr, technology officer of Merrill Lynch Private Client Group, became the architect that had to make sure that Merrill would make a true shift from the traditional sales approach into one of having the broker and the client genuinely co-produce value. Access to information would be paramount during these co-productive dialogues.

In 2002, Merrill signed a $1 billion, five-year deal with Thomson Financial to outsource its broker workstations. Thomson Financial is a provider of information and technology solutions to the financial community.

Merrill combined outsourcing and the concept of best of breed. Thomson acted as a partner and a general contractor. The expectation of Merrill was that Thomson would provide not only content, as that alone was seen as a fungible commodity, but they had to provide more value-added services. The idea was to create a next-generation operating model, to focus on Merrill's core resources, while partnering with best-in-class providers for other products and services. Commercial partnerships were seen to enable the sharing of development costs. So the Thomson deal was seen to represent significant savings for Merrill in addition to a dramatically improved retail platform for financial advisers over its previous proprietary platform.

The need for improved information transmission was a consequence of the broker/dealer having become more of a customer-oriented financial adviser, ultimately changing their data needs. Previously, these brokers/dealers may have had a telephone and quote screen on their desks but that primitive technology was not sufficient in the constantly changing economic climate. They needed a much more sophisticated set of tools. Those market-data providers that could create platforms including CRM and other tools, like Thomson, thus could step in and become collaborative partners for the financial services providers needing more comprehensive solutions.

The need for seamless information flows to support the broker asked for centralized and consistent data services. It was necessary to receive, store, and access information in a consistent way and to have a centralized information repository that could serve as many needs as feasible, and as cost-efficiently as possible. But cost discussions were less on the cost of data and more around the rising cost of making that data usable. What was spent on data was dwarfed by what had to be spent to implement that data. How to make information accessible and easily integrated into applications became much more of a problem. This, in part, led to a trend towards open solutions as opposed to proprietary technology, which could be difficult to integrate with third-party applications. So firms and institutions started to look to their preferred information provider to provide a broader range of information services. They were moving more toward tailored solutions, but in a very cost-effective manner. Merrill Lynch led the pack and became Wall Street's number one proponent of open standards, embracing such emerging technologies as Linux and web services. It had to look for possibilities to seamlessly connect applications without expensive and proprietary middleware. Partnerships with world-class providers at the infrastructure level, at the application level, and at the services layer were at the core of the technology strategy.

This also put new requirements on market-data vendors, such as Thomson and Reuters. Historically market-data people concentrated solely on real-time market data and were not particularly active in partnering with others parts of their clients' organization to identify what other content needed to be on the desktop. To an increasing degree they now had to understand how applications were used across the firms they were serving. They had to start serving multiple applications across the firm, and to develop a greater understanding of the content that the vendor was offering and match that to user needs.

But the vision of seamless information to the broker proved to be quite a challenge to implement. The original plan was to roll the whole suite in one go. The information on the website and desktop was to come through a single middle tier at Merrill Lynch facilitating the ability to collaborate. But due to considerable problems with the implementation it was decided in late 2003 to first roll out only the online aspects and postpone the desktop rollout.

The strategy to provide its brokers with constant access to relevant information proved to become a catch-up game. It was necessary to have the technology to be able to compete, but ultimately the trick was to obtain the technology at the lowest possible cost, because all competitors ended up having the same technological support available. But the core remained the same: the intimate, trustworthy advisory relationships that Merrill Lynch had built up with its customers over the decades. Orchestrating around this was the way to stay competitive. This meant using information even more efficiently, both to support the financial adviser, and to enable the customer to take a more active role in the orchestrated information-sharing relationship. In doing this Merrill Lynch had one significant advantage compared to many of its competitors: advice was a big part of the heritage.

Nokia: Building a Billion Business Portal – and Failing

Almost simultaneously with the decision of Merrill Lynch to completely overhaul its business model in response to the competition posed by online brokers such as Charles Schwab, Nokia also looked to the Internet as a source for additional growth and revenues.

Club Nokia had been set up in the mid-1990s as a website to provide detailed product information on Nokia cell phones and accessories, PCS wireless data products, and Nokia monitors. With the website, Nokia wanted to create a destination where people would come to learn more about Nokia products they already owned or were considering for purchase.

In the beginning of 1999 Nokia management started to look at the potential of Club Nokia becoming an integral part of the Nokia strategy to 'Put the Net in Your Pocket'. In June 1999 Nokia management was evaluating different options for how to further develop Club Nokia. Four alternatives were identified:

- Seeing Club Nokia as a channel to push products and services into the market – being a support tool providing product presentations and contact information.
- Positioning Club Nokia as a commercial portal offering products and services for sale in addition to providing product information etc.
- Developing Club Nokia into a transactional platform providing a wide range of product and services at very competitive costs.
- Building Club Nokia into a community portal based on interactive relationships between Nokia and individual end customers and customer groups. eBay was used here as a benchmark.

The recommendation in the presentation was to seriously evaluate the community portal alternative. For different reasons Nokia, however, decided to position Club Nokia as a multi-channel service including WAP, WWW, and SMS access with personalization as a key feature. Nokia wanted to focus on terminal enhancing and complementary services such as ring tones.

In spring 2001 Nokia lifted its profile regarding Club Nokia, and it was announced that the role of Club Nokia was first of all a customer loyalty tool, but it was also positioned as a business of its own. Club Nokia offered exclusive services to owners of Nokia cell phones in the Europe and Africa region. Proprietary Club Nokia web and WAP services could be accessed once the Nokia phone was registered with Club Nokia. Nokia's chairman and chief executive Jorma Ollila expected Nokia to sign Club Nokia billing agreements with more than 50 operators by the end of the year.[6]

In November 2001 10 million customers had signed up as Club Nokia members, and Nokia was aiming to increase that number to 50 million by 2004. The forecast was that Club Nokia would yield €1 billion in revenue in 2004. Such statements were starting to create counter reactions. In December 2001 *Mobile Telecommunications* wrote that Nokia was trying to do what Microsoft did in the computer world: establish open standards and a common platform, encourage a community of developers to produce applications and services, cherry-pick the best ones, and then integrate these into Nokia's offering.

In recognition of its waning popularity with the operator community, Nokia decided in September 2004 to discontinue its ring-tone business and canned Club Nokia in the format it had set forth four years earlier – canceling the initiative it had designed to generate a €1 billion source of revenue. It even joined the GSM Association, a step it had always resisted, keen to be seen as a willing partner to collaborate with the operators.

Nokia commented that it had decided to focus on handset manufacturing and would leave the provision of mobile content to the operators through their individual branded services, such as Vodafone Live!, T-Zones, Orange World, and O2 Active. But Club Nokia was still maintained as a way for consumers to resolve guarantee and warranty issues. Nokia also informed that it would continue to promote the Club Nokia brand as a customer loyalty venture.

The resistance from network operators who feared the handset maker was trying to compete for user revenues made Nokia take the decision to stop the service. Commercially, the decision was not difficult to make, as Club Nokia never became a major source of revenues. One industry observer noticed that the decision expressed Nokia's more flexible content strategy and denoted a humbler Finnish vendor.

When comparing the tactics of eBay and Nokia regarding how they have approached the challenge of building a customer community some key observations stand out. Firstly, eBay has been able to convince its community members that the evolution is driven by the eBay community, not by eBay the company. In the case of Nokia it was the company that tried to develop a more sophisticated business model to sell products and services. Secondly, the eBay community ethos is deeply engrained in the culture of the orchestrating company, and even personified in the CEO and the leading executives. Statements from Nokia were primarily directed to the financial markets and to the operators. Thirdly, eBay has created ways to separate different types of community members, and provide tangible incentives to really important ones, i.e. the 'power sellers,' the most active and reputable merchants. Fourthly, eBay has been able to institutionalize a fair process,[7] based on its feedback system. After each transaction, buyers and sellers get to rate each other. In that way every eBay member builds a reputation. Beside every member's auction ID is their feedback score. This feedback system is an attempt to secure good conduct in a community of self-interested individuals who may have short-term incentives to cheat one another. In the case of Club Nokia neither incentives for the most important community members nor any feedback system were put in place.

RECOUPING INVESTMENTS BY SHIFTING FOCUS FROM CONSUMERS TO CARRIERS

Nokia's lackluster performance in respect of Club Nokia showed the difficulty of Nokia in addressing the consumer market directly, as its roots were still very much in having a close relationship with the operators. This was dated back to the 1970s when Nokia had started the development of the first-generation analog mobile telephony standard called NMT, based on which it so successfully moved into becoming the market leader for 2G GSM.

It was therefore no surprise that at the same time as Nokia announced its withdrawal from aggressively pursuing its own direct penetration of the consumer market, it also announced that it was stepping up its services to the operators. This meant using some of the investments poured into Club Nokia to launch a new service, Preminet, a service to distribute certified Java- and Symbian-based mobile software. The ambition was that this should make it easier to sell, distribute, and buy cell-phone applications.

At the heart of Preminet, which had been in beta test with a number of carriers, was a master catalog of certified applications. Developers could get their applications into the catalog through a process that included relatively inexpensive certification testing.[8]

Cell-phone operators would access Preminet in the form of a Nokia-hosted service that, according to Nokia, could easily integrate into their existing delivery mechanisms including authentication and billing systems. Also available was a carrier-brandable, client-side, catalog-shopping application.

Developers would be able to submit their applications for certification using existing Nokia laboratories worldwide. For the past two years, rival Qualcomm had offered a similar system to certify and deliver BREW-based applications to operators offering its line of cell phones, with apparent success. The Nokia Preminet system, in contrast to the BREW model, was 'open' in that it supported third-party catalogs available from operators, so it could sit next to the carrier's other discovery mechanisms. BREW's rigorous application certification process for developers was also more expensive, at several thousand dollars per application, with Nokia's certification being one-tenth of that.

When launching the service Nokia already had in place a 'premier' catalog of several hundred certified applications, most of which were from members of its Forum Nokia Pro developers, and others of which were from software aggregators and publishers. Preminet thus started with 300 to 500 core content items. The setting of prices and carrier–developer revenue splits took place in the master catalog. Retailers and content providers retained the ability to negotiate individual prices.

This approach by Nokia was a gradual deviation from its once chosen strategy to minimize outsourcing (the ambition has been to keep it between 10% and 20% of handset sales). The in-house focus had enabled Nokia to establish the lowest-cost manufacturing in the mobile handset world. Managing the supply chain better than anybody else enabled Nokia to outperform competition both on efficiency and creativity for a number of years. Not until late 2003 did this change. Nokia was still the indisputable leader in efficiency, but started to be seriously challenged in respect of leadership in creativity and innovation.

The supply-chain efficiency paradigm of Nokia was based on integrating sales, manufacturing, and sourcing by an efficient information hub in the form of a single SAP instance covering the whole corporation. When design and R&D were at the early stages of creating a new panel, say, sourcing and manufacturing started figuring out how to supply the components and configure the production line, feeding information back to the designers on ways to create the same effect at lower cost. Critical to this approach was transparency of information between Nokia and its major suppliers. Nokia informed its vendors early whenever it altered demand estimates based on the latest retail results and consumer trends.

What was particular to Nokia was that already in the mid-1990s it became evident that the company would have to be able to cope with extremely large volumes of material items, and annual forecasted numbers reaching to tens of billions per year, more than any existing electronic device type ever. To handle this task Nokia Mobile Phones started to work on the unification of logistics operational and planning processes. As product life cycles shortened and the product range expanded it became evident that the whole life cycle of logistics aspects connected to new products had to be prepared together with the product itself. The logistics operations were defined to be like a transparent global pipe, where all material and product needs and availability were simultaneously known. The approach was to streamline the internal operations first, and only thereafter expand integration in the supply chain. An important decision was to introduce a concept called service classes.

Customers were classified in groups with their respective delivery needs, mainly as to delivery lot size, lead time, and punctuality. The purpose of the classification was to offer to each customer group the level of logistics performance and services, which would conform to the requirements of each group. In general the purpose was to optimize those logistics performance factors which would best support customers in their logistic efficiency. Corresponding categorizations were made for material suppliers as well. The ultimate goal was to improve logistics efficiency. The main identified efficiency drivers were asset performance, logistics costs, delivery performance, and flexibility.

The new operational mode required completely new functionality from the information systems. The systems had to serve global business operations through the time zones and languages nonstop, and practically without any breaks. Transparency requirements included company-wide, real-time access to product, customer, supplier and assets master data and data connected to these, such as order backlog, materials, costs, timing, product trace, quality and performance data. Information technology services were completely renewed and thousands of people had to change the way they worked to use the new tools. By mid-1999 the implementation of the transparent pipe strategy was completed.

Markku Rajaniemi, chief architect of Nokia System Landscape, noticed that Nokia used several application platforms in its business operations. However, it still needed true business process integration and efficient internal external collaboration. Efficiently managed vendor–customer and product–master-data was defined as a necessity for true business orchestration and collaboration. Rajaniemi saw orchestration of the supply chain as the natural following step once internal operations were streamlined. The benefits of the orchestration of the supply chain were classified in the groups of business speed, cost savings, and quality improvements in the functioning of interorganizational processes. To reap these benefits it was necessary to coordinate the logistics plans of the supply chain partners. The orchestration of the supply chain basically meant that the same transparent pipeline with the accompanying information system was opened up to the suppliers as well. The means of getting the supply chain parties working in a synchronized manner were largely the same that earlier had been applied internally within Nokia.[9]

Information transmission, or knowledge transfer, was an important form of learning in logistics. Club Nokia in turn was aimed at a totally new set of customers: end-customers or consumers. These consumers had completely different needs and requirements than the operators, whom Nokia had successfully served for decades. The team in charge of Club Nokia applied the familiar information transmission logic, and used existing knowledge. Through extensive interaction with leading Internet experts in the United States, they rejected the proposal suggesting a joint problem-solving strategy together with the customers. This would have implied a more emergent strategy in the form of an action learning process within the growing community. Such a problem-solving approach was in conflict with the information transmission ethos of Nokia. The information transmission ethos was strongly embedded in Nokia, and had brought Nokia into the number one position in cell phones. In retrospect it was hardly surprising that the Club Nokia concept did not succeed. The learning needed to build a community-based service was totally different from the existing learning culture. On the other hand the engineering-based information transmission culture was a prerequisite to build the superb logistics machine developed by Nokia. But this superb capability can also run the risk of becoming a rigidity, if it starts to stifle the design process.

When Nokia in 2003 was riding on the peak of its growth wave it had integrated the whole design and planning process with the efficiency objectives of the logistics. Retrospectively it proved that the focus had shifted too much in favor of the efficiency aspects of the business model. The wakening came when Nokia missed the clam-shell trend. Another factor was that Nokia was seen to have become too insensitive to its primary constituent, the operator. This clash was most notably illustrated in the relationship between Vodafone and Nokia. Subsequently Nokia had to seriously reconsider some of its strategic tenets. By late

2004 it looked like Nokia had decided to refocus on its core: providing operators with superb support, and relying on its own capabilities to fend off potential threats from invaders from Asia. The situation resembled to a large extent the conclusions made by Merrill Lynch management in early 1999. In the end technology will not alone decide the ultimate outcome, but wisely used technology can be an important ingredient in further strengthening the core. For Nokia the supremacy in serving telecom operators and handling the most complex supply chain in the world was the solid foundation from which it decided to move ahead.

LEADERSHIP IMPLICATIONS – THE VALUE OF AN ORCHESTRATION PLATFORM

Merrill Lynch Direct and the logistics collaboration of Nokia both used shared open information platforms to engage the external world in collaborative actions. In both cases content production was actively supported by internal operational processes of the respective company: by the financial consultants in Merrill Lynch, and by the supply chain managers at Nokia. These information platforms increased shared learning and creativity through active information transmission across organizations. The information platforms could be called orchestration platforms, tools to stimulate and intensify collaboration in networks.

The orchestration platform can improve the integration of the transparent information-sharing process with the other processes of the firm. It can also speed up and simplify the production of the information content both for the employees and the external collaboration partners. For Merrill Lynch this succeeded naturally as the financial consultants had already worked with such information. The same applied to the logistics information of Nokia. But when Nokia tried to start to engage consumers it had no existing process to fall back upon, and it was not prepared to actively stimulate the consumers to become engaged in the content provision process, in the same way that eBay did.

The first task when designing the orchestration platform is to specify the value-creating activities to be supported by the platform. For Merrill Lynch it was the financial services offered to its institutional clients, for Nokia it was the integrated supply chain whereby it could improve efficiency in its handling with its suppliers. One practical way to define the information content of the orchestration platform is by using the graphical representation of the value constellation as the basis when designing the orchestration platform. Using the auction house business introduced in Chapter 1 the design of the platform to support the auction business could, for example, be something like that suggested in Figure 4.1.

The design of the information architecture has to begin with the understanding of the information universe, which is relevant for the organization in question. For the auction house the

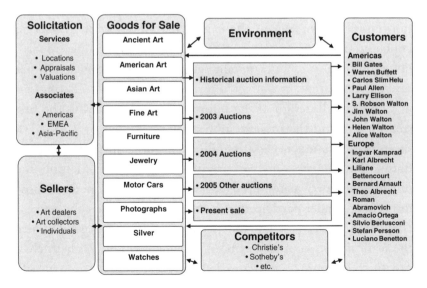

Figure 4.1 The orchestration platform of an auction house: illustration

analysis of the three-dimensional offering revealed that at least the following areas have to be monitored:

- the goods for sale;
- the expectations of the sellers;
- the price limits;
- how previous auctions have done;
- the results achieved by other recent competing auctions;
- the strength of demand in different geographical markets;
- the rumors about customers eager to grab some of the most valuable trophies on sale;
- the most loyal buyers in the recent past;
- small talk that has taken place during the pre-auction viewing;
- what has been reported by the other members of the sales and solicitation teams; and
- what is the overall sentiment that emerges from all this.

Figure 4.1 structures the 'big picture' and relevant information entities according to the value-creating logic of an auction company. In addition the architecture gives possibilities to drill down into specific information sets whenever more details are needed.

The overall design of the information architecture is the first step for making the orchestration platform a successful tool. All subsections are not necessarily addressed in detail right from the outset, but the content can be gradually built up letting the stakeholders participate in the enriching of the information repository. Stakeholder participation is exactly what makes the orchestration platforms of eBay and Amazon.com so successful. Once the critical base content has been provided, the users themselves can further improve and complement the content, to genuinely provide a means for collaboration and engagement, and support the orchestrator with their own creative input. The collective design and implementation also constitutes an action learning process, and this involves the participants in a joint learning experience. Simultaneously it strengthens the sense of belonging to an important group that is bringing the company forward.

What is essential in the initial stage of planning is to start from the market and customers. In Figure 4.1, the top billionaires of the 2005 Forbes list are used as illustrations to underline the importance of being able to cover the full spectrum from the overall strategic context to the detail of the individual customer, who ultimately brings in the revenues.

By combining both quantitative and qualitative information the platform expands the versatility of usage. A well-functioning orchestration platform thus supports both operational efficiency and provides relevant background information for creative sessions. Once the organization is confident with the data quality and the ability of the organization to constantly update the information, the next step is to consider how the information can be used to strengthen supplier and customer relationships.

A big design challenge is how to make compromises between the great amount of numerical information available from the auction and the need to create a customized set of information that is easy to understand and provides flexible opportunities to further drill down into details. Here the information architect has to work closely with the management and possibly even involve trusted external stakeholders to be able to make the right trade-offs. Designing a good orchestration platform is as much an art as the orchestration activity itself.

Both the auction business and the monitoring and management of an integrated supply chain are examples of using an orchestration platform for the purpose of providing transparent up-to-date information to a large number of users. In this respect the orchestration platform supports information transmission. But the orchestration platform can also support other forms of learning. In large decentralized organizations the access to fragmented information with the help of the orchestration platform can provide the clues to get access to other departments and individuals that may provide valuable help in problem solving. And if the orchestration platform is designed as an open portal with instant messaging features it can also provide the means for co-experiencing.

The next chapter will deal with learning challenges when the ambition is to develop capabilities to master continuous problem solving, and to make the problem-solving process the key success factor of the organization.

CHAPTER 5

PROBLEM SOLVING

P roblem solving within organizations is, to an extended degree, about groups engaging around problems that are not necessarily very clearly formulated at the beginning of the process. This means that problem solving is strongly influenced by both group learning and group decision making. Therefore learning will depend on how effectively the group is capable of making decisions relating to the problem.

Compared to individual decision making, group decision making is characterized by more people involved, more communication and information exchange, and different opinions, understandings and even conflicts. Consequently, the process of group decision making is a process for decision makers exchanging information and ideas to learn from each other and come to an agreement on the final outcome.

There is a growing amount of software solutions supporting group decision making. Enterprise collaboration, social software, group decision support etc. are some of the commercial notions related to such applications. What has been less discussed is how to support group decision making as a social process in a cultural context. Since decision making is a process of communication and learning, cultural impact has to be tracked down to the decision-makers' behavior, manner of communication, way of thinking, how information is processed, way of handling decision-making process, how conflicts appear and are resolved etc. Therefore, culture influences the whole process of decision making. Precisely because of this challenging cultural context of decision making and learning, it is no surprise that the development of e-learning has not progressed at the speed originally anticipated. Often software has been developed on too crude a level of granularity lacking a sense of familiarity and being too abstract.

An important issue relating to group behavior is the question of group leadership. For example, in problem solving in an autocratic or directive style, the leader maneuvers the whole process of decision making from defining the problem until choosing the final solution without much feedback or information from the other group members. If instead the group works more as a collective decision-making body the leader just shares his or her definition of the problem with the work group. Here it is the group who diagnoses, generates, evaluates and chooses the final solution. In such a situation the possibility to engage the group and to motivate the participants to actively contribute to the problem-solving process is a prerequisite. If the group is a self-organizing entity, then it is necessary to increase transparency and provide the minimal structures needed for good improvisation. Leadership is here emergent and appears alternately along the decision-making process. The whole process is then characterized by the possible shift of emerging leaders from one discussion issue to another. The whole group communicates, analyzes, discusses, and finally draws conclusions.

Research of management consulting companies has shown that utilizing the firm's existing knowledge resources to complete consulting tasks can backfire and undermine competitive performance. Their counter-intuitive finding was that the more codified knowledge a consulting team bidding for a contract utilized (regardless of task situation), the worse its chances of winning a bid. In other words: when the specific client problem requires a genuinely creative solution, then information transmission is not the proper learning approach.[1] Consequently knowledge that is valuable in one situation may be a liability in a different situation. So the crucial question is not how much firms know but how they use what they know.

In the case of Club Nokia, discussed in the previous chapter, it could be argued that using the knowledge built up around the product-based cell-phones business was a liability when designing the Club Nokia concept. The experience of handling the internal material flows was, however, very useful knowledge when Nokia implemented its orchestration strategy focusing on building a transparent supply chain management system for the extended enterprise.

Problem solving is thus a necessity for businesses facing demanding customers with individual needs. Such a case is the yachting industry. In the following we will look into the case of Nautor. This producer of the world-famous Swan yachts formed in the mid-1960s changed its business model to become a problem solver for customers, on top of being a superb builder of high-quality yachts.

Nautor: Reinventing the Rolls-Royce of the Seas[2]

Nautor was formed by a young Finnish entrepreneur in the mid-1960s. However, due to financial problems he had to sell the company in the beginning of the 1970s, and it became the subsidiary of a large pulp and paper corporation. Over a period of 25 years as a subsidiary of an industrial group Nautor was continuously producing high-quality yachts and kept its own market niche. But the company didn't make any major overhaul of its business model or its basic operating principles during this period. Neither did it make any profits. In April 1998 it was bought by a private consortium of Swan owners. The investors were led by long-standing Swan owner Leonardo Ferragamo, of fashion group Salvatore Ferragamo. He became the chairman of a company employing 325 people with a turnover of €27 million, and a very loyal customer base.

Ferragamo's first goal was to improve Nautor's efficiency. Luciano Scaramuccia was appointed as new managing director. He had previously been a senior manager at Italian yards such as Azimut-Benetti and Perini Navi.

Scaramuccia immediately addressed the problem of financial underachievement. His conviction was that Nautor should stay in Finland, but that the skill base would have to be expanded and flexibility would have to be increased. His first measure was to develop a network of small local subcontractors in order to increase Nautor's production flexibility.

Traditionally, the building of a Swan was accomplished with each part of the boat as a separate responsibility. A new element brought in by Scaramuccia was to treat each individual yacht as a project, with a single person responsible for shepherding the boat through the construction process, until the day the new owner accepted delivery. The project manager was a problem solver, balancing the wishes of the customer with the available resource base, including the network of subcontractors.

The new owners were impressed by the quality and craftsmanship of Nautor, and combined this with Ferragamo's experience and relationships from the fashion world. The product range was expanded into bigger and even more extravagant yachts. Previously 60-footers used to mark the top end of Swan's range. Nautor now offered 80-, 82- and 112-foot models. To further strengthen customer loyalty Nautor was also extending the after-sales services and community-building efforts through its ClubSwan program.

But Nautor hit the jackpot when finding a formula of how to combine the brand with the principles of true mass production. This new concept was introduced in May 2002. The standardized modularized Swan 45 concept enabled Nautor to produce a yacht in only 14 days. By September 2002 Nautor had already sold 30 of the €600000 Swan 45s. The new problem-solving attitude resulted not only in improved capabilities in addressing the needs of individual customers, but it also fostered a better collective problem-solving ability of the whole organization. Possibilities that previously had been neglected were found, and enabled the exploitation of new value-creating potentials.

In 2002 Nautor had a turnover of €82 million. The order book had grown by a multiple of five since Leonardo Ferragamo bought the company in 1998.

The capabilities of the reinvented Nautor are depicted in Figure 5.1.

The network approach was welcomed by the regional decision makers. In the fall 2000, a large delegation of small suppliers for the boat-building industry participated in the Interboat 2000 exhibition in Viareggio in Toscana, Italy, the home region of Scaramuccia. Led by the local Chamber of Commerce, the initiative aimed to broaden the international awareness of smaller enterprises in the boat-building cluster.

The new ownership also mobilized the local authorities to actively support the development of the company. In April 2000 it was announced that the city council had accepted to join the development of a new boating centre, BTC (Boat Technology Center), in its harbor area, including putting up

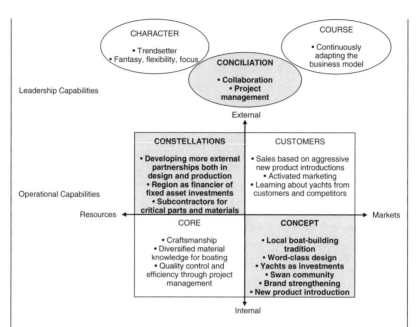

Figure 5.1 Capabilities of the reinvented Nautor

a large construction hall that would be able to handle the manufacturing of Swan yachts up to 200 feet. The new center was inaugurated in October 2002. The center also provided a physical node for the subcontracting network. The 45-footer was manufactured through a network of five key subcontractors. This way Nautor could both cut lead times and increase flexibility.

The problem-solving capabilities that developed within Nautor, and expanded to become a capability of the whole regional yacht-building cluster, were a way to strengthen the core of the organization. But even if they built on the existing core resources they were a distinct shift from an in-house mentality towards favoring the use of external resources whenever possible.

Nautor was a corporate turnaround: in scale and scope it was, of course, tiny compared to the turnaround of IBM, but many characteristics are shared by these two turnaround cases. They benefited from existing strengths, and in the face of increased competition, found ways to improve both efficiency and problem-solving skills.

IBM: Building a Problem-Solving Business

The sale of IBM's PC unit to Lenovo from China in December 2004 in many ways illustrates the remaking of IBM. In the early 1990s three-fifths of IBM's business was in computer hardware and roughly two-fifths was in software and services. In 2004 those numbers were more than reversed. When three-fifths of the business was manufacturing, management was basically supervisory: 'You do this. You do that.' But that no longer worked in a business that was primarily based on knowledge. So IBM's business model had changed dramatically.[3]

When Sam Palmisano became CEO of IBM in 2002, his message to his most demanding customers was: 'Give us your toughest problem!' But bringing this problem-solving ethos aggressively forward was dauntingly difficult. Former CEO Gerstner likened his efforts at turning around IBM to teaching an elephant to dance – and he pulled it off. Turning IBM into a genuine problem solver and not just a product and service provider asked for a whole new set of capabilities. But Palmisano was grateful for one legacy left to him by Lou Gerstner: the strategic approach that made IBM focus on the client. The new challenge was to shift from selling to the client towards solving the toughest problems of the client.[4]

Palmisano carefully picked the word 'client,' not 'customer,' when talking about the source of IBM's revenues. In the legal or accounting worlds, gaining a client could mean earning fees from him for life. IBM wanted to pull off the same gambit in computing. Those who hired IBM should think they were getting a company that planned not to sell to them but to continuously provide them with solutions.

Solutions for Palmisano represented aggressive on-the-fly team-building efforts. Solution status was not easy to come by: to qualify, a project had to involve IBM's Business Consulting Services, software, hardware, and a software application from one of IBM's partners, like enterprise software giant SAP or sales software leader Siebel Systems. In 2003 about one-third of IBM's sales to the financial services industry, which totaled $22 billion, were officially 'solutions'.

To transform IBM into a truly problem-solving company Palmisano saw in front of him a need to continue to push IBM's parts to work together ever more closely. The challenge in such a transformation was to have people from various parts of IBM to come together often enough to create such solutions. The execution challenge was to make this a core capability of the company. In July 2004 Palmisano admitted that this behavior was not yet systemic. It happened, for example, if it was a critical project or a very visible client.

An example of how IBM has developed its problem-solving capabilities is the healthcare sector. When entering the new millennium IBM had only a small presence in biotechnology. Even so, at the company's R&D labs some 150 scientists were focusing exclusively on computational biology. A researcher, Carol Kovac, got the job of creating a business unit targeting biotechnology and medical-research customers. Within three years the new unit generated over $1 billion in annual sales and included employees from all across IBM. In 2003, Kovac was given responsibility for all of IBM's $4.8 billion in healthcare industry work.

Kovac pushed aggressively to expand the presence of IBM within the healthcare industry. The Mayo Clinic, which for decades had maintained one of the world's largest and most complete sets of data about current and former patients, hired IBM to help assemble that information into a single, easily searchable database. Kovac's group did that, and also came up with other ideas. IBM and the Mayo doctors took the database a step further by cross-referencing the information with genetic profiles of patients with the help of IBM's Blue Gene super-computer. The Mayo doctors could benefit from advanced data-driven decision making, allowing for better and more individualized treatments. IBM in turn saw a chance to resell this particular service to others in the healthcare industry, an industry worth $1.6 trillion a year in the United States alone.

In the Nordic region IBM announced on December 1, 2004 that it had completed the acquisition of the 3000-person Maersk Data from AP Moller-Maersk in Denmark. One of the business units of Maersk Data, a company called Acure, had a strong foothold in healthcare. Through the acquisition, IBM was able to form a significant competence center in health and elderly care in Denmark and to be used to serve the whole North European region.

The competence center was fed with projects from different countries. An example is a project in one of the capital regions in the Nordic area, where IBM participated in a coalition to provide a solution to the logistics of medicine to elderly people staying at home. Here IBM energetically supported a public/private partnership. Even if IBM didn't take the leading role in the consortium, it actively supported the whole consortium in its efforts to find solutions to a multitude of legislative, political, and logistical problems. Support from the Danish competence center was also actively provided.

LEADERSHIP IMPLICATIONS – INSTITUTIONALIZING COLLECTIVE REGIONAL KNOWLEDGE BUILDING

Both the Nautor and the IBM case show how companies are actively engaging local addressable resources for the purpose of strengthening their problem-solving capacity. Institutionalizing the problem-solving capability has become one of the most distinguishing features of the business models of these companies.

Nautor had become an 'anchor tenant'[5] of the boat-building cluster in the region, and was therefore looked upon as role model by other companies. Luciano Scaramuccia recognized this, and was able to initiate collective actions that proved to be beneficial for both Nautor and the whole cluster. Scaramuccia had identified that there was limited networking among Nautor's subcontractors. He could compare to his previous experiences from the boat-building sector in Italy. He was therefore in collaboration with the chairman of the local Chamber of Commerce, coming up with the idea of providing the Finnish boat builders with a possibility to compare the Finnish yacht-building concept with the one in Northern Italy.

The Chamber of Commerce actively promoted the forging of links between the local boat builders and their counterparts in Viareggio, in the Toscana region of Italy. The Finnish boat-building capabilities were successfully combined with unique marketing and networking capabilities of the Viareggio area. This combination primarily strengthened Nautor, but also generated spillover effects that benefited other boat builders in the cluster.

Traditionally, marketing had been the single weakest part of the Finnish boat-building sector. In this respect the infusion of marketing skills into the region, based on the role of Ferragamo, was an immediate benefit not only to Nautor, but also to the whole region. One beneficiary was Baltic Yachts, an early 1970s spin-off from Nautor. Baltic Yachts evolved into one of the world's most respected producers of large one-off high-performance yachts up to and over the 200-foot range. The growth of Nautor and Baltic Yachts in turn was further strengthened by the building of additional regional infrastructures, like the Boat Technology Center. This accumulation of knowledge strengthened the collective problem-solving capability of the whole yacht-building cluster. This collective capability was something that each of its firms could draw upon when competing for orders on a global scale in this highly competitive market niche.

What is also worth noticing is that a large part of the 'knowledge infusion' that has come to the region has been through individuals that have not moved to the region, but have been actively seduced to support the knowledge development of the region, like the yacht designers and Leonardo Ferragamo, who influenced the development as the chairman of the Nautor board. Based on this, there is a need to thoroughly rethink the notion of capability building. The crucial point is not to physically attract people to work permanently within a firm or in a cluster, but to make sure that the critical knowledge is addressable.

Similarly, IBM has been able to mobilize regional interest in its development projects. Through IBM's infusion of key knowledge, local actors have subsequently shown a higher degree of commitment. In the mentioned project for the elderly citizens, the collaborating parties jointly developed creative solutions to provide a more efficient logistics process. This in turn gave IBM ideas on how to bring forward similar projects in other areas.

A leader can institutionalize collective regional problem solving. Subsequently the orchestration leader has to:

1. Provide incentives and immediate benefits to engage the network members in collaborative activities and to activate the network. This will exploit and leverage the resources and capabilities that exist in the region.

2. Initially secure enough facilitation to establish permanent shared problem-solving routines and enhance the creative capacity of the regional network. These dynamic capabilities form the basis for competitiveness and have to be constantly upgraded and thus approached from an evolutionary perspective.

3. Proactively facilitate knowledge exchanges within and outside the region. The firms in the region may need to have access to capabilities outside the region in order to update their own capabilities to remain competitive.

4. Engage the public sector, like the Chamber of Commerce, to encourage them to support the development by:
   - providing resources and infrastructures;
   - supporting and attracting relevant employers to the region;
   - developing an attractive living and learning environment for its inhabitants.

In the case of Nautor the new management entered a region that already had considerable knowledge in respect of yacht building. But what Scaramuccia and Ferragamo were able to do was to mobilize additional individuals to make the yachting industry of the region even more competitive. As the results improved more public attention was attained, which in turn made the process even more productive. Today the boat-building sector in the region has achieved increased national and international recognition, and both the local municipalities and the Finnish government are actively supporting the cluster. This has also benefited Nautor, and the spirit of Swan is more vibrant than ever.

What a Swan offers its users is ultimate experiences. In this respect the Italian owners also focused on the experience part in Nautor's marketing. So when organizing the Swan Cup at the rocky coastline of Sardinia's Costa Smeralda in the fall 2000, Mr. Ferragamo invited Claudia Schiffer, the supermodel, and Paul

Cayard, the well-known America's Cup sailor and skipper, to add a bit of celebrity buzz to the event. He also drew in sponsors such as Bulgari and Italian wine group Frescobaldi, while sprucing up the regattas in order to butter up potential clients. Building and shaping such experiences, and providing events that will positively influence the feelings and attitudes of present and future customers, is becoming increasingly important. The next chapter will take a deeper look into this phenomenon.

CHAPTER 6

CO-EXPERIENCING

As the previous chapter showed problem solving in business is becoming more and more focused on understanding the experiences around the products and services. This means that the problem-solving approach to learning, to an increasing amount, also includes elements relating to experiences. In problem solving, the problem is first defined and then relevant experiences are studied. When we talk about staging experiences we start from an event, the experience. If the event is successful, it may trigger the solution to some problems, and it may help to identify new problems, the solutions of which may provide even bigger benefits than solving the problems previously recognized.

Complex learning efforts exploring new domains of knowledge could be considered as learning journeys. Creative organizations seem to be able to constantly launch such journeys, and also come up with new interesting results, time after time. Based on the experiences from such efforts it looks like they best succeed if they are designed according to the principles of experience provision.

As the outcome cannot be envisioned at the outset, only some broad guidelines for the journey can be stipulated. However, what is important is that the process can be agreed upon in detail. To balance diverging and converging phases in the creative process there has to be a number of iterations that repeat the diverging–converging pattern to gradually deepen the understanding of the context, the whole, and its parts. In such a process a facilitator can be an important value-adding element. The role of the facilitator is twofold, supporting both intellectually and emotionally. Firstly, he has to be able to provide 'on-the-run syntheses' of the progress of the journey in order to keep the participants aligned with the overall development of the collaborative effort. This is the intellectual support. But he also has to find ways to connect to the different participants on the journey on an individual level, making them feel comfortable with the process and subsequently opening up and contributing to the learning process. This in turn is the emotional support.

To bring forward such learning journeys one has to use the initial insights, which form the basis for the journey; and establish some minimal structures, which form the rules for how to cooperate. These structures provide the unifying principles based on which the collaborative creative process can unfold. But these minimal structures only represent the intellectual foundation. In addition the emotional foundation will be manifested in terms of shared values and commitment among the participants rather than through formal structures.

The shared values among the participants usually represent some fairly broad principles providing coherence within the group. These principles refer to the purpose of the group and the domain in which this purpose is to be realized. The aim is not to direct the activities towards a predetermined outcome, but to motivate the participants and distinguish what is considered possible from what is considered impossible.

Another important observation relating to learning journeys is that different participants get different benefits out of the shared activities. Some participants may be able to connect what they learn to a prevailing very concrete problem in their own domain, and apply the new things learnt in this context. Others may be able to crystallize emergent ideas, which formerly were accumulated insights, into a firmer framework, thanks to associations rising from the collaborative learning efforts. This epitomizes the nature of open-ended processes. One of the main benefits of letting go is that unexpected benefits may unfold!

Staging the learning journey into clearly defined phases, and directing creative efforts to make intermediary learning events highly productive, has the side effect of mentally preparing the participants for something they will trust to be genuinely creative and rewarding. By being prescheduled, the learning events are known to all the participants. On the one hand, this enables individuals to relate themselves individually to these events. On the other hand, it also provides the facilitator with an opportunity to make last-minute adjustments and adapt the content of each event based on new information and identified expectations of the participants.

Staging an experience means attracting performers and facilitating performance. How the experience is staged and the time is paced is important. If problems are to be solved in 'due time,' performances have to be set up at a particular moment of time. An example of such a carefully staged experience was the launch of the Lagerfeld collection by H&M during the fall 2004.

H&M: Selling a Fashion Collection in 25 Minutes

H&M, the $8 billion Swedish fashion retailer, was looking to achieve balance between mass market and exclusivity. It had recognized that even if their collections could be considered as a smorgasbord of fashion, people were increasingly looking for ways to express their individuality. They were also consuming at a higher speed. H&M thus saw an opportunity to help drive consumer expectations, luxury or otherwise, toward the rare and the special. The ambition was to train consumers to expect new fashions on a daily basis. To display the same collection for three to six months was not possible any more. Although H&M still produced basics like black and white T-shirts in enormous quantities – hundreds of thousands of units – it had also started to cut as few as 100 pieces of some styles. The company also developed smaller retail formats focusing on women, men, or young people to adapt its mass concept to a niche world. But none of these efforts struck such a chord as the Lagerfeld collection.

On Friday, November 12, 2004 H&M launched its Karl Lagerfeld collection in about half of its 1000 locations in the US and Europe. Although the shipments of $49 blouses and $149 wool-cashmere coats were meant to last several weeks, many shops sold out their Lagerfeld merchandise by late afternoon the same day. As some of the smaller stores in the countryside sold a bit slower, garments were then reallocated from these stores to the busiest city stores.

The Karl Lagerfeld collection was a one-off collection and meant to be exclusive. But still the demand exceeded expectations. 'We've been operating this business for some 60 years and we've never seen anything like it. We are as surprised as the customer at the rapid sellout,' said Jörgen Andersson, H&M marketing director in an interview to fashion magazine *Women's Wear Daily*. What the collection proved was that the intention of H&M to combine fashion and quality at the best price worked very well, confirming the strength of the 'massclusivity' concept – offering an exclusive product, but on a limited-edition basis.[1]

For Karl Lagerfeld himself the big success was also a surprise. He commented that what was supposed to last two weeks was over in 25 minutes. He also felt sorry for the clients because he had been positive to the idea that everyone could wear Lagerfeld, even if he was flattered by the feeding frenzy for his designs.

The three hottest sellers were the Lagerfeld silhouette T-shirt for $19.90, the sequin jacket at $129, and the lace dress at $99.90.

A quintessential example of the burgeoning 'massclusivity' concept, the Karl Lagerfeld for H&M collection was trumpeted with a torrent of editorial features, massive billboards, and a two-minute television commercial.

When the collection was launched on November 12 there was a line of 'Karl-o-philes' standing outside the H&M store on the corner of 34th Street and Seventh Avenue waiting to storm in to grab what they could. The items, merchandised in a small area at the front of the shop, had to be restocked starting at 9:02. By 9:20, the store's stock was all out on the floor.

At the Fifth Avenue flagship, there were over 300 people in line for the 9 a.m. opening and in the first hour, 1500 pieces were sold. By 1 p.m., the store had sold between 1500 and 2000 pieces per hour. The collection was sold out by day's end.

By Sunday evening some items were already listed on eBay, including the Lagerfeld for H&M sunglasses, women's jeans, cocktail dresses, silhouette T-shirts, and sequin dresses. Women's jeans, originally priced at $59.90, were up to $75.

The objective with this new form of marketing is of course that a sense of exclusivity will spur sales. There are other variations on the same theme. Another fashion retailer, Comme des Garcons, establishes temporary stores. One shop was located under a bridge in Warsaw and designed to remain in business for only one year. This outpost of Comme des Garcons, one of its 'guerrilla' boutiques, met its monthly sales target in the first week of operation. And for H&M the rewards from the Lagerfeld campaign were handsome. The launch of Lagerfeld, in combination with favorable weather, bolstered sales in November by 24% according to the fourth-quarter financial statement, and sales for the full quarter soared 14.7%. In May 2005 it was announced that British designer Stella McCartney would be designing a one-time only line for H&M. Similar to Karl Lagerfeld's special line, the line would feature affordable clothing of a well-known designer.

Another way to nurture this perception of exclusivity but still maintain the mass production logic was developed by Germany's car manufacturer BMW when launching the new Mini Cooper in America. BMW recognized that the potential buyers could not be identified by their demographic variables, but instead based on their 'mindset'. They would be different ages, brand-conscious, but not interested in status. And they were very Internet-savvy. From a marketing perspective it was anticipated that they would like to discover things for themselves. Using PR stunts and a highly informative and interactive website, or what marketing people call 'guerrilla marketing,' people were intrigued and word of mouth established a growing interest in the product. Eighty-six percent of people buying a Mini in the United States used the company's website. Over the website they learnt that they could customize the car in respect of factory-fitted items such as body styles and colors, and dealer-fitted accessories, such as alternative lighting, audio systems and wheels. Ultimately, the customer ends up with an exclusive version, customized for him or her. The number of Minis sold in American in 2004 was around 36 000, more than three times the number of Minis sold during the entire eight years that the original Mini was on sale in America. The Mini factory at Oxford, UK, producing these cars has become BMW's most productive plant.[2]

Providing such experiences for the customers has become increasingly common, and especially the information and communication technology sector has embraced this path. One of the leading companies to stage such successful experiences is Apple.

Apple: Applying Experience Provision Tactics to High-Tech

When Steve Jobs rejoined Apple in 1997 his vision was to remake the company with software. He planned to build new exciting applications by inviting third-party software developers to develop software for such needs as editing home videos, managing photos, or managing a digital music box. One company he approached was Adobe, which he asked if they would be interesting in developing a Mac version of their consumer video-editing program. They refused. So Steve Jobs decided that Apple would do the development work.

In less than a year a department called Apple's Applications Software Division turned out two programs that capitalized on the iMac's ability to connect to digital camcorders: a video-editing program for professionals called Final Cut Pro and a simplified version for consumers called iMovie.[3]

Every time a new product came out, Steve Jobs orchestrated a spectacular event that helped to spur the media buzz around the company. Gradually users began to notice that the company was delivering truly innovative programs and continuously improving them. So using this continuous stream of skillfully promoted events became a way to systematically add value to the more mundane work done in the long term on the software platform.

Having previously neglected digital music, in the summer of 2000, Steve Jobs, the technological visionary of his generation, realized its potential. After this discovery he was afraid that it was too late, so he had to move fast. He ordered Mac hardware designers to incorporate CD-ROM burners as standard equipment in all Macs. And he was able to have his engineers put together the first version of iTunes in time for the annual Macworld trade show. The application simplified the importing and compression of songs. It also had sorting functionality that was superior to what other similar software could offer.

Once the software was ready the next step was to increase the visibility of Apple in the consumer market by making the decision to open its own chain of Apple stores. On May 19, 2001 the first store was opened at Tyson's Corner Galleria mall outside Washington.

But more was in the pipeline. In April 2001 Jobs asked Jon Rubinstein, the senior vice president for hardware development, to put together a SWAT team that could produce a device in time for the Christmas shopping season. Senior management had been talking about something like the iPod for about a year, but the team started with a clean sheet of paper. Rubinstein quickly recruited a handful of hardware and software engineers, including several from outside the company, without telling any of them exactly what they'd be working on until they signed up.[4]

On October 23, 2001 Apple announced the introduction of the iPod. In the announcement Steve Jobs predicted that Apple had invented a whole new category of digital music player, letting you put your entire music collection in your pocket and listen to it wherever you go. He stated that with iPod, listening to music would never be the same again.

The next announcement that further strengthened the platform came on April 28, 2003. Then Apple announced the opening of the iTunes Music Store. The announcement promised a revolutionary online music store that would let customers quickly find, purchase, and download the music they wanted for just 99 cents per song, without subscription fees. Jobs had been able to negotiate with the record companies to offer the consumers groundbreaking personal use rights, including burning songs onto an unlimited number of CDs for personal use, and listening to songs on an unlimited number of iPods. The deal covered all big record companies such as BMG, EMI, Sony Music Entertainment, Universal, and Warner.

The iTunes Music Store sold 275 000 tracks in the first 18 hours of operation, 1 million in the first six days, and 2 million tracks in 16 days. By 2005 it was selling 1 million a day.

The platform that Apple had built enabled it to increase partnering, to further leverage upon its software capabilities, but even more so to exploit its strong experience provision skills. One example is the way Apple launched the partnership with Motorola in cell phones.

In an analyst meeting in July 2004 Motorola CEO Ed Zander pulled a cell phone and an Apple iPod player out of his pocket and wished for a way to combine the two. Steve Jobs then appeared on a video screen behind Zander and said his wish had been granted. Motorola became the first company to license Apple's iTunes software for a device other than an iPod.

Another example is the way Apple benefited from its collaboration with Sony. When interviewed for *Fortune* magazine in February 2005 Jobs arranged to have a separate article on Sony in the same issue. The technology special article featured a picture of Sony's president Ando appearing at the Macworld trade fair. In March it was Jobs' turn to support Sony by announcing that Apple was backing Sony's Blu-ray format for the next generation of digital videodiscs, bolstering Sony's effort to dominate the $26 billion US market for DVDs and players.

The new strategy of Apple repositioned the company to become one of the most successful technology stocks after the

> Internet bubble burst. Apple's core strength was to bring very high technology to mere mortals in a way that surprised and delighted them and that they could figure out how to use. Combining this with mind-boggling experiences proved to be an extraordinary success formula.

High-profile media exposure has the consequence of making competitors more alert. In February 2005, it was announced that Microsoft and Nokia had teamed up to provide digital music using mobile devices. Nokia informed that it had agreed to use Microsoft's music formats on its handsets. The purpose was to change the trend of digital music being primarily carried around on portable players designed strictly for music, like the iPod. This announcement showed that Apple had forced Microsoft and Nokia to revise their strategies. The industrial giants had been seriously affected by the much smaller but nimbler Apple.

The success of Apple and the less rosy development of Sony also caused complications. When Apple launched its Japanese iTunes site in August 2005, without music from Sony BMG, this was a sign of a growing rift between the two companies. Sony was clearly unsatisfied with a deal that helped provide Apple with record earnings, whereas Sony itself had to launch a 'sledgehammer' strategy including elements of restructuring to revitalize the electronics business to return it to profitability, and to further integrate hardware and software to help differentiate the Sony products. Sony had, in a similar fashion to Apple, identified the key to future growth being in finding a way to bring entertainment and content together.

COMPOSING, ORCHESTRATING, AND CONTEMPLATING

The two examples of Karl Lagerfeld for H&M and Steve Jobs for Apple illustrate two different ways of handling composing and orchestration in business. Karl Lagerfeld was engaged as a composer of the design for H&M, but the orchestration role was kept by H&M. The end result was a good performance, and the collection was sold out. But it also meant that there was no continuity.

Karl Lagerfeld spent more than six months working on the range of affordable outfits for the Swedish store, even overseeing the massive advertisement campaign that accompanied the clothes. At the launch he said: 'You don't have to be rich to look good now.' When the Lagerfeld collection was launched on November 12, Lagerfeld voiced his disappointment with the fact that so many of his fans never had a chance to get one of these Lagerfeld pieces.

But this remark paled in comparison with the effect of his next comment. The designer – once heavily overweight himself until he lost over 40 kilograms – was reported as saying: 'What I really didn't like was that certain fashion sizes were made bigger. What I created was fashion for slim, slender people.' This, however, had never been agreed. H&M had clearly stipulated that the collection would be produced in sizes 34 to 44. But as the message was public, reactions followed. British MP Ann Widdecombe blasted the German fashionista saying most women are a size 14 or over, 'so why should they be denied the joy of his fashion?'

One month later, in December 2004, it was announced that Tommy Hilfiger, as part of the effort to turn itself around, had bought Karl Lagerfeld's brand, including the trademarks Karl Lagerfeld, Lagerfeld Gallery, KL and Lagerfeld.

Another example of the risk relating to the use of celebrities when staging performances materialized in the plan to make a collection together with designer Stella McCartney and supermodel Kate Moss. Just about a month before the planned launch in November 2005, Kate Moss became a paparazzi victim, over allegedly taking cocaine. H&M decided to abandon the planned advertisements featuring Moss, but launched the collection on November 10, worldwide.

So if Lagerfeld is the composer orchestrated by others, Steve Jobs is indeed the Beethoven of the business world, composing, orchestrating, contemplating, and performing. With the same attention to detail as Beethoven, Steve Jobs has an extraordinary skill in orchestrating both in the creative domain around the offerings and in the marketplace to stage the performances. In addition he has the sense for timing, knowing the importance of matching internal processes with the external potential.

LEADERSHIP IMPLICATIONS – EXPERIENCE PROVISION AS A TOOL TO DRIVE CHANGE

The examples provided here have shown that experience provision can be both a tool to increase the efficiency of the main strategy, such as the Lagerfeld collection did for H&M, and as the main strategy itself, as it seems to be for Apple under the leadership of Steve Jobs. A third possibility, and more often used by companies, is to see the experience provision approach as a tool to carry out successful change efforts.

One word of warning is necessary, however. For an organization without a culture, and a leadership naturally supporting the experience provision mindset, it is difficult to embrace this mode successfully. So did, for example, Nokia try to conquer the gaming market in the way that Apple had approached the MP3 players. But the cultural difference was gigantic. For Nokia this was one project among many others. The almost fanatic attention to detail by Apple top management, Steve Jobs included, when designing the user interface for the iPod was miles away from what Nokia could culturally mobilize. The N-Gage was technically launched with a similar attempt to create market buzz and excitement, but it failed compared to the iPod in two major ways. Technically it was heavily criticized. One reason was that the first version asked the user to remove the battery when changing the game. The other was that Nokia could only offer a limited number of games. The orchestration of a large amount of supporting actors was much more successfully done by Apple and Steve Jobs.

Irrespective of whether the experience provision approach is seen as a tool or as a strategy it entails a need for improvising skills. Once there is an explicit willingness to engage in a truly interactive way with the audience and to use the feedback mechanism to bring learning forward, then there has to be capacity to quickly adopt and fall into the rhythm of the larger community affected by and contributing to the shared experience.

In music, improvisation means composing and performing contemporaneously. Even if the orchestra is playing a pre-agreed piece of music, there is always a certain amount of improvisation or adaptation in the performance. This performative character of art is particularly apparent in jazz music. Jazz improvisation can be compared with organizational innovative activities.[5] This implies that there is a need for a balance between structure and flexibility in today's highly competitive business environment.

To be able to improvise, some minimal structures have to exist. The value of a minimal structure is that small structures such as simple melody, general assumptions, and incomplete expectations can all lead to large outcomes and effective action.[6] But improvisational freedom is only possible against a well-defined (and often simple) backdrop of rules and roles. As such, the process of 'jamming,' which jazz musicians engage in, is a kind of minimalist's view of organizing, of making do with minimal commonalities and elaborating simple structures in complex ways.[7]

Even if only few companies are ready to see experience provision as their strategy, many can benefit from using this as a tool to improve learning and increase commitment to joint activities. Staging experiences can be used as a means to speed up organizational change, and at the same time considerably improve the creative outcome of a change effort.

A typical organizational transformation process starts with the recognition of a need to change, e.g. due to a changing competitive context or because the present growth rate is too low. The first initializing phase is normally carried out with the management team, and a key task is to settle upon the basic questions regarding who will participate, which are the more detailed objectives, what is the overall timetable, and what will be the ambition level regarding resource utilization and depth of analyses. Once these preconditions are clear, a change program consisting of a number of workshops, events for shared experiences, can be put together, and announced to all the participants.

Each workshop is a staged event, where only limited input is predesigned by the organizer, the design team, normally including both top management representatives and experienced external facilitators.

Each workshop benefits from the contributions of the participants that have completed assignments prior to each event. The design team will have the results of the assignments only a couple of days before the actual event. Based on this material the detailed workshop agenda will be decided. The broad format of the program consisting of the separate events is predefined, but the details of the individual workshops are highly dependent on the contribution of the participants. Such a process has two major advantages. Firstly, it has a high motivation effect on the participants, as they will recognize that their input truly has an impact. Secondly, if the staging is well done the assignments and the work during the workshops will always reveal important knowledge presented by the participants. If the participants are not provided a structured way to present their experiences, this knowledge will likely remain unnoticed by the management. A typical program consisting of three workshops can include the activities described in the following.

The first workshop focuses on how to operationalize a particular challenge facing the company, for example changing the sales approach or speeding up the process of introducing new products. The workshop is staged based on the pre-assignments, with their detailed questions relating to the key strategic issues. The substantial input to the workshop is thus broad, and in some of the issues often quite deep as well. An experienced facilitator will rapidly recognize the most critical issues to propose for shared discussions during the workshop, and thus bring the operationalization efforts a considerable step forward.

The second workshop deepens the understanding of the threats and opportunities. By using scenarios the participants are encouraged to step out of their comfort zones to debate those issues that have been recognized as critical. In this workshop a shared consensus should start to emerge regarding which issues should be immediately addressed in order to raise the competitiveness of the company.

The purpose of the third workshop is to lay out the action plan. Depending on how radical the suggested changes are, there may be a need to initialize a separate collective effort in order to secure the success of the proposed actions. In such a case the next phase should be carried out as an action learning program, whereby the participants will work on their own business cases and the facilitators will provide on-demand coaching and access to external experiences and relevant benchmarking information. The same methodology of providing a series of experiences can also be used in collaboration with external stakeholders of the company, for example when developing the collaboration practices with dealers.

This chapter has shown that co-experiencing can provide value when dealing with issues that are broad in scope but not easily formulated into very concrete problems. The approach is efficient in the respect that it always stipulates the time table in advance, and makes sure that something will be delivered within this predefined timeframe. However, not all learning will take place in such a context that the broad outline can be defined upfront and a shared learning process can be laid out based on this outline. Increasingly learning processes only unfold as things proceed. One such evolution was initiated by a Finnish student of computer science in the early 1990s. His name was Linus Torvalds. How he succeeded in making history in the world of open source software will be dealt with in the next chapter.

CHAPTER 7

INSIGHT ACCUMULATION

*C*ompared with the three other types of learning, insight accumulation is much more ambiguous in its character. Referring to learning taking place in an emergent mode, whereby the insights gradually accumulate and form meaningful entities. This means that the learning context is important. The choice of context has an impact on the type of spontaneous but retrospectively important events, ideas, and coincidences that may occur.

Insights and intuition are problematic constructs in business. They are highly subjective, and difficult to grasp in advance. We can mostly rely only on ex-post explanations of individuals trying to make clear why they behaved as they did at a certain point in time. This, however, doesn't diminish the importance of these constructs. This part of decision making and leadership is getting increased attention. There is a growing need to make important decisions under time pressure based only on fragmentary facts.

Cognitive science suggests that people are more creative if the context where they pursue creative activities is perceived as a supportive and stimulating one. For organizations to be effective with their creative efforts they need to separate the creative tasks from those demanding efficiency and use of power. Providing support for positive learning experiences to unfold could thus also inspire to more 'blue sky thinking'.

The mobilizing of individuals to put their creativity to work is paramount to organizational learning. Success in achieving a creative atmosphere and committed individuals helps the organization prosper and grow. Such an atmosphere has definitely been established within the communities of Linux and eBay. Linus Torvalds, Pierre Omidyar, and Meg Whitman are household names when talking about how emergent behavior has reached unexpected proportions. Linux started in 1991 and eBay four years later. In this chapter we will look at how Linux emerged the way it did, and in Chapter 12 we will investigate eBay.

Linux: A Global Collaborative Community by Accident[1]

Linus Torvalds was born in Helsinki in 1969. His grandfather, a professor in statistics, introduced Torvalds to the fascinating world of computers when he was 11. When Torvalds was 16, he received a 32-bit Sinclair QL computer for which he started to develop more and more sophisticated programs. His interest was to solve problems that he encountered when using the computer. His sister described him as an 'intensive information control fanatic'. He didn't enjoy using the programs he had developed such as games, he was always chasing for the next application to be built, the next problem to be solved. But he felt very satisfied by being able to control every single small detail of what the computer could do.

In the fall of 1988 Torvalds started his computer science studies at the University of Helsinki. He was a diligent and energetic student for the first year, after which he entered the Finnish Army. Once he finished his military services in 1990 he read the book *Operating Systems: Design and Implementation.*[2] In this book Torvalds learnt about Minix, a teaching aid developed for Unix. Minix was a small Unix clone. As Torvalds started to understand Unix he got a big enthusiastic jolt, which has never subsided.

What intrigued Torvalds about Unix was its unique philosophy. It was a clean operating system, avoiding special cases and based on a process architecture having a core of six basic operations or system calls. You could build up any amount of complexity from the interactions of simple things. It thus represented an architecture based on simple building blocks, and its overall concept was based on intelligent design and good taste.

Torvalds bought a 33 MHz computer at the beginning of 1991. But even before getting the computer Torvalds had been following the Minix newsgroups online, so he knew from the very beginning what he could expect from the operating system. Having this first 'real' computer Torvalds could now for the first time totally devote himself to the beauty of programming. What made programming so engaging for Torvalds was the possibility to deeply understand how things work. He saw great commonalities between computer science and physics. Both are about how the world works at a rather fundamental level. The important difference for him was that in physics you are supposed to figure out how the world is made up. In computer science you create the world! Within the confines of the computer, you are the creator. You get to ultimately control everything that happens.

To Torvalds programming was a fascinating exercise in creativity, and creating an operating system was the ultimate challenge. He could combine his inner drive to control things with his strive to genuinely understand how things work. This made him the perfect individual to guide a group of developers building an operating system, something that would become apparent retrospectively.

During the period from April to August 1991 Torvalds hardly left his apartment, as he was working on the computer all the time when he was not sleeping. And on August 25, 1991, he posted a message on a newsgroup board where he mentioned that he was doing a (free) operating system, which he considered a hobby that would not become big and professional. He was just looking for feedback.

In early October Torvalds released version 0.02 and in November version 0.03. By then he felt that he had more or less achieved what he intended when he started his pet project, and he was considering leaving the project at that. But the increasing amount of positive feedback made him continue, and in late November he posted version 0.10. That was when there actually started to be a number of people using his operating system and doing things with it. By then people were starting to send Torvalds new features of the operating system.

In December the community of Linux users expanded, and Torvalds was receiving email from places that he had dreamed about visiting, like Australia and the United States. And he received a request from Germany about whether Linux could be compiled with a smaller compiler that wouldn't need as much memory. This feature was called page-to-disk. Torvalds didn't need this feature himself, but decided to make it. He worked on this during Christmas, and on December 25, it was done. This was the first feature Torvalds added to serve somebody else's needs. And he was proud of it. Adding the page-to-disk feature caused Linux to take off.

Suddenly there were people switching over from Minix to Linux. Linux didn't do everything Minix did, but it had one capability that people really cared about: with its page-to-disk feature you could run bigger programs than you had memory for. So in January 1992 Linux users grew from five, ten, twenty people to hundreds of unidentifiable people.

When Torvalds originally posted Linux he felt he was following in the footsteps of centuries of scientists and other academics who built their work on the foundations of others – on the shoulders of giants, in the words of Sir Isaac Newton. These values were for sure influenced by the fact that he had been brought up under the influence of a strictly academic grandfather and a diehard communist father. His attitude was well captured in the following expression from the email he sent out in October 1991: 'I've enjoyed doing it, and somebody might enjoy looking at it and even modifying it for their own needs.'

THE CENTRAL TENETS OF THE LINUX PHILOSOPHY – SHARING INFORMATION AND HAVING FUN

When initially posting his software on the newsgroup board Torvalds didn't want to sell it. But neither did he want to lose control, which meant he didn't want anybody else to sell it, either. He had made that clear in the copyright policy he had included in the copying file of the first version he uploaded in September 1991. As the copyright owner, he had made up the rules: one could use the operating systems for free, as long as one didn't sell it; and if one made any changes or improvement one had to make it available to everybody in source code (as opposed to binaries, which are inaccessible). If you didn't agree with these rules, you didn't have the right to copy the code or do anything with it.

In February 1992 it was not uncommon for those who attended Unix users' meetings to arrive armed with floppies containing Linux. People started to ask Torvalds if they could charge, say, five dollars just to cover the cost of the disk and their time. For Torvalds this posed a dilemma, as accepting such a request would have been accepting the violation of the copyright. So he started to rethink his Linux-is-not-for-sale stance. As the number of users had piled up he felt confident that nobody was going to be in a position to just take it and run with it, which had been his initial big fear. If anybody had tried to seize Linux and turn it into a commercial project, there would have been a strong backlash, and a growing community of hackers opposing it vividly.

The momentum had been established. On a daily basis, programmers from around the world were sharing their suggested changes, and because Linux had became so recognizable Torvalds felt comfortable allowing people to sell it. So when Torvalds posted version 0.12 he dumped the old copyright and adopted the general public license (GPL). The commercial aspect added through the new copyright clause was very minor, and didn't cause any negative reactions within the community.

Torvalds' achievements started to get more widespread reputation. He received invitations to be a speaker at conferences, and the development activities around Linux continued at an increased pace. He had to make the decisions regarding Linux fixes and upgrades, and he grew into his role as the leader of an expanding community. He directed the development forward by never accepting anything other than what he thought was the best technical solution being presented. This was also becoming visible to the people around him, and he gained respect and trust among his peers.

What had started from the messy bedroom of Linus Torvalds has become one of the most apparent symbols of the knowledge society. Torvalds describes this as letting the universe take care of itself, by making Linux available and then letting it self-organize. And it worked astonishingly well. But it was not an obvious and easy choice to make initially. It was a risky stance to take; however, it actually created more stability in the end.

When Linus Torvalds initiated his work on Linux he could not imagine that 10 years later (in January 2001) he would stand next to Sam Palmisano, then president of IBM, at the announcement of IBM having committed to invest $1 billion in Linux. Suddenly IBM salespeople had a disarming rejoinder for customers who were sure IBM was just trying to lock them into buying IBM forever. With Linux, Palmisano could tout IBM's commitment to openness and genuine problem solving – and have people believe it. What had started as a hobby had become a true driver for change in the society. Torvalds' voluntary network had forced the biggest actor in information technology to adapt.

When trying to analyze why Linux has become so successful, one explanation is that the information sharing within the community is highly effective. As the programmer cannot contribute without knowing the context wherein his contribution will be, it is an in-built property of the Linux community that the architecture is transparent and understandable. For organizations looking for possibilities to create similar benefits from sharing information openly the question is: Can the same attitude be built into a more traditional organization? The answer seems to be affirmative. One of the most acclaimed turnaround stories where information sharing has been raised as one of the key ingredients for success is that of the New York Police Department under the leadership of its then Police Commissioner Bill Bratton (1994–96).

The New York Police Department: Making Information Sharing an Imperative[3]

When Bill Bratton was appointed to head police forces in New York his first action was to require that all transit police officials – beginning with himself – would ride the subway to work, to meetings, and at night in order to shatter the staff's complacency. This was quite a shift for most of the officials who were not used to commuting to work, and traveled around in cars provided by the city. What they saw was not pleasant: aggressive beggars, gangs of youths jumping turnstiles and jostling people on the platforms, and homeless people sprawled on benches. Even if only a few major crimes took place in the subway, the whole place reeked of fear and disorder. With ugly reality staring them in the face, the transit force's senior managers could no longer deny the need for a change in their policing methods.

Bratton also systematically analyzed what efforts would bring in the best results. One of the management systems Bratton introduced was a crime-tracking system, which allowed police officers to look at maps of criminal activity and compare them with response rates and effectiveness. When resource allocation could be made more accurately, the next step was finding a way to motivate the organization towards a new way of working. The key influencers were brought into the process to create collective buy-in for the change. In the case of the NYPD's operating practices this buy-in came from the city's 76 precinct commanders. These were engaged in a semi-weekly strategy review meeting together with the most senior officials. Attendance was mandatory for all senior staff, including three-star chiefs, deputy commissioners, and borough chiefs. Bratton himself was there as often as possible. These meetings, to which media occasionally were invited, came to symbolize the NYPD's new determination and accountability.

At each meeting a selected precinct commander was called before a panel of the senior staff (the selected officer was given only two days' notice, in order to keep all the commanders on their toes). The commander in the spotlight was questioned by both the panel and other commanders about the precinct's performance. The role of the meetings was to introduce a culture of performance, and to provide a means for information sharing among the police leaders. The meetings also gave high achievers a chance to be recognized both for making improvements in their own precincts and for helping other commanders. It increased the organization's collective strength and ensured that people felt it was based on fair processes.

Bratton described his leadership principle as the community-policing philosophy. The results did not just come because of looking at response time and the number of arrests made, but were based on how successful partnerships in the community could prevent crime. With the help of the New York mayor, they claimed that they were able to slash crime by almost 50% in two years. They increased the number of police on the street and cracked down on even the smallest offences such as vandalism and graffiti. The approach was to hold officers to ethical values, increase department resources, and make the organization proud of its achievements.[4]

The changes initiated by Bratton did not evaporate once his mandate period was over in 1996. His work was continued by successors Howard Safir and Bernie Kerik. Crime rates continued to fall: statistics released in December 2002 revealed that New York's overall crime rate was the lowest among the 25 largest cities in the United States.

LEADERSHIP IMPLICATIONS – LEARNING-BASED CUSTOMER SEGMENTATION

When the business environment is undergoing rapid change one of the biggest mistakes leaders can do is to be too occupied with past experiences, and not be sensitive enough to the signals available about a radical change coming. Cyclical industries based on commodity prices, like housing, construction, metals etc. are full of evidence of this happening. In spite of existing comparable situations in history and indications about the risk of the same going to happen, decision makers neglect to see things as they are. Often the same mistakes are made again and again: the negative signals are considered only as temporary market disruptions, and leaders fail to make the necessary changes to adapt in a timely manner.

Finland faced such a situation of radical change when the Soviet Union collapsed. The country had been highly dependent on Soviet exports, and suddenly the customer disappeared. So if the breakdown of the Soviet Union meant an identity crisis for the US Army, it meant a financial crisis for the whole Finnish economy.

During the fall 1991 the Finnish unit of ABB started to pilot its own version of the customer focus program, initiated by CEO Percy Barnevik the year before. The work began in one of the units focusing on industrial heating and ventilation equipment. The first task initiated was a customer base analysis, whereby the buying behavior of the 30 largest customers was analyzed in detail for the period 1988–91. Based on this background material a workshop was held in November 1991. The workshop benefited from assignments prepared by the participants, thus following the co-experiencing principles presented in Chapter 6. Each participant had made his or her assignment reflect on the buying potential of one single customer that the participant knew very well.[5]

The participants, the 15 most senior salespeople of the company, presented their views on the business potential for three customer segments: domestic customers, Eastern European customers, and other export customers. Each participant indicated their views on business volume development (decrease, status quo, or increase) within the coming 3–5 years. When aggregating the results, it became evident for the participants that the potential of the domestic market was collectively perceived as far poorer than existing budgets and plans indicated. On the other hand, the collective view of the export potential was seen as much more promising than the existing corporate perception. The problem was that resources could not be deployed to develop the export opportunities, as most of the activities were allocated to the domestic business.

The results of this session created confusion among ABB management. The following three months were, to some extent, a crisis stage in the process. The future outlook of business opportunities presented in the workshop did not coincide with top management's view. To verify the results it was agreed to conduct in-depth interviews with the most important customers. The results of these interviews further supported the earlier, fairly pessimistic, domestic industry outlook.

Based on these findings, it was decided in February 1992 that ABB Finland should change its strategic goal formulation, and radically increase its deployment of resources to develop business opportunities in Eastern Europe, as well as focus more on export projects abroad.

In late 1991 the consensus of forecasts for the economic development in Finland for 1992 indicated something like zero growth or a small increase in the GDP. The actual result was that the economy contracted by more than 6%, followed by two additional years of contraction, by 3 and 2%, respectively.

Thanks to the fall 1991 project ABB Finland was one of the first Finnish companies to recognize the impending discontinuity.

The customer interviews helped management to re-evaluate the strategy, and to rapidly shift focus from domestic activities to more aggressively pursue export opportunities.

The ABB case also illustrates how different learning modes interact in successful learning setups. The starting point for the customer focus program was to gather information about the market by doing interviews (information acquisition). These results were then compared in a joint seminar (co-experiencing), which provided unexpected findings (insight accumulation). These findings were then further processed, and connected to the strategy formulation process. This led to a redefined export-focused strategy (problem solving).

The experiences from ABB Finland and the NYPD are similar in the respect that the transformation of the organization started with the managers being put in close interaction with their customers. Bill Bratton forced his lieutenants to ride the subway and face how crime affected the daily life of a New Yorker. In ABB a significant effort was put into interviewing the most important customers to figure out their buying potential. Another shared behavior was that both organizations benefited from sharing the experiences of the leading actors. They were brought together in events, where the experiences were debated and shared in order to stimulate learning and secure open information sharing. In this respect both organizations adopted the principles of open information sharing combined with periodical come togethers for the purpose of improving organizational learning. For the NYPD this routine was established in the form of the semi-weekly strategy review meetings, and in the case of ABB the learning in 1991–92 took place in the form of an action learning program.

In the industrial age the customer was mainly a target for selling. Customers were often grouped into segments according to how easily they were approachable from a sales or logistics perspective. One very simple distinction was domestic and export customers.

In the knowledge society customers also become important sources of information and learning. This poses an alternative dimension based upon which customers can be segmented. How valuable are they in respect of providing learning and development opportunities?

This perspective, the learning potential a customer provides, is of course not taking away the fact that customers are important as cash flow generators. So segmentation according to the sales potential is still valid. However, in more sophisticated segmentation schemes it is possible to include several dimensions, and then cluster the most significant customer groups according to several factors. In such a case one of the factors that should be considered is the potential value of the customer as a learning partner. There are four possible ways to relate to the customer in respect of how such learning partnerships can be developed.

The industrial thinking focuses on the product. Here information exchange is first and foremost about the supplier providing the customer with information about the product, and most of the information is bundled with the product. Some feedback is provided from the customer, e.g. in the form of customer surveys or customer satisfaction measurements.

Talking about solutions means that the supplier is more actively engaged in discussions about how the offering can be enhanced, and also engaging suppliers and other addressable resources in the shared task of providing the best possible solution for the customer. As the example in Chapter 6 showed the ambition of IBM is to be able to provide competitive solutions in a number of industries, health care being one of them. Here the learning is co-produced within the realm of the offering.

In ABB the customers were seen as sources of knowledge. Taking the account management perspective meant seeing the customer as a source of knowledge that provided an important contribution to the overall understanding of the future business outlook, in addition to being an important sales target. The information flow was thus truly bi-directional, which is the main difference between account management and product or solution focus.

The fourth possible way of looking upon customers is to see them not just as buyers of products and services and not only as knowledge sources regarding business potential, but on top of all this, as co-orchestrators, partners for co-learning about how to create value for the customer's customers. If the customer is defined in this way, then the collaboration partners share an aspiration to jointly become prime movers, creating markets that do not yet exist. Here the two actors together orchestrate a wider value constellation with the aim to mutually benefit, accepting that the constellation may evolve in an emergent fashion.

Recognizing shifts in the environment and swiftly reacting upon weak signals can be enhanced by seeing customers as a valuable source of knowledge. This is an important, but often overlooked, element of customer relationship management. Rethinking customer segmentation can therefore be one way to put the attention of the organization in this direction. If strengthening the interactions with the customers becomes a permanent routine it gradually may evolve into a key operational capability of the firm.

Part III will deal with this part of the leadership agenda; how to systematically build operational capabilities. But before that the notion of transitional objects and how they can support learning will be introduced in the next chapter.

CHAPTER 8

TRANSITIONAL OBJECTS

The research concerning transitional objects in the business world has discussed or adopted transitional objects without a clear definition, usually emphasizing the importance of transitional objects in relation to learning. Examples of what can constitute a transitional object include prototypes[1] and scenarios.[2] Transitional objects can also help to overcome the social defenses in information systems development and then models, methodologies, and pilot experiments can function as transitional objects.[3] Consultants as well as computer models can also be treated as transitional objects.[4]

When talking about transitional objects, there is another concept that deserves attention although less discussed, that is 'transitional space'. Transitional space is an area in which the individuals have internal changes and adapt to the external world.[5] The transitional space represents an area, where a psychologically supportive climate and transitional objects exist to help overcome difficulties with learning.[6]

The concept of transitional objects was first put forward by Donald Winnicott, a British pediatrician, child psychiatrist, and psychoanalyst, more than 50 years ago.[7] Transitional objects refer to an infant's first 'not-me possessions,' which present and bring the infant a sense of familiarity and security, comforting him or her and satisfying the needs of the mother when she is not available. For a child a transitional object can be a teddy bear, a security blanket, the fringe of a coverlet, or even a beloved diaper. When considering transitional objects for infants their main function is to enable children to undertake a degree of independence from the mother and move into another developmental stage of their lives.

There is a striking difference between transitional objects of early infancy (e.g. a blanket) and those in later childhood (e.g. dolls). The terms, primary and secondary transitional objects, distinguish the different functions and characteristics of early and later objects. Primary transitional objects are present in parent–infant interactions. During this period, transitional objects are concrete and at the same time represent the mother. Secondary transitional objects appear when children start to construct and enjoy fantasies.[8]

A transitional space or a transitional object can thus support individuals to associate 'the familiar with new, past with present, subjectivity with objectivity, inside with outside,' by bringing a sense of familiarity and security, comforting their anxiety, supporting them to cope with stress and pressure, and orienting them to explore the world.[9]

In most of the research done in the business world, transitional objects are adopted and applied from the psychological study directly without a clear definition. An exception to this is Wastell, who made an explicit definition of a transitional object:[10]

*A **transitional object** is some 'entity' enabling intellectual and emotional development by providing a temporary source of support allowing the learner to 'let go' a former, dependent relationship.*

Here, the dependency stated by Wastell could involve 'a person, an idea, a theory, or indeed a work-practice'. According to the definition, transitional objects have two functions – enabling both intellectual and emotional development. Intellectual development refers to the real learning in genuine problem solving; emotional development refers to the psychological supportive climate experienced by learners in the learning process. Transitional objects function as 'a temporary source of support,' showing the impermanent nature of transitional objects that might change with different learning contexts.

SUPPORTING LEARNING WITH TRANSITIONAL OBJECTS[11]

The definition of a transitional object emphasizes the learning that individuals can pursue, and how transitional objects foster this. The very fundamental function of transitional objects is to provide feelings of familiarity and security, which is realized by reducing complexity and thus instilling confidence and a sense of control. In this respect, the basic feature of a transitional object is simplification, that is, as simple as possible but simultaneously adequate enough with all key elements included. A transitional object thus makes the transformation from one state of cognition to another (i.e. learning) easier for an individual or a group. Depending on the situation the transitional object can support learning by facilitating the acquisition of new information, providing an improved way to structure the thinking, or by broadening the way of thinking, i.e. enabling 'thinking out of the box'.

Transitional objects can also be perceived as carriers of knowledge. Normann relates to this aspect when he refers to offerings as 'frozen knowledge' and genetic codes for learning. Such frozen knowledge gives the user a code for value-creating activities.[12]

Transitional objects can in the same way be seen as genetic codes for learning that can be instrumental in enabling learning. This means that transitional objects can be actively constructed by developers and users; and that they influence developers' and users' ways of thinking, preferences and decision, which in turn may lead to further improvement of the transitional objects. Transitional objects in this respect could also be seen as enablers of self-service, increasing the self-organizing capacity of individuals. A transitional object can thus support both individual learning and facilitate collective learning in a group. The role of a transitional object in a collaborative learning setup is illustrated in Figure 8.1.

In a real-world situation of concern, each person has his or her interpretation regarding the situation. The persons involved in the learning process possess a certain amount of knowledge. This aggregation of the knowledge of the individuals forms the shared knowledge stocks (t_0), which is the starting point of the learning journey. During the creative process, which can be supported by a facilitator, and include such events as brainstorming

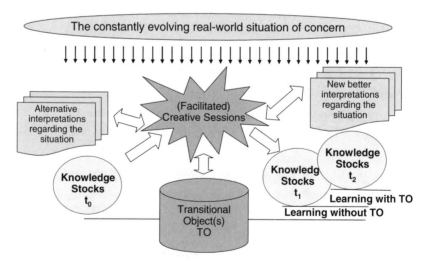

Figure 8.1 Learning and transitional objects

sessions, workshops etc., the individuals learn and acquire/create new knowledge and information. The knowledge stocks are thus expanded. If transitional objects are successfully adopted to assist and orient the learning, the knowledge stocks[13] consequently formed (t_2) will be on a higher level both in terms of comprehension and logicality, compared to the level achievable without using transitional objects (t_1).

The four learning contexts introduced in Part I will each pose different requirements on a transitional object, and subsequently the use of a transitional object cannot be approached with a 'one size fits all' mindset. In the following the possible applicability of transitional objects in the different learning contexts will be presented.

INFORMATION ACQUISITION AND TRANSITIONAL OBJECTS

Transitional objects can form platforms for information sharing and improve decision making. This becomes relevant when discussing information sharing across multiple levels of traditional echelons of command and control. Using such platforms one can make information sharing possible by networking the entire force down to the individual level. An underlying assumption of such information sharing is that it translates into shared situational awareness and self-synchronization through shared mental models of the current situation and of the desired end state, leading to an operational advantage. Through information sharing the improved information provision process will enable individuals to make more rapid and better decisions and actions.[14]

A multiyear assessment of the Joint Tactical Information Distribution System in the mid-1990s showed that networked F-15C and AWACS platforms – sharing a single tactical radar picture via data link – demonstrated a 100% increase in air-to-air combat power. Kill ratios in daytime engagements increased by a factor of 2.62 (from 3.10:1 to 8.11:1). Data were drawn from 10 000+ sorties and more than 15 000 flight hours.

The use of data links enabled the F-15 aircraft to send their radar information to each other and AWACS aircraft, and to view a common composite radar picture. If only one fighter's radar had picked up an enemy flight, every pilot – even if spread miles apart – could see 'red's' location. When AWACS' long-range data were added to the shared-information mix, every 'blue' fighter knew where all the incoming enemy aircraft were. With all pilots looking at the same radar picture, very little radio communication was needed. If aircrews are trying to share information via voice – at night, while pulling multiple gs, in adverse weather conditions – is compared to having a digital picture of what everybody sees, that is a dramatic improvement in warfighter situational awareness.[15]

In the February 1991 Gulf War 'Battle of 73 Easting,' the troop of nine M1 Abrams tanks and 12 M3 Bradley fighting vehicles destroyed the entire defensive belt in front of them, including 37 Iraqi T-72 tanks and 32 other armored vehicles, in about 40 minutes. The lead troop appears to have done this by maneuvering on the fly, using technologically enabled line-of-sight to exploit Iraqi errors.[16]

The following conclusion can be made regarding the benefits of technology when explaining why the Coalition's forces could perform so successfully compared to the Iraqis:

> If the Iraqis had attained Western standards of organizational performance, however, this analysis suggests that the results would have been radically different, even given the Coalition's advanced technology and high troop skills. Without errors to exploit, modern technology cannot provide anything like the lethality seen in 1991.
>
> This in turn suggests a broader hypothesis: that in general, late twentieth-century technology may be magnifying the effects

of skill differentials on the battlefield. If so, then a given skill imbalance may be much more important today than in the past, but combat outcomes for comparably skilled opponents may be little changed by new weaponry. The main effect of new technology may thus be to act as a wedge, gradually driving apart the real military power of states that can field skilled military organizations and those that cannot, but without changing fundamentally the outcomes of wars between equally skilled armies.[17]

Business consists of a constant flow of 'battles' in the form of interactions the firm has with customers, suppliers, and other stakeholders. This presents plentiful situations providing opportunities to exploit skill differentials. The role of transitional objects in the form of platforms for information sharing would thus provide a clear source of potential competitive advantage compared to more poorly equipped competitors. In a learning context characterized by a need for information transmission the most effective transitional object thus seems to be a common platform for information sharing.

PROBLEM SOLVING AND TRANSITIONAL OBJECTS

The study of the problem-solving tactics of photocopier repair technicians mentioned earlier showed that relying on the expertise of their colleagues in real time was the best support for learning. These findings would suggest that in complicated problem solving the expert as a transitional object is one considerable option. However, there are different types of problem to be solved, so a platform for information sharing is another option.

One supplier of agricultural machinery, CNH, has identified four types of problem-solving need, of which three are handled through largely automated information transmission:

- A technical information database: technical information, workflow information.
- A contact management system: point of contacts inside and outside the organization.
- A knowledge management system: symptoms, cures, and synonyms to help with search related to repair and service needs.

The fourth type includes problems that do not fall into any of the above-mentioned three categories. These are then escalated into a manual process where the field technician can access experts by calling the service center.

Problem solving in business is to an increasing degree asking for a group effort. Transitional objects supporting problem solving should therefore recognize and adapt to the cultural context wherein the group decision making will take place. If information-sharing platforms are developed, they have to recognize fine-grained cultural aspects to secure that the provision of familiarity and security is guaranteed. The role of an individual as a transitional object is compensating for the possible shortfalls of an information-sharing platform by providing such cultural sensitivity.

One example of problem-solving contexts where the social dimension is important is architecture. When, for example, Frank Gehry, the architect most known for the Guggenheim museum in Bilbao in Spain, was designing the new home of the Los Angeles Philharmonic he was in many ways the transitional object integrating the wishes of the Disney family, investors, and the music director. To facilitate the collective learning process Gehry built models and prototypes that could be evaluated by the other stakeholders. This illustrates that an individual performing the role of transitional object often uses different forms of tools like prototypes, models, scenarios etc.

What the individual provides is expertise. The expertise is often a mix of substantial and process-related ingredients. An architect primarily provides a strong contribution in the form of substance, whereas a consultant can be providing more of process support. Professor Richard Stacey has characterized this type of facilitation of complex open-ended learning as 'extraordinary management' and describes it as the use of intuitive, political, group-learning modes of decision making, and self-organizing forms of control in open-ended change situations. In light of this the most appropriate transitional object, when the learning challenge is about solving complicated problems, is a catalyzing expert that can champion the creative process and regulate the generation of ideas towards a solution.[18]

CO-EXPERIENCING AND TRANSITIONAL OBJECTS

One example of using co-experiencing as a way to engage customers was the introduction of the Karl Lagerfeld collection for H&M in November 2004 as presented in Chapter 6.

The launch of the collection had been nurtured by an extensive media campaign, including a two-minute commercial with Karl Lagerfeld himself acting. This would suggest that in this learning situation the transitional object was the event itself, or more precisely the perception that was generated through this event. The effect was that customers, when learning about the Lagerfeld collection from H&M, actually were associating H&M with a position more valuable and attractive than the previous brand image of H&M. The shared experience with other customers fighting to get a piece of the Lagerfeld collection strengthened this perception.

When considering learning in the experience provision context it seems like the emotional foundation is relatively more important than, for example, in problem solving. Because of this the event has to be designed properly to correspond to the relevant emotional states of the learners. The use of a well-known personality as a part of the concept is a way to be attuned to these emotional considerations.

An approach to engage customers similar to the one of H&M has also been used by Apple and Nokia. Apple's retail stores are designed to be stores around the customer's life experiences. Nokia in turn tries to reach out to music fans allowing their Nokia Theatre to bring the worlds of entertainment and mobility closer together. Here the learning is complementary to the shared experience the event provides. The customer is now not just a learner, but also a co-performer on stage. The firm is aiming at staging live performances, where improvisation plays a central role. The goal is of course to have this learning create increased awareness of Apple and Nokia products, and drive sales. But the sales effects are seen as derivative to the learning experiences, and thus facilitating such experiences is only indirectly connected to sales.

The learning events provide temporary transitional space for the participants. The brand or the celebrity involved in the event can further strengthen the individual's engagement in the learning process taking place in this transitional space. By being pre-scheduled, the learning event provides the organizer with an opportunity to carefully prepare, measure, and evaluate the outcome of the event. In the case of H&M the overwhelming success created commitment among management to repeat this type of campaign.

When the learning challenge is one of experience provision then an inspirational event can function as a transitional object, and the learning effects can be enhanced by the use of esteemed individuals, brands, or other artifacts.

INSIGHT ACCUMULATION AND TRANSITIONAL OBJECTS

When Linus Torvalds posted the first message on the Internet regarding his work on Linux he never planned for Linux to have a life outside his own computer. He also never planned to be the leader of a developers' community. It just happened by default. At some point a core group of five developers started generating most of the activity in the key areas of development. It made sense for them to serve as the filters and hold the responsibility for maintaining those areas.[19]

The Linux community developed into an intricate web of hundreds of thousands of participants relying on mailing lists and developers' conventions and corporate sponsorship in thousands of projects taking place at any one time. All this is possible because every developer is deeply engaged in active conversations with the rest of the community. These conversations can be seen to be the transitional object solidifying the Linux community.

The way the conversations within the Linux community are carried forward has evolved based on the ideology that Linus Torvalds had for Linux during its early stage. This ideology covered both the role of the members within the community, and the leadership principle. The rights of the members were regulated through the copyright policy whereas the leadership philosophy gradually emerged.

Within the Linux community the sharing of information is highly effective. The conversations over the Internet form the transitional object that provides the intellectual and emotional stimulation for the individuals that are members of the Linux community. Today these conversations take place in a way that is ingrained into the community. One of the important contributions of Linus Torvalds was to define the architecture or mechanism by which these conversations are carried out. Similar thoroughly defined and developed architectures for information and communication can be found in both eBay and Google. Also here the role of the architectures is to enable engaging conversations within the community. Different from Linux, eBay and Google have aimed at, and succeeded in, transforming their concepts into a business model with a sophisticated way to make money from these conversations.

When the learning challenge is to accumulate insights for the purpose of future direction setting then architectured conversations can provide the function of a transitional object.

APPROPRIATE TRANSITIONAL OBJECTS IN DIFFERENT LEARNING CONTEXTS

Many learning opportunities present a number of potential outcomes, the attainment of which depends on which learning approach is taken. Important questions to be asked are, for example:

- Is the case primarily about information transmission, or is information transmission only a prerequisite and the true learning challenge is about something else? (Here the experience from the management consultancies losing bids, when relying on information transmission, is a case in point.)
- Is the problem of such character that it has to be solved in its entity, or would an experience provision approach provide a better outcome?
- If the individuals are involved in the collective learning process, would they be more interested in solving individual problems, one at a time, or would they appreciate being invited to share the creation of the big picture and participate in continuous insight accumulation, framed by some shared aspirations?

Research has shown that joint problem solving plays a prominent role in capability acquisition within networks and alliances.[20] In this respect the role of transitional object is not just restricted to the internal settings of an organization, but should be considered more broadly in the context of the extended enterprise.

Another aspect relevant when considering appropriate learning approaches is the relating risks. As previously mentioned getting too reliant on having access to sufficient relevant information through information transmission can be detrimental, and prohibit genuine problem solving. Similar apprehensions have been voiced in relation to the benefits of the information-sharing platform within the concept of network-centric warfare.

Professor William Murray was an early expert who, in 1997, warned that even if technology can offer substantial leverage against future opponents, there is a risk of repeating the mistakes of the past. Americans have throughout history overestimated their technological superiority and underestimated the ability of its opponents to short-circuit the advantages. History suggests that the three most important elements if virtually all past revolutions in military affairs were not technological in nature, but rather conceptual, doctrinal, and intellectual.

Murray noticed that claims about information dominance miss the essential difference between information and knowledge. America did not need more information at Pearl Harbor, and he considered it as doubtful that America would need more information in the future. What is needed is a deeper understanding of the political context of war and the very different set of assumptions that American opponents may bring to it. The US Army requires knowledge of foreign languages, cultures, religious beliefs, and above all history – precisely what technocrats ignore because such knowledge cannot be quantified and measured. What matters most in war is what is in the mind of one's adversary, from command post to battlefield point of contact.[21]

Four years later, the information supremacy of America could not prohibit the attack on the World Trade Center. And even if Saddam Hussein could be defeated, re-establishing normal social order proved to be a significantly bigger challenge.

Another risk relates to the use of celebrities when staging performances. H&M faced the realization of such a risk when it had to replace Kate Moss when launching the Stella McCartney fall 2005 collection.

Leaders have to be alert to spotting learning opportunities, as organizational learning is increasingly a source of competitiveness. But at the same time more and more organizational learning takes place in the networks surrounding the enterprise, forcing individuals and firms to adapt to learning practices that may be different from the ones used within the enterprise. Different learning topics ask for different learning approaches, and any organization should carefully evaluate if it will be better off in applying different learning styles simultaneously, or by concentrating on becoming superior in applying some specific learning style. As learning is always an individual process, and the building blocks of organizational learning consist of individuals learning, the leadership of learning has to focus on how to motivate individuals to learn. Of growing importance is the design of appropriate information and communication architectures that provide support for learning. When doing this, transitional objects can provide means to establish more effective learning setups. However, which type of transitional object to use, depends on the learning context.

This chapter represents the conclusion of the evaluation of different learning contexts. As was initially said, learning is the foundation for firm success, and the role of learning is to enable the building of necessary capabilities for the firm. The next part of the book will look into how the capabilities enabling operational excellence are built.

PART III

BUILDING CAPABILITIES

*P*rime movers impose their structures on the environment and at the same time renew the model for success in that particular business. Prime movers can surface based on a new physical product, which sells itself. Ford represented a prime mover of this type with the T-Ford. GM changed the rules of the game within the car industry Ford had created. The customer was offered additional value beyond the car as just an artifact needed for its own sake. The color, the design, the image of the car became new value-adding ingredients.

Toyota brought the car industry one step forward and designed a model for combining resources much more flexibly in order to be better at giving the customer what he or she wanted and to make more money in the car industry than any of its competitors.

What Toyota was doing was to become a prime mover based on an orchestration approach, which very effectively supplemented and strengthened its own core resources. This form of capability building will be described more in detail in Chapter 9. The main question here is what to consider as core and what can better be performed by third parties. Based on this division of responsibilities the orchestrator has to design the principles for interaction between itself and the other members of the value constellation and to consider how to simultaneously drive efficiency and nurture creativity. The evolution of the market for cell phones will be used to illustrate how to build capabilities around the core resources.

Toyota has been very good at blending its own activities with those carried out by its collaborative partners. The more an industry is maturing, the more it will reward efficiency, and competitive advantage will be based on the ability to handle the resource allocation issue better than competitors. For a business not that mature there are greater possibilities to stand out from the pack. Chapter 10 illustrates this possibility. It exemplifies how a radical but quite simple innovation can create huge differences. This can happen anywhere, at any time. The example to show this is Nautor, the producer of the 'Rolls-Royce of the Seas,' which was founded 40 years ago. The founder, a young entrepreneur, was orchestrating and combining his own leadership skills with external capabilities. Astonishing results followed.

How firms can activate their customers and in this way strengthen their loyalty is the message of Chapter 11. It is even possible that the customers form self-organized communities. To provide the context for such customer communities to evolve is one way to build operational capabilities and become a prime mover. This can be a complementary value-creating proposition in addition to focusing on providing high-quality products and services. Two companies, Games Workshop and Harley-Davidson, have been very successful in doing this.

Chapter 12 brings the scope of orchestrating for value creation even further away from traditional industrial thinking. Here we will discuss how value can be created by aggregating resources, and nurturing active self-organization. The foundation for this can be found in the cooperative movement. The Spanish employee-owned cooperative Mondragon is highly successful and has over €10 billion in turnover. This can be compared with a more modern version of a resource-based community, eBay. What can be found is that both share a very strong ethos going beyond just making money. Still both organizations are very profitable.

Operational capabilities have to be built. How this building process takes place is explained in Chapter 13. The process follows a logical sequence of initialization, operationalization, crystallization, and commercialization – the IOCC framework.

When building capabilities some basic considerations have to be taken into account.

Firstly, there are at any time different options to consider. Whether to focus on the core resources, the offering concepts, the customer interactions, or the value constellations is always context specific. How much effort should be put on each option at different times has to be related both to the external surroundings of the firm, and the resources available to undertake different initiatives.

Secondly, capability building demands a certain amount of effort from the top management of the firm in the form of change management, constellation alignment, and internal coordination. Management has to be aware of this and make sure that the necessary resource allocations for this are available.

Thirdly, the question of how to organize the capability-building process is crucial. If there is not a clear vision of the future offerings available, then the process should be initiated in an emergent mode with the specific intention to engage in conversations, internally and externally, to generate the insights about how the future offerings should look. If there is a clear offering vision, then the implementation can be directed towards the capability-building efforts needed to develop, produce, and deliver the new offerings.

Fourthly, if the change process requires reorganization, management should be aware that such a change process demands considerably more efforts in respect of providing: (i) strong facts to support the need for change and (ii) an emotionally encouraging climate. Only through such measures can management gain credibility in front of, and support from, the rest of the organization.

Fifthly, aggressively building a new operational capability changes some of the business processes, as this is the way to be able to come up with new offerings, which is the only valid reason for entering a process of capability building.

Sixthly, capability building looks for long-term impact. The systemic structure embedded in the critical firm capabilities is highly idiosyncratic, and therefore difficult to imitate by competitors. This often provides the opportunity to achieve a sustainable competitive advantage.

The ambition with this third part of the book is to present an exposé of how firm capabilities more and more are replaced with capabilities in networks. Nevertheless the same challenges for how to mobilize change remain when building the capabilities. The ultimate outcome of a capability-building effort is that organizational behavior will change. If the capability resides in a network, this means that the network behavior has to be changed. Such change has to be orchestrated.

CHAPTER 9

CORE RESOURCES

A firm's resource leveragability often depends on the possibility of combining its own resources with resources of other firms within the value constellation. If for some reason these complementary resources are not available, the result can be disastrous. As shown in Chapter 3 Toyota was seriously affected by a fire in the Aisin Seiki plant. In this case all members in the value constellation were unified to reduce the damage. Three years later another fire created a situation where somebody had to lose, and the stakes were high.

Philips: What a Difference a Fire Can Make[1]

At about 8 p.m. on March 17, 2000, a lightning bolt hit an electric line in New Mexico, causing power fluctuations throughout the state. It was caused either by a sudden drop or a surge in power – authorities don't know which. This lightning bolt started a blaze in the Philips semiconductor plant in Albuquerque. Philips workers quickly smothered the flames, the plant burned for just 10 minutes, but the damage was done. Far away in Northern Europe, this fire touched off a corporate crisis that shifted the balance of power between two of Europe's biggest electronics companies, both major players in the cell-phone industry.

Both Nokia and Ericsson bought computer chips from the factory. The flow of those chips, crucial components in the cell phones that Nokia and Ericsson sold around the world, suddenly stopped. Philips needed weeks to get the plant back up to capacity. With cell-phone sales booming around the world, neither Nokia nor Ericsson could afford to wait.

But how the two companies responded to the crisis couldn't have been more different. Nokia officials outside Helsinki noticed a glitch in the flow of chips even before Philips told the company there was a problem. Within two weeks, a team of 30 Nokia officials fanned out over Europe, Asia, and the US to patch together a solution. They redesigned chips on the fly, sped up a project to boost production, and flexed the company's muscle to squeeze more out of other suppliers.

Ericsson moved far more slowly. And it was less prepared for the problem in the first place. Unlike Nokia, the company didn't have other suppliers of the same radio frequency chips. In the end, Ericsson came up millions of chips short of what it needed for a key new product, and lost more than €500 million in potential revenue, according to company officials (although an insurance claim against the fire made up for some of that). 'We did not have a Plan B,' conceded Jan Ahrenbring, Ericsson's marketing director for consumer goods.

On Friday, January 26, 2001 the fallout from the New Mexico fire and other component, marketing, and design problems for Ericsson reached a climax, as Ericsson announced plans to retreat from the phone handset production market. It said it planned to outsource all its handset manufacturing to Flextronics, and team up with Sony to form a joint venture, SonyEricsson, in cell phones. Ericsson said a slew of component shortages, a wrong product mix, and marketing problems sparked a loss of €1.8 billion in 2000 for the company's cellphone division. The news sent Ericsson shares falling by 13.5% and shook other high-tech stocks around the world.

The way Nokia cushioned the losses from the Albuquerque fire was totally in line with the orchestrated supply chain strategy that it had built up for years. Let's take a look at how this capability had been built.

EXCELLENCE IN EXECUTION – BUILDING A SUPERIOR SUPPLY CHAIN STRATEGY

Nokia, founded in 1865, started its more determined push into electronics and mobile telephony in the 1970s when it entered a consortium participating in the development of the standard for the first-generation mobile technology, NMT (Nordisk Mobil Telefoni). This development resulted in the opening of an analog mobile telecommunications network in the Nordic countries in 1982.

Quite rapidly Nokia found that developing technologically was not enough. The cooperation around the NMT standard had established a mindset to see the telecommunications industry as a relationship-based learning ecosystem and not as a transactions-centered technology business. Close and long-lasting cooperation with customers, and to some degree also with competitors, manifested this. Already in the 1980s Nokia was in a competitive environment.[2] Nokia's customers were the most sophisticated customers one could learn from in the world. This 'sophistication differential' gave Nokia and Ericsson unequaled co-productive R&D advantages.

The 'closed' environment of worldwide communications paradoxically moved the Nordic actors to be 'open' with each other. By the time that the world's telecommunications started to become deregulated and privatized, Nokia and Ericsson had acquired networking and orchestration skills that others were at pain to comprehend. The capabilities, based on which Nokia's success in the telecommunication field emerged, formed during the 1960s–80s, are summarized in Figure 9.1.

Figure 9.1 indicates the most important resources and processes. Close collaboration with the external research community was an important part of the capability-building activities. In this respect Nokia could benefit from the high level of technical education in Finland. In cities with a university level of education in electronics Nokia established its own development center. These developed into the most important employer in each of these cities. The symbiotic relationship between Nokia and the local research community exemplifies how successful firms cultivate regional competitiveness and create broader capabilities in the networks where they are active, as was suggested in Chapter 5.

The technological capabilities that Nokia had built up over the years would probably not have been fully exploited if Nokia had not been forced to make some very tough strategic decisions in the beginning of the 1990s. One of these decisions, once the board had rejected a proposal of a merger between Nokia and Ericsson, was to appoint Jorma Ollila as the new CEO of the company in the beginning of 1992.

Ollila laid out the premises for a new strategy built on four premises: 'Focus,' 'Global,' 'Telecom-Oriented,' 'High Value-Added'. This strategy was later labeled as 'Excellence in Execution'. Mastering complex systems was the dominant mindset. Using information as a means to be more efficient and effective

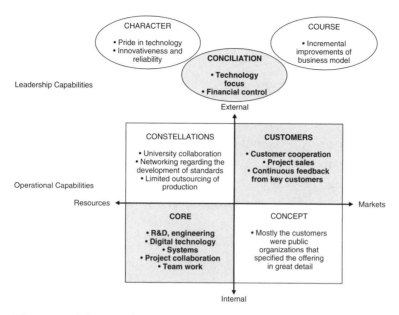

Figure 9.1 Initial capabilities of Nokia in the field of telecommunications

was a main ingredient of the strategy. Superior supply chain management became the most important capability by which Nokia differentiated itself from competition.

The right timing and speed were the cornerstones of the supply chain. In the mid-1990s Nokia recognized that the cell-phone market started to resemble the computer business. The product cycles were getting shorter and technology was changing rapidly. To handle this Nokia had to manage its logistics for plants and distribution centers on a regional basis, but following global strategies and processes. The regional logistics managers were meeting about six times a year to discuss supply chain issues. These meetings were overseen by a team of global logistics managers from headquarters in Finland.

An office in Singapore oversaw logistics for the Far East, while a Dallas office managed the Americas. Logistics for Europe,

Africa, and the Middle East was managed from Nokia's head office in Finland. The sourcing strategy for each component that came into a Nokia plant was reviewed by the company's supply chain management team. This team determined if the components should be sourced from a global, regional, or local supplier. As the price of cell-phone components decreased about 15 to 20% each year Nokia could not afford to operate long supply chains or maintain large inventories.[3]

Increasingly Nokia also started to consider third parties for manufacturing, distribution, and handling whenever it made economic sense. So could Elcoteq; the Finnish electronics manufacturing services company announced in December 1998 that it would set up a full-service electronics manufacturing services joint venture in China with Nanxin Industrial Development Corporation. The venture bought Nokia's joint venture Dongguan Nokia Mobile Phone's cell-phone accessories manufacture and subassemblies. The deal enabled Nokia to focus on its local resources in China and meet the growing demand for cell phones, while ensuring the supply of accessories. In a similar fashion, other Finnish contract manufacturers like Perlos, Elektrobit, and Aspocomp have followed Nokia around the world and carried out successful internationalization strategies.

Nokia saw its suppliers as resources that could be accessed on demand to achieve execution supremacy. Nokia dictated how the supply network should move, defined the offerings, provided some of the production input, and complemented it by a substantial resource input in respect of R&D. Taking this type of an extended enterprise view also meant that Nokia had become very skilled at monitoring its supply chain. Nokia could therefore rapidly detect the disturbance in Albuquerque, and react faster than any of its competitors.

Making a comparison between how Nokia handled its problem with the way the fire at the plant of the Aisin Seiki division of Toyota in February 1997 (see Chapter 3) was handled reveals both differences and similarities. In the Toyota case the network capability emerged based on a collaborative effort, because all participants were part of the same Toyota community. In the Albuquerque case the fire created a conflict of interest among several players, most notably Nokia and Ericsson. So if a collective orchestration mindset evolved in the Toyota case, the Albuquerque fire created a situation where Nokia had to take command. The choreography was laid out by Nokia, and designed to serve first and foremost Nokia. Nokia officials were very demanding on Philips and insisted to be given highest priority. Nokia went so far that it demanded that in this area of operation Nokia and Philips should be managed as one company.

However, looking into how rapidly actions could be taken, the recovery for Nokia and Toyota were very similar. So if the Aisin Seiki recovery was an orchestrated process relying on a lot of bottom-up self-organization, then Nokia recovered from the fire in a top-down highly structured and administered way. But in spite of completely different governance mechanisms, the creativity and speed by which recovery took place were comparable.

Nokia orchestrated the events subsequent to the fire not only to maximize its own benefit, but also to outperform its competitor Ericsson. This enabled Nokia to further cement its position as the number one producer of cell phones in the world.

THE INFLUENCE OF DIGITAL CONVERGENCE ON THE CELL-PHONE MARKET

Only a couple years later Nokia was facing a new challenge. Digital convergence had suddenly changed the role of cell phones. They now had become fashionable multimedia devices. One company to spot this was Samsung, which in the mid-1990s began to increase its focus on digital convergence. When Yun Jong-Yong was elected new CEO of Samsung Electronics in 1996 he decided to invest heavily in technology, design, and human resources. He hired 300 US-educated MBA graduates and 700 PhD-level engineers in order to reposition Samsung as a top-end producer of high-quality digital products, such as color-screen cell phones, notebook computers, and camcorders. Samsung made all of these products and the chips needed to operate them. Samsung was therefore aggressively seeking to get maximum benefit out of digital convergence.[4]

The strategy of Samsung assumed an increasing need to understand and respond to rapidly changing consumer expectations. Due to digital convergence, products were merging to perform multiple functions, as well as being interconnected within the home, the mobile, and the office space. Samsung, in order to be flexible and responsive, decided not to base its product creation on platforms. Instead Samsung took a 'Darwinian approach' to building many one-off models: it had internal R&D and also subcontracted to a range of design houses, picking the best ideas from each.

The combination of being the most vertically integrated handset vendor and at the same time having a market-led product portfolio created some big successes for Samsung in the mobile telephone market during the first half of 2004. The business was characterized by rapid growth and turbulence. The environment was highly competitive, but there was also competitive behavior of companies that was aimed at creating new businesses. Product life cycles were very short, and there was strong standardization- and technology-based competition. These tendencies emphasized the importance of the right timing, as well as the speed of bringing new innovations to the global market place.

Nokia had traditionally been very good at identifying market trends, and adapt its product portfolio to changes in customer preferences. But this time Nokia was hurt, as its product range proved to have weaknesses in the mid-price range. To achieve operational excellence Nokia had developed a modular product architecture allowing Nokia to fit capabilities and customer-specific offering requirements more effectively than most of its competitors. This modular product architecture was, within certain limits, quite flexible. But it had some key design parameters, outside which the efficiency of the integrated supply chain was substantially reduced. One such design parameter was the form of the cell phone, the so-called 'candy bar' design. The whole supply chain was best suited to rapidly design, modify, produce, and deliver products based on the candy bar format. Nokia hesitated to promote the clamshells, as this would reduce its comparative advantage. The time it took to readjust to this new imperative from the market meant a loss of 5 percentage points from a 34% market share to 29%.

Samsung, without such constraints, was therefore able to quickly exploit the void left by Nokia, rapidly gaining market share. Samsung had waited for others to develop the winning technology; then improved on it, and pumped out a greater variety of finished products faster than anyone else. With clam-shell cell phones this strategy worked very well.

Samsung was, however, still production-wise a vertically integrated company, producing LCDs, chips etc. Indeed it was opening up its supply chain in the early design phase to have the flexibility to adapt to fashion trends in cell phones. But in the actual production phase Samsung was a highly integrated opera-tor, with much less external production resources involved com-pared to, for example, Nokia. Combining a creative and flexible design phase with an effective mass production was not an easy trick to pull off. So, already at the end of 2004, Samsung reported disappointing results from its cell-phone business, and one of the reasons mentioned was production problems. This in turn proved that Nokia had an upper hand on Samsung when supply chain capabilities started to count.

Retrospectively it is interesting to ask why clamshell designs took off with such frenzy in late 2003. Clamshell designs had been on the market for quite a while, so why did this trend only now take off? One possible explanation is that the combination of camera functionality and clamshell design triggered customer interest. Somebody has even suggested that taking pictures is much easier with a clamshell, where the user can adjust the screen to see how the picture will look when holding the camera-phone. This is not possible with a 'candy bar' design. Whatever the ultimate cause of the surge in demand was, it undoubtedly verified the impact of digital convergence on the mobile handset market. Now the handset wasn't just a phone any more, but a digital multipurpose device and the customer preferences were more unpredictable than ever. In such a situation it became important to thoroughly rethink how the market should be defined.

Nokia and Samsung offered two different approaches on how to balance efficiency and creativity. The product is a compromise between constantly evolving new technology, persistently shifting fashion-inspired consumer tastes, and a need to keep production costs competitive. Nokia kept its focus on supply chain efficiency whereas Samsung opted for more flexibility in respect of responding to rapidly changing customer preferences. Samsung got some quick wins, but during 2005 Nokia showed that it was regaining market shares, as did Motorola. And when the manufacturers competed vigorously against each other operators, with Vodafone as the leading proponent, were refining their strategies to reduce the power of the phone companies to a minimum.

WHO WILL OWN THE CUSTOMER?

Arun Sarin, CEO of Vodafone, announced in December 2003 that in the same way that fast food was associated with McDonald's and soft drink with Coca-Cola he wanted people to associate cell products and services with Vodafone.

To achieve this ambition Sarin wanted the customers to be attached to the service package delivered by Vodafone. And if possible, he would like to see the branded mobile handsets getting less consumer attention.

The way to focus customers' attention on the services of Vodafone was to introduce new service concepts. A highly successful one had been Vodafone Live, the group's data services portal. Figures for 2003 showed that customers who used Vodafone Live spent at least 7% more than other subscribers.

But this concept was just the beginning of Sarin's vision. The key to success was seen to be the ability to offer exclusive content, such as branded music downloads and film clips. Following the example of British Sky Broadcasting in pay television, Vodafone was expecting customers to pay a premium for sought-after content.

The total Vodafone offering was to include both services and physical content. A Vodafone-branded Sharp phone, for example, became one of its early top-selling handsets for its Vodafone Live service. Having Vodafone-branded handsets provided the twin benefits of increasing Vodafone's purchasing power with manufacturers and building customer loyalty.

Moreover the goal was to develop a standard Vodafone 'look and feel' on all handsets. If customers could be persuaded to ask for a 'Vodafone handset' rather than, say, a Nokia product, it would greatly enhance Vodafone's branding and pricing power. This ambition of course was putting Vodafone in head-to-head conflict with leading handset manufacturers. A similar conflict arose when Nokia through its Club Nokia had tried to offer ring tones and other content directly to handset customers. The question is whether the concept of 'owning the customer' in this type of business is valid or not. Could it be so, that there will never be a very high degree of brand loyalty in respect of mobile services and mobile phones?

The question of customer ownership shows how digital convergence has altered the competitive context for the whole telecommunications industry. Changes are taking place all the time.

Active big players such as Microsoft, Vodafone, Nokia, Motorola, and Samsung are constantly shifting their priorities within different collaboration contexts. Competing alliances are looking for ways to provide the customers with new attractive offerings. The mobile telecom operators push the idea forward of more comprehensive service concepts, and try to force hardware and software providers to align more around the concepts they come up with. At the same time hardware and software companies are busy finding collaboration arrangements that will strengthen their positions in the face of the carriers.

The worst-case scenario for handset makers is that the operators truly will succeed with conquering the ownership of the customer. If that happens then the cell-phone market will start to resemble the apparel market. What this means can be illustrated by the way Levi Strauss & Co. has had to adapt in the face of the dominance of large retailers.

Levi's: Facing the Toughness of Globalization

Levi Strauss & Co. had had a period of 10 consecutive years of record sales between 1986 and 1996. Revenues had grown from $2.7 billion to $7.1 billion. But times were changing. In 1997 Levi's revenues dropped for the first time in 13 years to $6.9 billion, in 1998 sales shrank 13% to $6 billion, and the decline continued in 1999 to $5.1 billion.

Demand for blue jeans in general had slumped as Baby Boomers had aged, and were less likely to buy jeans. Levi had been hit especially hard because its two biggest customers, J.C. Penney and Sears, had each launched their own highly successful lines of private-label jeans, which directly competed with Levi for shelf space. In February 1997 Levi's decided to cut 20% of its 36 000 workforce and in November the same year it was announced that Levi would close 11 of its 37 plants in the US and Canada.[5] By the beginning of 2005 the work-force had diminished to 8850, and 2004 revenues amounted to $4.1 billion, unchanged from the year before.

The challenge was cost competition. For example, in 1997, private-label brands, including J.C. Penney's Arizona label and the Sears' Canyon River Blues brand, were priced significantly lower than Levi's – about $19.99 compared with at least $29 for Levi's. The fact was that there had been enough improve-ment in fabric-cutting technology overseas so that the factories there could produce a comparable garment to Levi's 501 for under $8.

The average consumer had become more focused on price than the status conferred by a label, leaving Levi awkwardly wedged between private-label brands sold by Sears, Roebuck & Co. and others for $10 to $25 and designer models priced above $50 a pair. Many of those rival products were made overseas.

In September 1999 Philip Marineau, an ex-Pepsi Co exec-utive, became president and chief executive officer. His role was to revitalize the Levi's brand. He entered an industry that faced extremely brutal conditions. What Marineau had to do was to try to turn around a company in a very difficult envi-ronment with an enormous amount of debt.

Marineau undertook an ambitious strategy to slash the time it took to get the products to market, improve the fit and design of the jeans and patch relations with retailers unhappy over a history of poor service.[6] In 2003 he decided to shut the doors of the last North American manufacturing plants. Simul-taneously the Levi Strauss Signature brand was launched to the mass channel in the US and other countries. Li & Fung was selected as a main supplier for the new brand. In the space of a few weeks during the summer, the company filled nearly 3000 US Wal-Mart stores with men's, women's, and children's Levi Strauss Signature products. Improvements that had been made in the delivery capabilities enabled Levi's to meet the stringent customer service expectations of the world's largest retailer.

By the end of 2003 the Levi Strauss Signature brands were expanded to Canada, Australia, and Japan. In early 2004 it was rolled out to Target stores in the United States and hit retail shelves at select mass merchants in the UK, France, and Germany. With the entry into the mass-market channel, Levi's could offer casual apparel that spanned the whole consumer market, from lower-priced Levi Strauss Signature jeans for the value-conscious shopper to premium priced Levis Vintage jeans for the connoisseur of vintage-inspired clothing.

Wal-Mart publicly praised the sales of the Signature line. The goal was to reach the 160 million consumers who shop in discount stores each week, and reduce Levi's exposure to troubled department stores, which were losing share to mass merchants and specialty stores. Levi's badly needed the volume that only a big retailer like Wal-Mart could provide to offset the decline in its main 501 jeans business.

In order to meet the intensifying competition due to globalization Marineau had to be extremely focused on costs, and especially labor costs had to be squeezed to the minimum. This is illustrated by the decline of the Levi's workforce from 36000 to fewer than 9000 in seven years and the closure of 37 factories. This transformation meant that Levi's had become a contract manufacturer focusing on marketing and distribution.

So there are parallels between the apparel and telecom industries. Both are global and driven by fashion. Telecom is still more shaped by technology and innovation, but the threat exists that some day one of the carriers will become the Wal-Mart of mobile telephony using superior bargaining power to force equipment manufacturers to even more relentless efficiency improvements and cost reductions.

LEADERSHIP IMPLICATIONS – INDUSTRY MAPPING

For many companies fashion-like rapid fluctuations in consumer demand is a new acquaintance in the competitive landscape. The clamshell case is just one example of how an industry may become less and less predictable. Another trend is that many industries also face the convergence challenge, meaning a radically widening industrial scope to watch.

For telecom firms digital convergence puts more attention on the consumer experience. However, the role the customer is taking in the co-production process has also changed. Some customers want the service provider to package everything for them, whereas other customers want to select themselves. Of course this also has an impact on the price levels.

Companies have to play a catch-up game. If Nokia has been outstanding in supply chain efficiency, other competitors have to bring their own supply chain costs down. In the same way Nokia furiously pushed its new product development efforts to match the demand of clamshell phones. Simultaneously everybody is jockeying for an optimal position for what is expected to be the next major trend. For example, in February 2005 Nokia and Microsoft announced an agreement enabling Nokia customers to access their Windows email software from their phones. Four months later Nokia made another announcement saying it had agreed to collaborate with Apple in open source browser development. Apple in turn had earlier agreed with Motorola to launch the iTunes service on Motorola phones.

As these examples show the industry map gets quite complicated. What is the proper definition of the industry becomes the

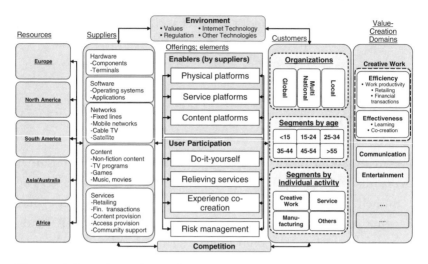

Figure 9.2   Industrial map for digital convergence

key question. Figure 9.2 shows one way to map the digitally converging information and communications industry. The map is based on the value constellations approach, and depicts the matching of appropriate resources with value-creation domains.

The industry map indicates that on one side there is the value-creation perspective, depicted in two dimensions, the domains and the customer segments. The other side is the resource dimension, again seen from two perspectives, the physical location of the tangible resources, and the way they are organized into companies, categorized into traditional industry classifications. These two perspectives meet through the offerings. The offerings can be seen as enablers of value creation (which is the perspective of the supply side), but can also be seen as co-produced entities (being the customer perspective).

An industry map is one example of a transitional object, but it can also become a means for systematic evaluation of what is the appropriate scope for the intelligence activities of the firm. As the existing industry definitions become obsolete a key question is what is the process whereby it is defined what are the relevant boundaries at any given point of time. Apple radically enlarged the boundaries of what could be considered as relevant industry boundaries for them. The computer manufacturer became a major actor in the music business. This in turn forced many other companies to rethink their own industry definitions as well.

CHAPTER 10

OFFERING CONCEPTS

*I*ncreasingly offerings are co-created with customers. At the same time the resources needed to design and provide these offerings more seldom can be found within one single company. Orchestrating and mobilizing third parties thus becomes a prerequisite for success. Such orchestration was also the path chosen by Levi Strauss to make the transformation to survive the increased cost squeeze of the late 1990s (see previous chapter).

Like Levi's, many established companies were born in an industrial setting, with a legacy of carrying out a majority of the value-creating activities within the boundaries of the firm. External relations are then primarily devoted to secure sufficient interactions with customers to generate revenues. When the founder of Nautor, Pekka Koskenkylä, started to think about establishing a business, he was by necessity right from the beginning in the orchestrating mode. He masterminded the orchestration of a number of crucial capabilities forming a business that in 40 years has produced almost 2000 of the most prestigious yachts in the world. Koskenkylä proved that a business can be designed based on an orchestration philosophy right from the beginning. This chapter will reveal how this was done.

After having looked into how the Swan was born we will investigate how one company, IDEO, has made continuous development of new offering concepts its sole reason for existence, and also how Nike is combining creativity with efficiency in its own offerings. In the light of these examples it is evident that tracking and understanding rapidly changing customer preferences is becoming more and more important. This applies irrespectively if offering design is the core business function, or if it is one critical capability of the firm.

Nautor: How a Swan was Born[1]

The Ostrobothnia area on the west coast of Finland has a long tradition of boat building. Earlier, when Finland was a part of Sweden, shipwrights traveled north from Stockholm to build the nation's naval vessels. Since then the area has maintained its boat-building tradition, which in the mid-1960s also caught the interest of Pekka Koskenkylä. In 1966 he founded a company called Nautor, which by the end of 2004 had produced more than 1800 Swan yachts, considered the Rolls-Royce of the seas, and bought by wealthy people from all over the world, as the price range is from €600 000 upwards.

When Koskenkylä at the age of 28 in 1965 arrived in Ostrobothnia it was estimated that around 100 people earned their living from boat-building activities. In the year 2004 there were about 1500 people in the area that earned their income from boat building. This development of a vibrant boat-building cluster was possible because of the successful interaction between strong individuals, companies and regional actors.

The innovation that Koskenkylä came up with was to combine the long Ostrobothnian boat-building traditions with world-class design, and develop a new approach to yacht building: production yachts made from glass-reinforced plastic fiber.

The legend tells that when Pekka Koskenkylä started he was so ignorant about the business and sailboats in general, that he did not know any yacht designers – not even the most famous. Therefore he went to the local yacht club and asked who was the best designer in the world. He was told that it was Sparkman & Stephens. After having contacted Sparkman & Stephens, Koskenkylä met with Rod Stephens for the first time in Helsinki in September 1966. They made an agreement that Stephens would provide the drawings of the 36-foot sloop, which was to be marketed as the Swan 36. Koskenkylä would be in charge of arranging production facilities and sales.

When Stephens paid his first visit to the factory he could witness the most beautifully prepared plug, all painted and polished and ready to be used to make the mold for the first fiberglass deck. Based on this experience Stephens understood that the Nautor people and Koskenkylä in particular were very serious in their desire to make everything as good as possible, and the commitment from Sparkman & Stephens was cemented. A couple of years later many builders were knocking on their door, but Sparkman & Stephens remained loyal to Nautor and did not give out competing designs.

To secure high quality Koskenkylä trusted Rod Stephens to provide the necessary expertise to the Nautor organization. Stephens' work for Nautor was absolutely essential. Because of his long experience in both sailing and building he knew how to build yachts. Especially in the case of Nautor it would have been difficult to obtain the high-quality reputation of which Swans have always been known without Rod Stephens' keen interest and frequent visits.

The role Koskenkylä took upon himself was to continuously work on improving the offering. He went to boat shows to learn more about yachts and to promote Nautor and solicit orders. Apart from looking at equipment he would pretend to be a buyer and be very interested in looking at all the details. He was trying to figure out how everything was made. And he was successful. The local skilled labor, access to one of the best yacht designers in the world, and glass fiber as material for high-performing yachts formed a unique offering.

The collaboration between Nautor and Stephens was very special. Once Stephens told Koskenkylä that the fact that Nautor knew so little had one big advantage. The people were not set in their ways. Other older yards would argue with him, that they had for the part 20 years done things so and so and did not feel that Stephens' comments were right. Instead Nautor needed all his know-how and took it on with no resistance.

During its first year of operation Nautor delivered four boats. In the beginning the only tangible thing Koskenkylä could offer a prospective buyer was the name and reputation of Sparkman & Stephens. Retrospectively Koskenkylä argued that it is difficult to understand how superior in reputation they were compared to other yacht designers. This reputation was built on winning races such as the America's Cup. Then Nautor came from Finland, the first to produce Sparkman & Stephens designed boats not only in a series at a very reasonable price, but also in a new and stronger material than wood.

On the top of being price competitive, the Swans were also lighter and therefore had a better chance of winning races. The fourth Swan 36 to be produced was named *Casse Tete*. It was sold at the London Boat Show in January 1968, and entered the English Cowes Week races in July the same year. It won six of the seven races. Nautor had a tremendous amount of free publicity in the major newspapers including *The Times*. The client was extremely happy. Demand surged.

The strength of Koskenkylä was to complement his own skills with two additional complementary skill sets: the craftsmanship of the local workforce and the design, production and marketing knowledge of Sparkman & Stephens. This meant a mutually reinforcing positive development process boosting the success of the Swans. Of course this was not a foolproof recipe for success. These initial capabilities of Nautor are illustrated in Figure 10.1.

When the production volumes of Nautor increased in the early 1970s, Nautor became more and more dependent on suppliers and subcontractors. One year for instance the mast and rigging makers in England were late in deliveries. First they were only a few weeks late, but then it turned out to be months. It was spring and there were a lot of boats to deliver. The customers were angry. Some were staying in the local hotel with crews.

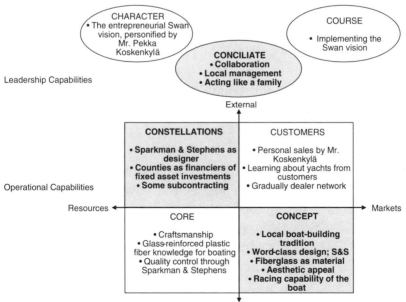

Figure 10.1   Initial Nautor capabilities

Their expenses were mounting day by day and their summer vacation running out. The mast makers were in the UK, but Koskenkylä was in Finland, so he got the heat. In addition, the bank was getting nervous, because the clients naturally would not make the last payment because of the delay of the delivery. Koskenkylä felt that because of its remote location Nautor was the last to get the orders delivered whenever suppliers had delivery problems.

The Nautor case shows the potential of a disruptive technology,[2] glass-reinforced plastic fiber, combined with an innovative orchestration approach. In such a case, the offering concept forming the basis for prime movership can be owned by one single entrepreneur, such as Pekka Koskenkylä. He not only identified the market potential for a disruptive technology, fiberglass as material, combined with mass production for luxury yachts, but also he recognized that he had to enter the market with a visible brand, and found the designer Sparkman & Stevens. He could see that the access to highly skilled labor could be advantageously arranged by inviting the adjacent counties to become sponsors for building the premises he needed for production. In five years he went from scratch to become the biggest boat yard in the world, building offshore yachts from 40 feet upwards, having over 300 employees, and operating from three separate factories.

As a skillful orchestrator Koskenkylä was able to attract the necessary resources to make his vision come true. But the danger is that when such an influential person leaves the company the capability to come up with constantly new concepts disappears. This was unfortunately what happened with Nautor, and not until 25 years after Koskenkylä handed over the leadership did the company start to regain its creative spirit under the new Italian leadership, as described in Chapter 5.

Another company that has been very successful in building its offering design capability and institutionalizing concept design as the foundation of its strategy is IDEO. How this has been done is portrayed in the following.

IDEO: Co-producing Value with the Customer

IDEO is an industrial design firm that provides product development and branding for a wide range of clients. It also offers packaging design, product research, and strategic consulting services. The company has designed such famous name products as TiVo's digital video recorder, the Oral-B soft-grip toothbrush for children, Crest's stand-up tube of toothpaste, the Palm V personal digital assistant, as well as the interiors for Amtrak's Acela high-speed train. IDEO also provides executive training and education services to help companies become more innovative. IDEO earned $62 million in revenues in 2004 and employed 350 people.

IDEO aims at providing better products and services to consumers. It applies an open-ended process consisting of five steps:

- Observation of the consumer experience, usually teamed up with the corporate client.
- Brainstorming: analyzing data gathered by observing people.
- Rapid prototyping, to help everyone visualize possible solutions.
- Refining: engaging the client and focus on the outcome of the process and getting agreement from all stakeholders, especially from top-level executives involved.
- Implementing by tapping all IDEO resources to secure the success of the new product or service.

The IDEO process corresponds to the *IOCC* framework, which will be presented in more detail in Chapter 13. Through observation and brainstorming the *initialization* is handled, the *operationalization* phase takes place by rapid prototyping, *crystallization* in IDEO-speak is refining, and finally *commercialization* is equivalent to implementation.

The central tenet of the IDEO approach is to systematically engage a broad set of expertise into studying the actual customer experience, learn from that, and ultimately come up with a better way to provide this experience. One example of how IDEO does this is the way it helped Kaiser Permanente.[3]

Kaiser Permanente is the largest health maintenance organization in the US. It was developing a long-range growth plan in 2003 that would attract more patients and cut costs. Kaiser had hundreds of medical offices in hospitals and thought it might have to replace many of them with expensive next-generation buildings. It hired IDEO for help.

Kaiser nurses, doctors, and facilities managers teamed up with IDEO's social scientists, designers, architects, and engineers and observed patients as they made their way through their medical facilities. At times, they played the role of patient themselves.

Together they came up with some surprising insights. IDEO's architects revealed that patients and family often became annoyed well before seeing a doctor because checking in was a nightmare and waiting rooms were uncomfortable. They also showed that Kaiser's doctors and medical assistants sat too far apart. People, especially the young, the old, and immigrants, visited doctors with a parent or friend. This second person was often not allowed to stay with the patient, leaving the afflicted alienated and anxious. Another area for criticism was that patients often had to wait alone in the examination rooms for up to 20 minutes half-naked, with nothing to do.

The recommendation of IDEO, after just seven weeks of work, was to overhaul the patient experience. Kaiser did not need to build new facilities. But it had to look into how to provide more comfortable waiting rooms and larger examination rooms. Kaiser realized that they had to think about how they were designing human experiences, not buildings.

The way IDEO worked meant that the Kaiser representatives had participated in the whole process, all the consumer research, analysis, and the decisions that went into the final solution. As the process was complete there was no need to think about how to get the top-level buy-in, the client representatives had already been involved, they knew what to do, and how to do it quickly.

IDEO has developed a culture of creativity. IDEO's designers produce a continuous stream of creative work as they are constantly exposed to creative dialogues evaluating clients' current products and possible improvements, drawing new designs, building and testing prototypes, and brainstorming. An important part of the success formula of IDEO is to use prototypes as transitional objects. IDEO CEO Tim Brown explains as follows:

> Design thinking is inherently a prototyping process. Once you spot a promising idea, you build it. The prototype is typically a drawing, model, or film that describes a product, system, or service. We build these models to create a close approximation of the finished product or process: the goal is to elicit feedback that helps us work through the problem we're trying to solve. In a sense, we build to think.[4]

Both Nautor and IDEO had their strategy built on concept design right from the beginning. But also more traditional companies, focusing on the physical product, have lately had to put more attention on their offering concepts. Nokia had to adapt and improve its concept design capability when facing the clamshell trend. Levi's in turn had to totally transform from having been a production-based company to becoming a design and marketing organization. Levi's is in this respect starting to resemble Nike, which for a long time has been a superb orchestrator, mastering both the area of concept design and efficient aggregation of global resources. One particularly interesting case is how Nike conquered a leading spot in the soccer industry, starting from scratch in the mid-1990s.

Nike: Conquering the Soccer Field

When the US hosted the World Cup in 1994, Nike's global soccer sales were $45 million. But a team of Nike executives persuaded top management that soccer was the company's future. Today Nike has a 25% share of the global soccer market. In 2004, for the first time, Nike's share of the soccer shoe market in Europe, 35%, exceeded Adidas, at 31%. Nike achieved this fast growth in part by using what can be described as 'outsize marketing tactics'. This means that Nike invested considerably more than the competition by having the most visible athletes promote the Nike brand. They did this with Michael Jordan in basketball and with Tiger Woods in golf. In soccer the first bet was on the prestigious Manchester United club. Nike closed an unprecedented $450 million 14-year deal with the club to run its merchandising and uniform operation.[5]

Subsequently soccer marketing gained increased attention. What Joaquin Hidalgo, at that time global soccer brand director for Nike, recognized was that the soccer market required a different approach from what any other brand had taken before. The focus had to be on how to get inspiration from the younger consumer who was growing up with Nike. A multiple media approach was used to drive the brand connection Nike was after. By using television, the Internet, cell phones, and video games Nike got in touch with the customer. The interest was caught by having some of the game's greatest stars – Ronaldo, Luis Figo, and Thierry Henry – as Nike mannequins.[6]

Another example of the attempts to get in touch with the young soccer fans was the global campaign arranged in connection with the 2002 FIFA World Cup in Seoul, South Korea. The company erected 40 Nike Park 'soccer cages' around the globe. In these 30-foot by 80-foot cages young athletes competed in three-on-three contests that made soccer seem as fast-paced as basketball. This game was called 'Scorpion Knock Out,' and was accompanied by stealthy scorpion-shaped logos rolled out on billboards and in magazine advertisements.[7]

But what really caught the headlines of the 2002 World Cup was the success of the US team, which also became a success for Nike.

Very few had expected that the US team jersey would emerge as the national must-have souvenir of the 2002 summer. But after the US had beaten Mexico and advanced to the quarterfinals to play against Germany everyone suddenly wanted to wear a piece of the soccer action. These high-tech jerseys, dubbed the 'Cool Motion Jersey,' and retailing for $89.99 sold out from coast to coast in the United States.

The jersey illustrates another feature of the Nike concept: obsession with technology. The Cool Motion Jersey had two layers and took several years to develop. The bottom layer absorbed sweat, and the top layer had tiny vents to help keep the bottom layer dry.

Mixing sports and fashion in a subtle way was another important part of the concept. Just before the European soccer championships in 2004, Nike launched its Total 90 III, a shoe that drew inspiration from cars used in the Le Mans 24-hour road race. Nike had realized that millions of children around the globe play casual pickup soccer games in the street and developed the shoe especially for them. That insight may not have impressed soccer purists, and was also putting pressure on major rival Adidas. Nike suddenly redrew what was to be considered as the relevant industry map of soccer. By doing this Nike repeated the formula that had worked in basketball. Just as Nike made basketball shoes into an off-the-court fashion statement, its Total 90s were designed to become fashion accessories for folks who may never get closer to a soccer pitch than the stands.

Nike has also constantly promoted soccer as a core element of its success. For example, Philip H. Knight, chairman of the board, in his letter to the shareholders in the 2005 annual report, underlined Nike's emphasis on soccer. Without mentioning Adidas it informed that Nike was the soccer footwear market-share leader in Europe equipping FC Barcelona, Juventus, PSV Eindhoven, and Arsenal. Ronaldo was named FIFA Player of the Year. Thierry Henry won Europe's Golden Boot Award. Both of course were wearing Nike gear.

LEADERSHIP IMPLICATIONS – BALANCING EFFICIENCY AND CREATIVITY

What the Nike case shows is the need for balancing creativity with efficiency. So even if Nike is a leading brand and one of the most creative companies in the fashion industry, the basis for success is the extremely efficient supply chain. Almost all of Nike apparel production is manufactured outside of the United States by independent contract manufacturers located in around 40 countries, such as Bangladesh, China, Honduras, India, Indonesia, Malaysia, Mexico, Pakistan, Sri Lanka, Taiwan, Thailand, Turkey, and Vietnam.

Levi Strauss & Co. was in the 1990s seen as a forerunner in adapting a creative approach to design. In a *Harvard Business Review* article the Levi's design philosophy was praised to spur innovation in two ways. One was based on close interaction with customers. The other was continuous development of in-depth knowledge about the finishing process, which in large part determines the look and feel of the garment. Levi's was seen as guiding flows of conversations. The notion of a conversation was more than just a metaphor. The designer was encouraged to become immersed in the culture of a specific customer segment, to live the life of the customer. The designer was expected to shop at the stores where the customers shop, eat in their restaurants, dance in their clubs, listen to their radio stations, read their magazines – all in an effort to pick out new trends.[8]

But Levi's could not fight against the brutal forces of globalization and subsequent price squeezes. Levi's learnt that it had moved too far in the creative direction on the efficiency–creativity continuum. As was described in Chapter 9, the new CEO, Philip Marineau, had to drastically refocus the company on improving efficiency, closing factories, and reducing personnel. But still its design and marketing capabilities remained its most valuable assets.

Nokia had developed a modular product architecture, which became too rigid to adapt to the clamshell trend, whereas Samsung couldn't fully benefit from its clamshell market victories due to lack of sufficient supply chain capabilities when demand surged.

Nautor also stumbled. Once Koskenkylä left Nautor in the early 1970s, the focus of the new management was on internal efficiency. This made the organization more bureaucratic. In the 1980s management tried to put more emphasis on marketing, and the service network was extended to provide better services in respect of spare parts and supply all over the globe. But still, in Nautor's own 25-year anniversary publication in 1991 it was admitted that Nautor had become quite conservative. The emphasis on quality was causing excess weight, which was further emphasized by sticking to old materials and not using, e.g. composites as some of the competitors were already doing at that time. When balancing creativity and efficiency, Nautor had clearly leaned too much towards the efficiency part. The new owners would skillfully and rapidly correct this imbalance, and create a successful turnaround as described in Chapter 5.

So this and previous chapters have shown that leaders have to continuously ask themselves if they are balancing efficiency and creativity in an optimal way. As markets shift more quickly than before, it seems to be more of a rule than an exception that past success formulas become obsolete faster than ever. And the shifts can be both ways asking for either increased emphasis on efficiency, or demanding the ability to come up with fresh creative approaches.

To manage this balancing act two different processes have to be carried on simultaneously. How efficiency is developed is by definition measurable against predefined goals, whereas a truly creative output cannot necessarily be identified at the outset. Because of this the mindset and the atmosphere are poles apart for these two undertakings. This does not mean, however, that there is a need for different individuals to carry out these two parts of the strategic agenda. Of course there are managers who by nature are more attuned to one of the modes, but most well-educated managers can intellectually and emotionally adjust to both modes. What is important, however, is that these discussions are separated both time-wise, and preferably also space-wise. To free up people to be creative it is vital to provide a setting, which is different from the daily micromanagement environment. The setup has to inspire the minds to think more about options and possibilities and not so much about constraints and rigidities. This also encourages a more open social process, where the values and not the strict command and control structures rule. Using some forms of transitional objects can further improve the results of the process.

Many companies are struggling with how to pursue the balancing between efficiency and creativity. One company facing this was a global equipment manufacturer. In the early 2000s this company recognized that most of its growth had been based on acquisitions, and hardly any organic growth had taken place for 10 years. At the same time management had to meet constant cost pressures as the industry in general was moving manufacturing from high-cost locations in Europe and the United States to lower cost countries in Eastern Europe and Asia.

When kicking off a project to look into opportunities for organic growth the first brainstorming session with the management team was scheduled the evening before the budget review meeting. Entering the room it was easy to sense the pressure the top executives felt in front of the upcoming tough budget discussions the following day. It turned out that it was impossible to get the participants into a creative mode. Everybody was unintentionally thinking about the expected difficult discussions the following day.

In spite of not being successful in coming up with new ideas about how to attack the strategic challenges, the process ahead was agreed upon. The following meetings were held with better possibilities to create the necessary creative atmosphere. Three months later, based on thorough analyses and extensive involvement in the action learning process, the management team was prepared to present the new strategy to the board, and the new organization was announced only five months after the first meeting.

Two major findings came out from the project. Firstly, the access to a shared fact base proved extremely important to balance between activities aiming at cost reductions, and other activities driving top-line growth. The use of this fact base was later institutionalized into an orchestration platform providing improved situational awareness across the company. Secondly, the subtasks related to respective streams, efficiency and creativity were largely carried out as different subprojects. This enhanced considerably the efficiency of both streams. The learning from the first management meeting proved that these efforts need different atmospheres. One year down the road from the organizational change the company was reporting considerable increases in the order backlog, and significantly higher profits.

So any leader is continuously confronted with a balancing act, and has to find a way of how to delicately do many things in parallel. But as the above example showed, a large organization can also radically change its way of working in a relatively short period of time, providing it uses a sound methodology for how to balance efficiency and creativity. In this case the business was still very much in the industrial context, but used a 'knowledge society' approach to actively share knowledge and mobilize collaboration across units and continents. However, this company didn't really initiate radical changes in how to interact with the customers. That is, however, a path some companies have embarked upon. The next chapter will look into how such companies have been successfully making community building among their customers a key operational capability.

CHAPTER 11

CUSTOMER INTERACTIONS

A community is according to *Webster's* dictionary any group living in the same area or having interests, work etc. in common. The key words here are group, interests, common. From history, the notion of community has traditionally referred to something in common that provides the individual with some benefits. These benefits are not necessarily evaluated by the member of the community according to economic criteria, but still the members perceive these services as valuable and meaningful. Of course religious communities are the strongest communities that have emerged.

However, the *Webster* definition defines the role of the community member as passive. It is enough to live in the same area or have the same interests. However, from the perspective of customer communities, the community will not evolve and prosper without some active behavior of the members. Communities can emerge ('bottom-up') or can be consciously built up ('top-down'), but in any case communities will not prosper without conscious action by some individuals who have an interest in the formation of the community.

A community-building effort has the objective of creating a sense of belonging among its members based on the shared interest. Thus communities are basically evolving groups of people, who feel that they belong to each other and want to communicate and act together based on a common purpose. In the case of Levi's, 501 owners all over the world may at least at certain points in history have had a strong community feeling, inspired by such jeans cult figures as James Dean. But the challenge for Levi's is how to engage these individuals in common actions that will generate economic returns to Levi's. The same challenge was faced by Nokia when trying to mobilize its customers to form a customer community with the help of Club Nokia.

A community keeps together a group of people only if they share some complementary interest in addition to money. If money is the only common factor we only have a group with common commercial interests.

American psychologist Abraham Maslow suggested that individuals have needs which are satisfied in a hierarchical way.[1] Physiological, safety, social, self-esteem, and self-actualization needs were suggested as forming the pyramid of needs. These needs are much in line with the values suggested by Zetterberg (see Chapter 1). What Maslow adds is a perspective of hierarchy. The two first steps of the Maslow pyramid, physiological and security needs, hierarchically form our base for existence. As long as we are not sure of having enough food and shelter other needs remain irrelevant. Once this need is satisfied we want to make certain that we can continue our life in a safe environment.

This basic need for safety is one easily overlooked issue relating to the knowledge society. One way Maslow expressed the issue of safety was 'freedom from fear'. This was an important part of the social context wherein Linus Torvalds made his historic contribution to the open source movement in the early 1990s:

> My single regular social event in those days was the weekly students' meeting, Spektrum, where I mingled with other science majors. These social encounters created far more anxiety than anything connected with technology.
>
> 'What was I worrying about?' Just social life in general. Maybe worry is the wrong word, there was more emotional impact. Just thinking about girls. Linux wasn't that important to me at the time. To some degree, it still isn't. To some degree I can still ignore it.
>
> In those early years at the university, the social thing was very important. It wasn't as if I worried about my hunchback and people laughing about it. It was more like wanting to have friends and things. One of the reasons I liked Spektrum so much was that it was a framework for being social without having to be social. That was the evening I was social and every other evening I sat in front of the computer . . .
>
> The things that I got really upset about, and what still makes me upset, is not the technology per se but the social interactions around it.[2]

Professionals thus have high incentives to engage in active communication and collaboration with other professionals. Cell phones, the Internet, email, video conferencing are technologies facilitating such collaboration. This means much better ability for groups to work together and participate, in spite of separate physical locations. Of course much of the collaboration takes place under the auspices of the extended enterprise. But there is also an increased engagement of self-organized individuals participating in professional communities in their free time. Companies like IBM and Nokia even encourage part of their employees to use their work time to participate in open source activities, keep web-logs and be socially active in the virtual space. Also governments are linking electronically to their citizens and companies to promote commerce, become more efficient, and enhance services through value co-creation.

Individuals engaging collaboratively choose with whom they interact, who they trust. When making these choices they often consider the values of the other party. But these values are not just societal values imposed on individuals based on what the society considers as recommendable according to a religion or any other ethical or moral norms. In addition there are other value-laden considerations related to how to interact, how the collaborative environment is sharing pain and gain, how risks are divided and so on.

In the cases of Amazon and eBay, customer communities have emerged simultaneously with the development of the transaction platform. These companies are supporting groups of people sharing some common interest and being prepared to communicate and act within this group. What makes these communities vibrant is that the nodal firm provides their members with economic value on top of the same learning and communal benefits provided to members of the open source community. Both Amazon and eBay further strengthen the communal element of their business models by explicitly encouraging and rewarding group interaction. Amazon provides incentives to individuals who contribute with book reviews, and eBay ranks its most active members based on peer ratings. This means that the individual community members continuously provide Amazon and eBay with enriching content, which can be considered as part payments for the goods and services purchased. From a community perspective Amazon and eBay, however, are not primarily cultivating customer communities, but they are building platforms enabling resource aggregation. Indeed as a byproduct, communities do evolve, but they are not first and foremost customer communities from the perspective of Amazon and eBay, instead they are aggregated resources. In this respect their orchestration approach is one of cultivating the value constellation, not customer community building. This is underscored by eBay's CEO Meg Whitman stating that the community brings eBay forward. It is not eBay that brings the community forward. So eBay is not explicitly cultivating its customer community, it is enabling resources to self-organize into communities. We will show how such resource aggregation is facilitated in the next chapter.

For a community (either a customer or resource community) to prosper, enough members have to be prepared to use their time to sustain the community ethos. If this communal interest can be aligned with clear benefits for the individual, this may strengthen the concept. However, the more the economic logic dominates, the larger is the risk that the individual will perceive that there is a conflict of interest between the nodal actor, the orchestrator, and the individual.

In a customer community there is always a central node, an economic actor whose interest is to gain economic benefits from the community. This implies that this actor is allowed to collect some fees for its services, either as a transaction fee, or by including the costs of the community cultivation in the pricing of the products and services.

The first customer communities were formed as cooperatives. The nodal actor was a separate legal entity, but collectively owned by the customers. So the customers were actually formalizing the rules regarding risk sharing etc. through the formation of the cooperative. In the following we shall briefly look at the history behind this form of customer collectivism.

A HISTORICAL PREVIEW OF CUSTOMER COMMUNITIES

The roots of the first customer cooperatives can be found in the colonial United States. The objective behind forming a cooperative was to band together and gain economic clout. One of the earliest cooperatives was established in 1752 by Benjamin Franklin and is in operation to this day – the Philadelphia Contributorship for the Insurance of Homes from Loss by Fire. It is the oldest continuing cooperative in the United States.

From colonial times on, most early American cooperatives were formed primarily for the benefit of farmers. Some cooperatives helped farmers keep their costs low through joint purchases of supplies, such as feed, equipment, tools, or seed. Some marketing cooperatives helped farmers obtain the best prices for their goods by combining their crops and selling in large quantities. Others provided storage or processing services, such as grain elevators or cheese making.

If the early cooperatives in the United States were formed in the agrarian context, the rapid growth of cooperatives in Europe during the latter half of the nineteenth century had its roots in the Lancashire textile town of Rochdale, England. Here, in 1844, harsh living conditions and inadequate consumer protection – the adulteration of food by private traders was widespread – inspired 28 working men to adopt a new approach to the supply of food and other goods, and the provision of social and educational facilities for ordinary working people by setting up a retail cooperative society, the Rochdale Equitable Pioneers Society.

These 28 Rochdale men scraped together a meager capital and opened a shop in Toad Lane, where they sold wholesome food at reasonable prices. A share of the profit or surplus as they preferred to call it, was returned to members in proportion to their purchases – the famous cooperative dividend or 'divi'. The pioneers and other early cooperators owed much of their inspiration to the cooperative writings of Dr. William King, a Brighton physician and philanthropist, and Robert Owen, a Welsh manufacturer and social reformer. From the decisions and practices of the pioneers, based on the Owenite theories of cooperation, the Rochdale principles of cooperation were formulated. These included: voluntary and open membership; democratic control –

one member, one vote; payment of limited interest on capital; surplus allocated in proportion to members' purchases – the dividend; and educational facilities for members and workers.

The Rochdale Pioneers Society was not the very first cooperative, but Rochdale formulated the principles of cooperation that became a model for the formation of similar cooperative societies throughout the United Kingdom and around the world. By 1880, national membership of consumer societies had reached over half a million people – a figure that was to triple to 1 700 000 by the turn of the century.

A spur to this remarkable growth was the establishment in 1863 of the Co-operative Wholesale Society (CWS). This society, supported in its early years by a strong band of activists from the Rochdale Society, quickly developed into a major food importer, establishing supply chains for Irish butter, Danish bacon, Indian tea, and American wheat at prices working people could afford. Within a relatively short time the CWS opened depots on five continents, buying directly from the growers; it built its own fleet of ships; and it established factories to produce and sell on to societies the vast range of products which a more prosperous working class was now demanding.

But cooperatives are not the only forms of customer communities. There are also firms that have successfully built customer communities. These firms have nurtured their customer relationships and encouraged the customers to start to self-organize into true communities. In the following we will look into two such firms in greater detail. The first case, Games Workshop, shows the evolution of a traditional product-based company into a large global network of highly dedicated enthusiasts. The interesting thing with Games Workshop is that the emergence of the large community has happened with only limited guidance from the top, from Games Workshop itself.

The second case, Harley-Davidson, also illustrates how aficionados of a product may expand this appreciation of the artifact in question to become a lifestyle. In the case of Harley-Davidson this has developed into a cult, and a highly successful business. But contrary to the case of Games Workshop this has been the deliberate strategy of the top management of Harley-Davidson, and the formation of the user groups is strongly endorsed by the company.

Games Workshop: a Community of Gaming Enthusiasts

Games Workshop Group Plc, founded in 1979, designs and manufactures model soldiers, game systems, and accessories for tabletop war gaming. Games Workshop is a vertically integrated business, retaining control over every aspect of design, manufacture, and distribution of the models and rulebooks. Products are sold through its own chain of about 300 Games Workshop hobby stores and 4000 other toy and hobby shops around the world. Its 2004 revenues amounted to $278 million, an increase of 31% from the previous year, and it employed 3200 people.

The business of Games Workshop is basically about marketing a hobby based upon tabletop gaming with model soldiers. At the heart of the hobby, nurtured by Games Workshop, are the millions of gamers, who spend their time collecting, creating, painting, and building up the armies which they go on to command on a carefully prepared tabletop battlefield. Popular game lines include Warhammer, Warhammer 40 000, and The Lord of the Rings. Games Workshop also publishes a monthly hobby magazine called *White Dwarf*, available in five languages.

The company designs and makes miniature figures, in 35 000 shapes and sizes, that belong to different warrior races. They have such names as Orc Boyz and weapons such as

Warplock Jezzails. The fantasy war games where these minia-ture figures are used can go on for days.

One of the most striking features of the communities around Games Workshop is the way the individuals are engaged both within the community and on their own. Competition isn't the main thing in Warhammer. It is the painting, the collecting of models, the strategy, and tactics.

What intrigues people to join the Games Workshop com-munity is the escapist framework of the hobby. Unlike a tra-ditional board game, Warhammer requires its players to handpaint hundreds of tiny metal or plastic figurines, to con-struct miniature buildings, trees and hills for their tabletop battlefields, and to pore through an endless supply of official manuals and novels describing the rich, though fanciful, origin of the various races depicted in the game.[3]

Most of the true gamers spend a lot of hours preparing their gaming equipment, painting the tiny soldiers, weapons, and vehicles that get moved around on the battlefield. Paint-ing, in fact, is what many players particularly enjoy about the war-gaming pastime.

To encourage new customers to join the community the personnel at the Games Workshop stores offer free lessons and unlimited free play. They also provide free painting clinics and tournaments. The store can afford this largess, because visitors who take up the hobby tend to buy all their soldiers, scenery, rule books, and other game supplies at the shop.

So Games Workshop, for all its commercial aspects, func-tions largely as a club for its community members, adults and children included. Drop-in play is encouraged, and a bulletin board enables players to seek competitors for games in or outside the store.

To further strengthen its community spirit Games Work-shop created Warhammer World, a war-gaming arena in Lenton, Nottingham, in 1997. These facilities have allowed the UK business to stage increasing numbers of gaming tournaments and special events. Today Lenton has become a place of pilgrimage for gamers from around the world.

One of the deepest and most striking aspects of the Games Workshop hobby is the camaraderie of sharing the experience with others. Around the world millions of players forming the gaming community meet in the Games Workshop hobby stores, in their homes, and at clubs to hone and test their skills as military commanders.

An example of a member of the Games Workshop community is Brad Gordon from Windsor in Brisbane, who works full-time at the Games Workshop in Chemside.[4]

Brad is not married, rents a unit with friends, enjoys rock concerts, watching *Harry Potter* movies, and playing games. He has played tabletop games for years, and likes to get together with friends for a game. Brad has recognized that in the shop there are a large number of fathers who bring their sons to play miniature figurine games. More often than not it is the father who is really interested. The number of people aspiring to stay young and ignore the natural aging process is on the rise, and they represent an important market segment for Games Workshop.

To understand Games Workshop, according to Tom Kirby, chairman and chief executive, it is essential to discuss the broader points of selling not on a mass scale but in a 'niche' or 'sliver' field with a small number of potential customers. The challenge for Games Workshop is thus not to try to get everybody to buy the products but to reach out and find the people who want them, anywhere in the world. The 1.5 million customers of Games Workshop are predominantly similar. Two-thirds are teenagers and a vast majority is male. They come from middle-class families that are reasonably wealthy.[5]

Games Workshop appeals to people who have a hobby, which is to do with fantasy, and can afford to pay for it. One can't persuade people to play with Games Workshop figures if they don't want to; in most countries with a certain level of income per person, enough people exist who are interested to make it worthwhile for Games Workshop to sell its products to them. In this business the cultural differences between countries around the world are not as great as some people may think. The average customer spends hundreds of euros a year on models and books. Games Workshop only needs to add a relatively small number a year to continue to expand.

EMBODIED VALUES AS NURTURERS OF CUSTOMER COMMUNITIES

The interesting thing with Games Workshop is that the business initiated a strong community, without Games Workshop actively pursuing a community-building strategy from the beginning. As the business has grown, the local country organizations to a varying degree support community activities on the country level. In the UK, Games Workshop has organized an online community, where Games Workshop fanatics can get together to trade secrets, evaluate new products, investigate other cool websites about Games Workshop, or just socialize. But this is the way the community is defined in the UK. In other countries there are different ways to support the communities.

So the way Games Workshop management defines its role within the community is to promote the hobby. And Games Workshop is very picky about what is a hobby. A hobby is something people make time for. It is not a pastime and therefore not usually analogous to watching TV or playing computer games. With most hobbies, it involves commitment, collection, craft or manual skills, and imagination. Someone who is involved in the Games Workshop hobby collects large numbers of miniatures, paints them, modifies them, builds terrain, and games with them in the imaginary universe. This involves huge amounts of time.

Games Workshop hobbyists play war games with large numbers of metal or plastic miniatures that they have carefully chosen and, usually, painstakingly painted, on a tabletop face to face with their friends. It is a social and convivial activity loved by hobbyists the world over. The job of Games Workshop revolves around the ability to recruit new gamers (of all ages) and keep them in the hobby.

So the way Games Workshop works is that the company produces the artifacts, the figurines and the accessories related to the game, the literature through which gaming is explained, and any new elements of the game. Subsequently gamers are attracted by the social and escapist experiences enabled by the game. Some of these gamers also choose to work for Games Workshop in their retail outlets, and others become voluntary organizers of local gaming communities. The community evolves as an open-ended self-organized process among Games Workshop enthusiasts. Now with Internet support Games Workshop can more effectively reach new gamers, which is one of the explanations of the sustained growth. With the help of the Internet Games Workshop can also better stimulate enthusiasts, which in turn increases repeat purchasing.

Initially Games Workshop was a pure product company producing games and accessories for games. Gradually it has increased its measures to build communities. The focus seems to be on combining the virtual and real world, emphasizing the value-added aspects of the social interactions between the gamers when physically meeting. An explicit statement on the company website says that a hobby is different from a pastime, such as playing computer games. This means that Games Workshop first of all wants to build real-world communities, and that online communication is a means to improve the way these real-world communities function. In this respect Games Workshop has been able to deploy new technology to speed up and broaden its reach to existing and potentially new gamers. But its original mission has remained unchanged: provide the means for the hobby, tabletop war gaming, and promote this hobby to generate an increase in the number of gamers.

Games Workshop nurtures its communities in two ways. Firstly, the attachment the community members have to the physical artifact sold by the company is the basis. This means that a regular stream of beloved artifacts, such as figurines and other accessories, is the main attraction that Games Workshop provides for its hobbyists. This engages them in their escapist self-occupying activities, which provides the basis for their shared interest in the community. Secondly, the socializing enabled through these artifacts is encouraged by the way the whole business is run. The role of the physical meeting places is important here. The company has to be a steward of how the local camaraderie evolves, and secure that fanatical community members are accepting and appreciating the way the company manages its legacy.

Harley Owners Group; Fulfilling the American Dream

If Games Workshop has been able to create a global community of hobbyists around its products, it is still dwarfed in the visibility of its community in comparison with Harley-Davidson. Harley-Davidson, founded by William S. Harley and Arthur Davidson in 1903, has become a global 8000-people company listed on the New York Stock Exchange. Harley-Davidson positions itself as a customer-oriented company, building on long-lasting customer relationships while selling motorcycles, highlighted by the mission statement of the company: 'We fulfill dreams'. A publication for Harley-Davidson enthusiasts states that a Harley-Davidson motorcycle is a thing of beauty, the image of cool combined with the power and performance of fine engineering.

In 2003 Harley-Davidson sold over 290 000 motorcycles, with $4.6 billion in sales and a net income of $761 million. Parts & Accessories and Merchandise represented $920 million (22%) of the revenues. The offerings of Harley-Davidson consist of the motorcycles, finance, additional merchandise, and the provision of a wide distributor/rental/repair network. On top of that Harley-Davidson is very clear about its community-building interests. One explicit corporate function is to support its customer outreach program, called the Harley Owners Group (HOG).

The Harley Owners Group is a factory-sponsored enthusiast club, formed in 1983 partly to neutralize and control the negative influence of the outlaw biker gangs. HOG is open to all Harley-Davidson owners, with a free one-year membership included in the purchase of a new motorcycle. In 2004 the number of members amounted to over 900 000. The satisfaction among the membership is very high, represented by a score of 3.7 out of 4, and a renewal rate of 75%. HOG operates in Northern America, Europe, Asia, and South Pacific.

HOG provides its members with a large array of programs and ownership benefits, which include the *HogTales*® magazine, the Fly & Ride program (which allows the member to rent a Harley motorcycle at numerous locations worldwide), insurance, roadside assistance, and safety education. The club also organizes larger rallies, i.e. gatherings for several hundreds or even thousands of enthusiasts throughout the world. HOG is the largest factory-sponsored motorcycle organization in the world.

HOG brings together people loving and riding their motorcycles. The division to chapters enables the enthusiasts to meet other similar people in a local context, whereas nationwide or even global rallies gather the most active members of the group. The rallies always have participation by the employees and management of the company, which allows them to stay in close contact with their customers enabling co-experiencing.

Also the merchandise and memorabilia help members to recognize other members, and see their history even in an arbitrary location on the road. Meeting a fellow rider with a pin from the same rally that you participated in, brings a feeling of having something in common even if the person him/herself is unfamiliar. By telling its members about suitable routes and destinations, and arranging renting and assistance, HOG can greatly increase the possibility of these kinds of encounters.

In the same way as Games Workshop, the HOG communities are also organized on a local level, but with a higher level of corporate guidance. Local activities may include monthly meetings, dinner rides, parades, observation runs, toy runs, holiday events, safe rider programs, charity events, or volunteering as chapter officials.

The products of Games Workshop and Harley-Davidson are esthetically appealing to the customers. Another strong value-adding element is the socializing opportunities provided through the shared interest around the physical products. If the local communities have a high level of activity they successively start to become value adding in their own right. This value-adding element is produced by and for the members of the communities. For the manufacturers again such communities become important sources of ideas about how to improve the quality of both the physical products and the related services. Some financial incentives may also be attached to the membership of the communities. So may certain products (such as memorabilia etc.) be available at a discounted price for members only.

Both Games Workshop and Harley-Davidson communities also function as a marketing tool promoting the product among like-minded enthusiasts. When, for example, the Japanese motor-cycle manufacturers entered the US market in the 1960s and 1970s with technically sophisticated products, they managed to attract the young customers. The traditional products of Harley-Davidson were seen by many as outdated and old-fashioned compared to Honda, Yamaha, Suzuki, Kawasaki etc. By concentrating on the value of its esthetics Harley-Davidson has managed to expand its market share. It is not only the classical design of the bike but also the spirit attached to the Harley-Davidson and the way of living as a Harley-Davidson owner that are important. Some Harley-Davidson owners can even be recognized without being near a bike, from all the merchandise and clothes they are wearing.

Allan Girdler is such an enthusiast. He has written a history of Harley-Davidson. In the introduction of his book he proudly announces that in case any Norwegian, Danish, Swedish, or Finnish moms wonder who taught their kids to say 'Harley-Davidson is Number One' in English, it was him, riding an FLH (a flagship model of Harley-Davidson) to North Cape, Europe's northernmost landfall.[6]

Both Games Workshop and Harley-Davidson have been building communities around their products for decades. Through these communities they promote the uniqueness of the brand and sponsor the idea of product superiority. Especially Harley-Davidson has endorsed this community involvement as a main part of their way of working, starting from the management team, who themselves live the 'genuine Harley-Davidson' life.

Games Workshop has not built the community as systematically from a marketing point of view as Harley-Davidson. Instead Games Workshop has focused on providing continuously new products and support, which delight its gaming enthusiast. The strength of these communities is based on the admiration the customers have for the products and the values these products embody. In the case of Harley-Davidson, the bike is a means for a dream coming true, and for Games Workshop the hobby provides a stimulating, escapist relaxation. As long as the products continue to manifest strong positive values among the users, the communities will remain pulsating and dynamic.

LEADERSHIP IMPLICATIONS – CO-ALIGNING THE STRATEGY WITH MAJOR CUSTOMERS

If a company is looking for the opportunity to develop its customer interaction capabilities, one option is to nurture community building among the customers. The Games Workshop and Harley-Davidson cases show how this can be done: create such a superior product that the product itself largely becomes the object of admiration of the customers. Unfortunately, only a few companies have products that are so clearly distinguishable from the competition that they stand out as unquestioned attractors of admiration. Nokia tried to do this with Club Nokia, but failed. So just relying on the superiority of the products is not the answer for most companies. What then can be done? The following shows how one company systematically built its customer interaction capabilities around one specific customer.

In the mid-1990s a leading European producer of fine paper was reviewing its strategy in order to develop a more customer-oriented business model.[7]

For one of the main product categories, copier papers, the two largest customers were Xerox and Canon. In-depth analyses indicated that there was a substantial potential to deepen the relationship with Canon. The company decided to form a Europe-wide partnership with Canon. To define a more comprehensive service package the company decided to engage representatives from Canon as a resource pool that could support the efforts.

The account executive on the domestic market had built very good relationships with the local Canon organization. These relationships enabled the company to mobilize a co-sponsored seminar for all European Canon units. In this seminar 12 Canon representatives and the entire management team of the fine paper unit attended. The seminar confirmed that the potential existed, and that an opportunity to co-produce value existed. Canon was indeed interested in working more closely with the company and to jointly make competitive offerings available across Europe. The management of the paper producer decided to allocate more resources to further develop the Canon relationship. On top of this, the management team also addressed some specific issues that related to the offerings presented to Canon. After this occasion the business relationship developed very favorably, and in two years volumes had increased by 50%.

In this case the customer was identified as a resource to participate in joint offering development. Using the three-dimensional offering concept it was apparent that the offering was broader than just the physical paper product. To better evaluate which offering elements should be emphasized, the customer, Canon, provided a highly valuable source of knowledge. Based on a better understanding of the customer's value creation, the offering was supported by a multi-million dollar investment in sheeting and packaging operations, as well as considerable investments in human resources. Thanks to the close collaboration with the customer, the paper producer was able to partly shape the value constellation in which it wanted to be a significant actor. The learning from the customer also improved the decision making regarding which resources and capabilities to develop to increase competitiveness.

What the paper manufacturer also achieved was to get access to the large Canon customer base. Even if these customers didn't share the same strong community characteristics as, for example, Harley-Davidson owners, it was still a fairly coherent group, thanks to the strength of the Canon brand. By closely interacting with Canon the paper producer could more effectively learn about the expectations of this quite sizable market segment. This improved considerably the offering design process, which in turn created higher customer satisfaction and increased sales.

The above case shows that customer interaction capabilities can be developed in several ways. But common to all of them is that two particular issues have to be looked into. Firstly, how can the linking with the customer be improved, i.e. creating an optimal way of interacting to conduct the daily business transactions? Secondly, what possibilities are there to use the customer as a source of knowledge and a participant in the capability-building constellation? These two elements combine the efficiency and creativity elements. The above case showed that by designing the customer interaction properly the paper producer could achieve both these goals simultaneously. It learnt a lot from Canon, and at the same time the sales increased significantly.

Building customer communities is nothing new, and can take place in almost any setting. For example, Shouldice Hospital in Thornhill, Ontario, Canada, has built its customer community systematically since 1947. The hospital reports a 99% success rate with over 270 000 hernia repairs. They know this because they follow up every patient. Every year they contact 130 000 patients, and each year their annual patient reunion in downtown Toronto, a gala event including dinner and entertainment, attracts up to 1500 patients.[8] When founder, Dr. Edward Earle Shouldice, organized the first get-together he saw this as a splendid opportunity for annual checkups and building research data. And besides learning from the patients, the get-togethers also create a large number of patient evangelists, the apostles of Shouldice.

Building customer-interaction capabilities has many similarities with the cultivation of value constellations. In the next chapter we will look further into examples of how value constellations can be developed in practice.

CHAPTER 12

VALUE CONSTELLATIONS

*I*n the industrial age individuals grouped together for protection, either to have insurance against the 'Higher Powers,' which could cause disaster on the farm, or against profit-seeking capitalists. Today individuals more often group together for the purpose of creating, learning, and fulfilling their own inner ambitions. The idea to expand the opportunities for people to participate in the relationship economy provides the opportunity for a community to act based on a strong inner drive. This drive can direct the activities in a much more flexible way than original cooperatives, which were formed based on a certain industrial activity like milk cooperatives, food retailers or mutual insurance companies. Mobilizing such an individual drive has throughout history resulted in remarkable achievements. So if the Linux movement is a result of collective action other notable historical accomplishments based on collaborative work include the pyramids in Egypt, the Great Wall of China, the Taj Mahal in India, and the Moai Statues on Easter Island.

Often these creations have been constructed driven by fear, as defensive strategies, in order to avoid punishment from a Higher Power, or to protect the population from outside aggressors. But as the example of the Taj Mahal shows other values can motivate great achievements as well. Shah Jehan ordered the Taj Mahal to be built in honor of his wife. So great was the emperor's love for his wife that he ordered the building of the most beautiful mausoleum on earth for her.

Although it is not known for certain who planned the Taj, the name of an Indian architect of Persian descent, Ustad Ahmad Lahori, has been cited in many sources. As soon as construction began in 1630, masons, craftsmen, sculptors, and calligraphers were summoned from Persia, the Ottoman Empire, and Europe to work on the masterpiece.

The Taj Mahal was made possible by involving a large number of individuals and asking for considerable efforts and sustained performance. Significant for such a professional achievements is the strong anchoring in something outside the realm of personal gain. The driving force can be found in the values based on which the work is seen to be important. These values unite large numbers of individuals in the face of seemingly impossible tasks.

We have recently witnessed the emergence of resource aggregators like eBay and Amazon.com that have skillfully motivated individuals with an entrepreneurial spirit to engage in a collaborative value creation effort, whereby these companies capture part of the collectively created value. This formula is not new, and one of the most vibrant pre-Internet businesses built in this way is the Spanish cooperative, Mondragon, which was established already in the 1950s.

Mondragon Corporacion Cooperativa: Cooperation as Business Strategy[1]

The Mondragon Corporacion Cooperativa (MCC) began in the town of Mondragon in 1956 when a group of five young engineers were encouraged by their priest, Father José Mariá Arizmendiarrieta, to set up a cooperative to make paraffin cooking stoves. Using his vision the five young students built a financial base for the MCC.

By 1959 they had already formed a bank. Today the bank is not only the bank for the cooperatives but is also run as a cooperative itself. MCC has grown to include more than 200 employee-owned companies and entities organized in three sectors: financial, industrial, and distribution; and its own retailer Eroski.

Grupo Eroski is the second biggest Spanish food retailer. It owns and franchises more than 1200 supermarkets and 55 hypermarkets throughout the country and the Balearic and Canary Islands. The company also runs a travel agency. In 2004 Grupo Eroski employed more than 30000 people, of which about 12000 were owners.

The main focus of the association of the Mondragon co-operatives is the creation of owner-employee jobs to expand opportunities for people to participate in the relationship economy. Statistics show the Mondragon cooperatives to be twice as profitable as the average corporation in Spain with employee productivity surpassing any other Spanish organization.

The MCC includes numerous community and employee-based programs. The social systems include health care, housing, social security, primary and post secondary education, training and retraining, and unemployment insurance. Extensive efforts to retrain or relocate workers who are affected by changes that occur in the wider economy is an essential component of its program. The educational system has over 40 schools and a college; there is also a student relationship cooperative, which allows working students to cover their tuition and living expenses for their private high school and college education while having the experience of running their own cooperative.

MCC views capital as a means to an end: the goal is a happy and productive work environment and capital is only a tool. Of the annual net profits 10% is donated to charity and 40% is retained in the collective internal account. This internal account is regarded as the portion of profits that is collectively owned and managed for the common good: if the cooperative ceased to exist, this portion would go to charity. The remaining 50% is open for use by the owner employees.

Another unique aspect of MCC is the way it deals with the establishment of new companies and the repayment of debt. MCC always begins a new enterprise with a group of people who are friends, never with just one person. It sees the natural bonds of friendship as a building block on which successful ventures are built. The new enterprise and the MCC bank agree to stay together until the business is profitable. The members of the new group put up twice the membership fees that others will invest and the bank loans any additional capital necessary at a normal interest rate. If the business runs into trouble the bank will loan additional capital at roughly half the initial rate. If the company is still in financial trouble the interest rate will be dropped to zero, and if more assistance is needed the bank may donate capital to the business. The role of the bank is to secure that the business becomes successful and is able to repay much of the loans, even if the company has to go through drastic changes like new managers or new product lines.

One reason for the success of the MCC seems to be that it recognizes that ordinary people may be able to provide an astonishing amount of creativity and collective insights, once they feel that they truly belong to a community, both intellectually and emotionally.

MCC has been influenced by two main factors: its leaders' strong commitment to the Basque region and culture, and the drive of its initiator, Don José Mariá Arizmendiarrieta. Don José Mariá, as a young priest, began his ministry in Mondragon in 1941. The history of Mondragon shows a period of 15 years with Don José Mariá promoting the vision and possibilities of worker cooperatives, without having any practical examples to refer to. Once the first cooperative was established, Don José Mariá and his followers adopted an approach that set out to integrate economic, social, political, and cultural developments as part of a strategy of reclaiming and revitalizing a part of their region as its primary aim. Cooperation is not an ideology at MCC – it is a business strategy and it seems to work.

The scale of MCC and its regional influence is considerable. Independent cooperatives extend from manufacturing to banking and from farming to retail distribution. It includes a center for university-level education and an array of specialized institutions ranging from a research center to its own social insurance and welfare agency. Within the industrial and manufacturing sector there is a wide span of activity. Domestic appliances have formed the most important product category, but there are others including car components, machine tools, building materials, casting and dies.

The establishment of its own research center was very significant in creating the common ethos within MCC. This provides the existing and potential cooperatives with the stimulus, experience, and guidance of 'high quality' industrial and commercial research advice.

What can be seen from the MCC case is that community behavior can be appealing to the individual, and can be a powerful source contributing to economic success. The more traditional nineteenth-century cooperatives were formed in a defensive spirit, they wanted to protect the cooperative members from something. The MCC started from individuals and groups of friends, and the value-creating ideas of these individuals.

Mondragon is a pioneer in adapting the cooperative idea in a learning context. The first era of cooperatives in the United States was built on the realities of the agrarian society, providing protection against risks due to the unpredictability of nature. The second era of cooperatives emerging in the UK was reforming the cooperative thinking to adapt to the industrial society and reduce poverty and remove material distress, forced upon individual citizens by scrupulous capitalists. Don José Mariá in turn was a pioneer in understanding the emerging nature of the knowledge society. He developed a cooperative concept that was benefited from the needs of individuals to simultaneously learn and contribute to a larger community. By using this property of the individual as the building block a successful network encompassing 70 000 employees has evolved.

What Don José Mariá was doing was to set up a framework enabling a self-organized process to emerge and then to be nurtured. He redefined the logic of expansion of the cooperative from linear, industrial thinking into one of nonlinear expansion enabling resources to be aggregated organically. So instead of having existing businesses planning their growth targets, the community logic allows totally new businesses to join and emerge. Another very powerful insight by Don José Mariá was to have a transparent logic of value appropriation. The formula of 10–40–50 openly and clearly tells every individual how the organization economically functions. Because of this, limited energy and coordination efforts are needed to discuss who is getting what from the possible profits. Ownership, power, and value creation are all in the hands of the community, and they form an integrated whole.

The Mondragon model recognizes the benefits of providing creative individuals with the incentives and the power to bring the community forward. In this respect it strengthens the original idea behind the cooperative movement, the idea that the individual has multiple organizational roles. Early consumer cooperatives emphasized the role of the individual as both a consumer and an owner of the cooperative. In the Mondragon model the cooperative first and foremost recognizes the role of the individual as a knowledgeable worker, and on top of that his potential as an entrepreneur. This ability of the individual is combined with his potential to be an owner and decision maker in the cooperative. This recognizes the importance of the individuals as not primarily consumers, or destroyers of goods, but as knowledge generators, or creators of value.

eBay – Providing a Community Platform for Resource Aggregation

Games Workshop and Harley-Davidson have created communities through the affection created by their products. eBay is different. eBay is a community platform. The company only provides the means for the community to evolve. In this respect the ideas of the founder Pierre Omidyar resemble what Don José Mariá Arizmendiarrieta laid out as principles when he encouraged the formation of the Mondragon cooperative.

The eBay community is guided by five fundamental values:

- We believe people are basically good.
- We believe everyone has something to contribute.

- We believe that an honest, open environment can bring out the best in people.
- We recognize and respect everyone as a unique individual.
- We encourage you to treat others the way you want to be treated.

eBay is firmly committed to these principles and believes that community members should also honor them – whether buying, selling, or chatting with eBay friends.

The company formed by Pierre Omidyar in 1995 began as a trading site for nerds, the newly jobless, and bored home-bound parents to sell sub-prime goods: collectibles and attic trash. But it quickly grew into a teeming metropolis, with its own laws and norms, such as a feedback system in which buyers and sellers rate each other on each transaction. When that wasn't quite enough, eBay formed its own police force to patrol the listings for fraud and to kick out offenders.

eBay manages a community where the customers themselves organize into chapters based on their own interests. The communities are emerging among the members. eBay's management provides the infrastructure so that this can happen. This means that management must take a somewhat laissez-faire approach. The nurturing of the community has to be based on cooperation and finesse, not coercion and force. To make sure eBay doesn't do something that incurs the wrath of its citizens and incites a revolt, eBay's executives work more like civil servants than corporate managers. They poll the populace through online town hall meetings and provide services to keep them happy – and business humming. What also is important is the way the culture and the ethos of the company become personified. In this respect Meg Whitman as the CEO has had an important role in nurturing the organization with proper values.[2]

This collaborative approach has offered awesome benefits. As buyers and sellers flock to the site, they not only feed on it, but also nourish it. By rating each other on transactions, for instance, both buyers and sellers build up reputations they then strive to maintain, setting a standard of behavior that reinforces eBay's appeal. But pushing through reforms is tough because eBay's millions of passionate and clamorous users demand a voice in all major decisions. These users can easily organize themselves and go elsewhere if eBay management tries to enforce something they don't like.

eBay combines two very powerful elements provided by the Internet. Firstly, it is a very cost-effective way of handling transactions in goods with small markets. Secondly, it provides an opportunity for learning and socializing. This community-building function of eBay goes far beyond just selling and buying merchandise.

eBay is much more than retail therapy. For mothers the main attraction of eBay is that they can shop without taking the children. So shopping is much easier online, and can be more fun too. Every auction combines the intoxication of gambling with the thrill of thriftiness. eBay was never meant to be just another cyber-shopping site. From the very beginning, it aimed at combining community and commerce, or in the words of eBay co-founder Jeff Skoll, 'heart and wallet'. The other co-founder Pierre Omidyar wanted eBay to be a place where people made real connections with each other, and where a social contract prevailed.

The eBay community is full of stories about individuals who have started a completely new life thanks to eBay. Two important categories of major influencers are recognizable: the eBay merchants and the virtual personalities. Both categories are important elements, which enable the resource aggregation process to organically evolve.

The eBay merchants have seen eBay as the platform for a new career and have become well-earning super sellers. They have often shifted from a traditional career in a big organization to become entrepreneurs in the eBay universe. By the end of 2004 it was estimated that almost half a million people were engaged full time as eBay merchants, being the drivers of the commercial buzz around eBay.

The virtual personalities can be exemplified by Uncle Griff, 'a 50-something cross-dressing dairy farmer who lives with his mother' – even though she's been dead for 30 years. This virtual character has become wildly popular online. He welcomes new neighbors to the community and generally lives the Omidyar ideal: he makes eBay a place where good people want to gather.[3]

Both eBay merchants and virtual personalities are needed to continue to make eBay as popular as it became during its first 10 years of existence.

The strategy of eBay is to continuously enable millions of people to thrive and conduct business in an open marketplace. eBay and Mondragon are identical when it comes to two main principles. Firstly, the role of the center is to enable a self-organized process to emerge. Secondly, to establish trust there is a transparent mechanism for value appropriation, whereby the majority of the surplus goes to the network members. In the Mondragon case the business is more traditional and the network members are the workers and owners of the cooperative. eBay has reconfigured the value-creating system, and the workers are now independent entrepreneurs. Nevertheless, the success of both organizations is based on having a business model, which stimulates individuals to work for themselves and simultaneously contribute to something they have in common with other members of the network.

eBay is very focused on measuring and adapting: how many people are visiting the site, how many of those then register to become users etc. Get your arms around the data, the thinking goes, and you can decide where to spend money, where more people are needed, and which projects aren't working. To be able to control one has to be able to measure.[4]

The people who do the measuring tackle their mission with intensity. The most important group is what eBay calls category managers, who carve up eBay's major categories and subcategories. In 2004 there were some 20+ of the former and more than 30 000 of the latter, for example collectibles; sports; jewelry and watches; and motors. The category managers spend their days obsessively measuring, tweaking, and promoting their fiefdoms, but they have only indirect control of their products. They can't order more toothpaste onto store shelves. What they can do is endlessly try to eke out small wins in their categories – say, a slight jump in scrap-metal listings or new bidders for comic books. To get there, they use marketing and merchandising schemes such as enhancing the presentation of their users' products and giving them tools to buy and sell better.

Ultimately the future of eBay seems to be dependent on how well it succeeds in maintaining its values and having a sustained value match with its community. Pierre Omidyar wanted eBay to operate according to the moral values he subscribed to in his own life: that people are basically good, and given the chance to do right, they generally will. Adam Cohen in the book *The Perfect Store*, the history of eBay, sees this as the paradox at the heart of eBay: idealism made it profitable. Jeff Skoll had already explained this in a 1999 *Fortune* interview where he stated that beyond fulfilling a financial function trade also satisfies another human need – social contact. In the course of a transaction, a buyer and seller may find common interests, exchange gossip, and even develop a relationship.

eBay encourages its community members to meet physically, e.g. in its yearly eBay Live! Reunion. In 2004 more than 10 000 members showed up in the June meeting in New Orleans. Some of the participants even admitted an addiction to online trading.

eBay wants to differentiate from its competitors by underlining the values of openness, trust, and respect among its members. The members of the eBay community are attracted by the values, which also provide reduced risks for the customers. The members feel that a mutual relationship built on trust and respect is a good and firm ground for business. Through the feedback the individuals conducting a trade are providing, each community member gets evaluated in respect of trustworthiness. If you as a member accept these values you assume all other members also accept them, even if criminal elements may try to exploit this openness.

Still, eBay has had to admit that not all individuals are good. One big threat against the Internet-enabled community-based business model is the impact of unreliable and criminal elements in the virtual space. In January 2005 *The Sunday Times Magazine* found eBay auctions under way for illegal flick knives, pornography, pirated software, obviously fake designer labels, and junk email addresses, all supposedly banned by eBay. And a reseller was offering five 'big-bud cannabis seeds,' with bidding at £6.61. An eBay representative admitted that 'the trust and safety' values were difficult to live up to due to the volume of transactions.

THE EVOLVING NATURE OF COMMUNITIES

Communities have always existed as a natural part of the society. Traditional strong communities are the church, the village, the family etc. As noticed in earlier chapters the Internet is now providing an additional forum for communities to emerge. In some cases the Internet provides a means for existing communities to find an additional arena to grow and prosper. Both Games Workshop and Harley-Davidson are examples of communities born in the real world that are now living a much more active and dynamic life thanks to the virtual possibilities. eBay, of course, was born in the virtual world, but has also expanded its activities in the real world. So is eBay endorsing the opening up of I-Sold-It stores, where people can go to a physical location and sell things. eBay itself has no plans of going into that business, but eBay management is excited that such new phenomena are growing up around the eBay platform in every part of the United States.

eBay has in some instances been compared to Wal-Mart, and it has been questioned whether Wal-Mart is the ultimate competitor for eBay. This comparison is interesting, and also relevant, as eBay and Wal-Mart partly perform similar tasks but use two completely different business models. eBay provides an efficient transaction platform for entrepreneurs to engage in value-creating activities, and relies on the market for logistics services to provide an efficient way for the goods to move from the seller to the buyer. Wal-Mart also provides the buyer with goods, but in turn has built its own competitive advantage based on its in-house global logistics process. Both operate with the resource market following an open architecture philosophy. As the example of Levi's showed, Wal-Mart is prepared to develop joint processes with leading suppliers in the same way that eBay tries to support its super sellers, the critical nodes of the eBay community.

How its communities are evolving is something which even eBay management admits is to a large extent impossible to predict in detail. But it is clear that the network behavior in this form of self-organization is one of the corner stones for successful communities.

ETHOS – THE GLUE OF A RESOURCE COMMUNITY

A youngish man, who looks like a graduate student, sits on the floor of his unpretentious dorm-like room, spooning Thai noodles from a plastic container. His glasses are smudged, his clothes are wrinkled, his hair is tousled like a boy's. But when he talks, people listen. Certainly no person on the campus can talk about the future, as he does, with the riveting authority of someone who not only knows what's in store for tomorrow but also is a major force in shaping that future as well.

In the above way did the *Playboy* magazine introduce Bill Gates in a featured interview in July 1994. After having explained the notion of 'digital convergence' (for which he acknowledged John Sculley to have been the one to do the popularizing) he was asked to sum up the Microsoft ethos in one sentence. His answer was: '*Let's use our heads and think and do better software than anyone else.*' Even if many have questioned whether Microsoft truly does better software than anyone else, the ethos embodied in Bill Gates and his view on what Microsoft is, and how it will move forward has helped to create the most vibrant company-driven developer community in the world. What is interesting here is to notice that the same community-building principles, as described in the previous chapter regarding customer communities, also apply to Microsoft when building its resource community. Microsoft develops the main part of the content, which is then provided to the developer community for testing in the form of beta versions, and the knowledge exchange going on between Microsoft and the community provides considerable added value to Microsoft. The Microsoft solution providers, which have grown with Microsoft, subscribe to the ethos of the Microsoft ecosystem as expressed by Bill Gates more than 10 years ago.

This is why the notion of ethos is a valuable construct when discussing community building. Ethos is an element of the organization, which is neither fully under the control of, nor restricted by, the organization. The ethos is the incarnation of what the organization stands for in the broader context. It embodies how the organization has become part of its environment, an environment influencing it and providing nutrition. But this environment is also influenced by the organization, to a varying degree. In the case of Microsoft to such a high degree that even the Federal Trade Commission has had to question whether this influence is too big. Ethos can be defined as follows:

Ethos is the guiding belief, standards, or ideas that characterize or pervade a group, a community, a people, or an ideology.[5]

Subsequently ethos is the spirit that motivates the ideas, customs, or practices of people. According to Atkins ethos comprises the complex and fundamental values that underlie, permeate, or actuate major patterns of thought and behavior in any particular culture, society, or institution. Originally ethos is Greek for character.

Microsoft is an organization, whose ethos has its origin in the aspirations of a strong visionary founder. If this individual is successful, the ethos gets institutionalized, and starts a life of its own. This has also been observed when searching for what is distinctive of companies known for their quality ethos. What was found was that the 'special something,' underpinning quality culture, is not so easily named. Rather, it seemed to be a function of fuzzy elements that might be described using words such as depth, language, confidence, risk, and respect. Major changes in attitudes and mindsets are not easy to achieve. For example, in the procurement function the skilled use of simultaneous partnership and pressure elements to get desired results is not easily taught, as it is more an art than a science. To get the right culture in place it is important to select respected individuals who can serve as role models for the new ways of doing business. A new culture will gradually emerge as an increasing number of individuals begin to emulate behaviors of these successful role models to achieve similar results.[6]

The power of a strong ethos is illustrated by the seeming paradox of life in terrorist groups: despite the anti–authoritarian ethos, the cadre demands unquestioning compliance and rejects dissent in any form. The way to get rid of doubt is to expel or eliminate the doubters. On the other hand, terrorists whose only sense of significance comes from being terrorists, cannot be forced to give up terrorism, for to do so would be to lose their very reason for being. But this is very similar to what the most elitist military units try to establish. The US Marine Corps present themselves as a calling, not a job. Marines commit themselves to serve the nation and to accept risks and sacrifice on its behalf. The Marine culture emphasizes self-sacrifice, discipline, courage, physical rigor, and loyalty to comrades and country.

Ethos has become a topic of increasing interest when considering why and how certain communities have prospered, and others have not. A possible explanation is that one key ingredient of successful communities is that their, at least retrospectively, attractive ethos has been built into the network right from the start. The ethos has evolved from having been an integral part of the originator(s) to gradually become institutionalized and further shaped through the interaction between the organization and its environment.

When comparing Wal-Mart and eBay one big difference is that Wal-Mart is based purely on an economic model, whereas eBay at least tries to build an ethos into the network, which goes beyond just economic rationale. Wal-Mart has a substantially longer history, and its business model has proven to be very competitive and sustainable. During the beginning of 2005 eBay did not live up to the expectations in respect of growth and profit making. So again the two elements of creativity versus efficiency play out. Whether the eBay model is providing enough efficiency to expand significantly into new product and customer categories remains to be seen. The ethos of eBay has been referred to as one of its most decisive success factors. What yet is unproven is how far the collective efforts of the eBay community can invade the markets built through the engineering and logistics expertise of the leading retailers. eBay has already captured a considerable part of the second-hand car market in the United States, so there is evidence that the eBay platform in certain categories is considered highly attractive by the customers, also when it moves outside the primary focus area of collectibles and sub-prime goods.

LEADERSHIP IMPLICATIONS – BUILDING NEW VALUE CONSTELLATIONS

When building new value constellations the question of how the orchestrator relates to the network becomes important. The external interactions are sources of learning, and the network members are contributors to competitiveness. This means that managers and leaders have to more consciously evaluate with whom to interact. Supplier networks can be used to learn faster and, subsequently, choosing with whom to collaborate becomes a strategic issue.[7] The example of the paper producer in the previous chapter showed that customers can also function as resources that can be addressed for shared learning and offering development. In this respect the members in a value constellation can have multiple roles, depending on the circumstances. What counts is the optimal learning setting at different moments in time.

One consideration when building value constellations is whether it is possible to specify in detail the task of each member. If the task is predefined, the role of the member is one of 'execution'. If, however, the orchestrator dynamically interacts with the member, and they jointly define how the specific value-creating tasks will be handled, the role of the member is 'co-creative'.

Another issue relating to the orchestrator–member relationship is the question of use of power and governance. The relationship between the orchestrator and the network member also relates to the financial context of the value-creating activities. By engaging network members the orchestrator will have to give up some of the financial gains for the benefit of the members. The orchestrator will therefore have to solve the issue of value appropriation. One possibility is to have a formal contract as the governance mode. If the member is engaged to provide critical knowledge in the co-production of the offering, the orchestrator may have difficulties in formulating a successful contract. In such a situation the orchestrator may be better off by engaging in a relationship based on trust.

The Linux community has from a production perspective been based on trust, but from a usage point of view it is clearly governed by the copyright agreement. In this respect trust and contracts can both exist within the same constellation. The way that Linus Torvalds in his first email put forward the simple principles based on which trust was established can be summarized in three points:

1. He positioned what he intended to do in a humble way, i.e. provided the basis for the orchestrated process.
2. He described what the content was, without trying to oversell – rather the opposite.
3. He invited people to give him feedback on what he had done and what features most people wanted from the system.

These simple principles form the basis for the building of an emergent value constellation. The first challenge is how to establish trust. The initiator has to communicate an interest to enter collaboration with the potential members of the community. This requires a long-term perspective and a conscious effort not to overpromise. The second theme is to present some concrete results, the seed capital for the work process to get started and the knowledge exchange to gain some meaning. And last but definitely not the least the orchestrator has to be prepared to listen to the community members, and be open to incorporate their suggestions into future work to show them that their efforts have mattered.

When adhered to, these three principles encourage continuous learning with the network members as co-creators of value. These principles also illustrate the importance of different learning processes. In between the leader has to handle problem solving, as Linus Torvalds has been doing for the Linux community as the main orchestrator. Another role is to enable co-experiencing, which in the Linux community happens, for example, in different fairs and exhibitions. Information transmission is continuously supporting the ongoing real work and the feedback posted on new functionalities. Finally insight accumulation is something which continuously surrounds the orchestrator as things evolve, and the orchestrator tries to navigate and find out what is important and what is not. An example of this was the decision by Linus Torvalds to change the copyright, and allow commercial activities around Linux at the beginning of 1992.

Orchestration in the form of building a value constellation has to focus on establishing the actual work environment. Linux has established routines for continuous improvements of the software. Games Workshop, for example, has combined the resource development perspective by guiding the members in their gaming social interactions. This also strengthens customer relationships. As the gaming communities get stronger, they also become fertile ground for additional sales of product and services offered by Games Workshop. As the work proceeds the community evolves as a byproduct of the work being done and the learning taking place. The community capital is built up based on all the small steps that form the co-created results of the interaction between the orchestrator and the community members.

The four categories of operational capabilities, and their concrete outcomes: the core resources; the offering concepts; the customer interactions; and the value constellations have now been presented. All these capabilities need capability management; they have to be built, leveraged, and maintained over time. In the next chapter we will portray how to direct the building of new capabilities.

CHAPTER 13

THE IOCC FRAMEWORK

*T*he propositions presented so far in the book suggest that leaders have to engage people in learning in order to initiate new offering ideas. To design, produce, and provide these offerings, new capabilities are needed. Only by building these new capabilities can the commercial benefits of the original ideas be captured. But how such capabilities are built varies from case to case. The engineers rebuilding the valve production capability in the Toyota supplier network, and the Linux developers, are examples of collective action resulting in capabilities being built in networks. A key requirement for such an emergent action to take place is shared awareness of what is going on. This means that individuals can understand the context wherein they have a role to play, carry out their individual task, and then make others aware of the fact that the task is completed. By everybody acting in this same way a highly disciplined collective creative effort can be accomplished. But the Toyota and the Linux cases also suggest that the speed by which the capabilities are built is by no means self-evident.

Common to any capability-building activity is that during the process individuals have to learn, and in order to learn they have to make decisions about how to do things differently from how they did in the past. If the decision making is taking place in a highly competitive – or as in the military, lethal – environment, then improving decision-making speed is vital. Consequently this has been a topic of great interest for military strategists.

In 1986 Colonel John Boyd gave a presentation on patterns of successful military operations. He concluded that those that had been successful had been able to observe–orient–decide–act more inconspicuously, more quickly, and with more irregularity compared to the opponents. This formed a basis to keep or gain initiative as well as shape and shift the main effort: to repeatedly and unexpectedly penetrate vulnerabilities and weaknesses exposed by that effort or other efforts that tie up, divert, or drain away adversary attention (and strength) elsewhere. This was the first time Boyd introduced the notion of the observe–orient–decide–act (or OODA loop), the conceptual basis for the principles of network-centric warfare.

Boyd hypothesized that all intelligent organisms and organizations undergo a continuous cycle of interaction with their environment. Boyd broke this cycle down to four interrelated and overlapping processes through which one cycles continuously:[1]

- Observation: the collection of *data* by means of the *senses*.
- Orientation: the analysis and synthesis of data to form one's current *mental* perspective.
- Decision: the determination of a course of action based on one's current mental perspective.
- Action: the physical playing out of decisions.

This decision cycle is the OODA loop. Boyd emphasized that this decision cycle is the central mechanism enabling adaptation (apart from natural selection) and is therefore critical to survival.

In his conceptualization Boyd considered 'observe,' 'decide,' and 'act' as self-explanatory. The key issue was 'orient'. By 'orient,' Boyd meant analysis and synthesis based on new information, previous experience, cultural tradition, and genetic heritage, to shape the way we interact with the environment – hence orientation shapes the way we observe, the way we decide, and the way we act. Boyd viewed time (and its reciprocal, speed) as the critical element of decision making at all levels of operational command and control. Operational success, in Boyd's view, depends on being inside the opponent's decision cycle – that is, completing the OODA loop faster than the opponent.

The way effective capability building in networks takes place is by a combination of directed, nurtured, and self-organized individual action based on the availability of accurate, detailed, and real-time information for the individuals participating in the collaborative action. In this respect building capabilities means that the leader has to facilitate the network members with the opportunities to complete their OODA loops as fast as possible.

A key requirement of leadership for capability building is to provide the network members with shared information fostering shared situational awareness. This in turn is the basis for self-synchronization, in which coordination proceeds without overt communication. Having shared information and common mental models of the current state and the desired end state is the key to effective OODA loops at the individual level. To provide such self-synchronization the leader has to shift the balance between bottom-up organization and top-down control in favor of bottom-up organization.

Network-centric operations and the associated self-synchronization thus put a premium on the performance of individuals and small teams throughout the network. A critical component of such performance is the ability to integrate information, anticipate, and plan.

These ideas suggest that when building a new way of working, there are some logical steps that the organization has to go through. If the OODA loop represents the logic of how decisions are made at the level of the individual, there is a similar cycle describing how ideas mature in an organization. This cycle can be described as the initialization–operationalization–crystallization–commercialization or IOCC framework.

The Olympic Games institutionalized its IOC (the International Olympic Committee), an industrial construct. Here we introduce a knowledge construct: the IOCC framework. The difference between the two is illustrative. Traditionally it was important to establish permanent organizations, committees. In the knowledge society the concept is more important, and the organizational structures may change and adopt. IOCC is a framework about how to manage and lead change: a framework for dynamism. This is what ultimately orchestration is about: feeling, sensing, living, and instigating change – and enjoying it.

If the individual can benefit from shared awareness when performing tasks in a collaborative network from a clearly defined mission, organizations often face situations where the mission is less clear, and the collective action is much more looking for what to do next, instead of considering how to perform a well-defined task. One such example was the US Army and its identity crisis after the Cold War was over.

The US Army; Re-Establishing Legitimacy

Initialization
In 1989, when the Berlin Wall came down, the US Army had to redefine its mission. The Army was an organization that had been optimized to defeat a single threat – the Soviet Union. Suddenly this threat was disappearing as a means to

mobilize such a large force of military power, which the United States had supported during the whole period of the Cold War. The legitimate question was: In the absence of world-class enemies, how could the United States keep its world-class armed forces gainfully employed?

The Army was faced with a much different world, posing challenges that promised to be difficult. Over 500 000 people had to leave the Army, almost 600 installations were closed, tactical nuclear weapons were removed, and chemical weapons had to be destroyed.

In 1991, the Army started to rewrite its basic vision and doctrine to include military operations other than war, peace-keeping, and a prototype doctrine for thinking about the future. The new doctrine was the basis for translating ideas into new or modified weaponry, organizational designs, tactical concepts, and training and leader development programs. The ambition was that the vision could be used to focus the energy of the whole military. The articulation and dissemination of the vision was seen by the Army as nearly as important as the vision itself. Unless a vision can be shared, it cannot be brought to bear. This phase of the development could be called the initialization phase of the transformation process.

Operationalization

The process of rewriting the doctrine took almost two years. Then it was put to work at the national training centers. At the end of each exercise there were tasks, conditions, and standards, which were reflected upon once the exercise was over. This was seen as a way to transform the Army into a learning organization. The ambition was to drive people to think about the future and to experiment in the field, in the training centers, and in simulations, using the doctrine as the basis to experiment with organizing around information, not equipment.

The challenge was described by General Gordon R. Sullivan as follows:

> To demonstrate the power of our ideas about the future, we had to create a model – something people could see and touch. We had to provide proof that change was real, useful, and purposeful, so we created a series of experiments designed to bring people together to enable them to understand what this new Information Age will enable us to do. We had to create something not unlike a 'Grecian urn.' You can read Keats' poem for hours and not really understand what a Grecian urn looks like. Until you hold one in your hands, the magic escapes you. So it is with change – in some cases you have to create prototypes in order to create disciples. Proof is essential to making change happen.[2]

In many ways the Persian Gulf crisis provided the Army with legitimacy for a new role, and demonstrated anew the real value of having large, superbly trained and equipped professional forces on hand ready to respond to emergencies. So the 'business case' for change was established, and the prototype was tested. This can be described as the operationalization phase of the transformation.

Crystallization

However, the Army was at the same time facing much more scrutiny from the outside world in respect of its role and integrity. Drug trade-related corruption in the Coast Guard caught the attention of the press. It was also questioned how well equipped the Army would be to nurture peace instead of winning battles. In combat, the leader emphasizes maximum force to protect his own troops; while the peace-keeping unit stresses minimum force to protect the public. To provide peace, appropriate military units would have to be permanently retrained and reorganized. The challenge was how to adjust the organization and organizational ethos. The organizational legacies of the Cold War era had to adapt to the opportunities of the new geopolitical situation.

In the mid-1990s the Clinton administration had serious doubts regarding the future role of the US military. David Reiff, a senior fellow at the World Policy Institute, stated that the reality was that the consensus about what the United States should stand for, where it should act, and where it should refrain from trying to affect events had broken down. To Reiff, warnings about the coming clash with militant Islam and suggesting that chaos in the Third World had replaced communism as the gravest danger to US security, had an obvious, vulgar appeal. He questioned the future role of the Army. Was the continued support for military expenditures justifiable?[3]

In December 1997 Colonel Michael Lehnert provided, in retrospect, a strikingly good analysis of the new character of terrorism. He saw terrorism as an enemy force multiplier. It is asymmetrical warfare in its classic form. Whether ballistic weapons with precision strike capability could be added to the terrorist arsenal should be a cause for concern.[4]

To an increasing degree the Army now had to cope with how to handle information and deal with moral issues. Its traditional strong foothold was in the physical domain, which by and large represented the thinking of the industrial society. What now was needed was to be able to cope with unfamiliar purposes and methods, those peculiar requirements manifested in operations other than war. Most important was mental agility, expanding the range of operations into unfamiliar realms and the imagination to use Army capabilities for purposes for which they were not designed.

Network-centric warfare and network-centric operations emerged in the late 1990s as the new concepts based on which the US Army was moving into the information age. This perspective was primarily built on technological leaps in sensors, networked communications, precision weapons, and in their application to the problems of expeditionary warfare.

But even if new technology could be successfully used for intelligence activities on the battlefield, there was also a need for improved strategic intelligence. This was not easy, and, for example, the CIA was incapable of addressing the new problems of the post-Cold War period. Even with a budget of $30 billion a year the CIA could not provide the intelligence capability that the new world order demanded. With the attacks on the World Trade Center on September 11, 2001, it became evident that the world's greatest intelligence organizations had not been able to protect America. The Cold War was gone, but the world was by no means safe. Even America was vulnerable. But it was not paralyzed. On September 11, President George W. Bush declared that America would stand united to win the war against terrorism.

Commercialization
In the days of the Cold War, the Army justified a force structure by the threat defined by the Soviet Union. Generations of Pentagon warriors testified to Congress by comparing weapons systems to Soviet tanks, planes, ships, and missiles, and debating their numbers and their individual merits. The change now was that the number of weapons systems was less important than the right weapon, at the right time, in the right place. Precision and initiative, not volume, provided the advantage, and this precision is required in recognition of the advantages of asymmetrical as opposed to counterforce warfare.

The war on terrorism brought back the need to revitalize the warrior ethos of the Army. The primary mission of the military was to fight and win America's wars. But as Afghanistan and Iraq had shown, a new dimension had to be added. The US Army should also be able to build peace once it had won the wars.

THE IOCC FRAMEWORK

Executives long felt comfortable with Chandler's proposition that 'structure follows strategy'. Recently this dictum has been opposed, for example by Jim Collins, the author of the best-selling book *Good to Great*, saying that first one should decide upon who and then what.[5] Are these apparent conflicting views on the sequencing of strategizing and organizing representing a genuinely unsolvable paradox, or are these perspectives reconcilable?

The orchestration examples presented so far in this book suggest that most new businesses or business models emerge gradually. When Stevens came up with his idea about starting a barter relationship, Robinson got the inspiration to progressively build his entrepreneurial activities. When Baron de Coubertin defined the principles for the new Olympic Games he could not envision the proportions this new movement would reach, even if he could build his vision on facts about how the Olympics were organized in ancient times. When the Cold War was over it was debated for years whether terrorism posed a real threat on America or not, and how the US Army should adapt to the new situation.

In the case of the US Army the whole American society was involved in a shared dialogue regarding the future of the military. The shared learning was influenced by many individuals, and, of course, external events, such as the Gulf War and 9/11, which were important catalysts that brought the process forward.

Emergent learning processes can thus be observed, but with various durations. The re-establishing of the valve production capacity of the Toyota production system was completed in six days, whereas the post–Cold War transformation process of the US Army lasted for more than a decade. Both, however, shared the same phases of initialization, operationalization, crystallization, and commercialization. In the following the nature of each phase will be laid out.

During the initialization phase the idea appears for the first time. It can be triggered by an external event, it can be initiated by a single individual, or the idea may pop up in a brainstorming session with many people present. In the Toyota–Aisin case the initialization was very clear and concrete, the fire. For the US Army the need for change appeared more subtly.

Phase two marks the shift from an idea into a more concrete vision of a new state, an offering, a product, or a service. This vision then starts to have organizational impacts. In the US Army this meant the debate about how to adapt the military forces to the withdrawal of the threat from the Soviet Union. In the Toyota–Aisin case it was the emerging role configuration leading to the orchestrated processes whereby the production capacity could be built.

The third phase is about crystallization. This means building the necessary capabilities into the network, which are needed to carry out the new way of working. As normally more than one actor is needed in the new setup, the actor is no longer the internal organization, but a community of collaborating actors. The crystallization phase means working simultaneously with alternative views of the future, but with one dominating perspective starting to evolve. In the Toyota–Aisin case this was the phase when the production processes started to materialize, and in the US Army when the new doctrine became operational – ultimately catalyzed by 9/11.

The fourth phase is commercialization. In this phase tasks become very operational. Success can be measured on how well clearly defined objectives can be met, be they cashflow from a new business venture, or success in war in respect of a reorganized army. In the Toyota–Aisin case the results were very clearly measurable. In the case of the US Army, the performance will ultimately be judged by the people. How the voters will approve the results is what constitutes the measurable outcome of the success of the US Army.

The evolutionary path described here thus consists of four distinct phases: initialization, operationalization, crystallization, and commercialization.

In many of today's firms strategizing has replaced strategy: the verb is more important than the noun. Strategizing is continuously taking place in the form of different orchestration initiatives where probes, experiments, and trials are carried out in collaboration with an array of actors joined by an emergent vision of some new value-creating opportunity. Thus there is also a need to monitor the continuous flow of new ideas forming the strategizing process, and insights have to be systematically collected and tracked.

The IOCC framework indicates that most strategic issues are emergent, and that the tradition of first making strategy, whereby structure follows, has to be reinterpreted. In Figure 13.1 the traditional definition of strategy would mean the outcome of the operationalization phase. The offering vision is thus equal to what normally is perceived as the strategy. Structure is then both preceding the structure (the choice of individuals to participate in the initialization phase) and following the strategy (the participants in the constellation that will be formed to build the needed capabilities). So structure does follow strategy if we think about the formalized structure, but it precedes strategy when thinking

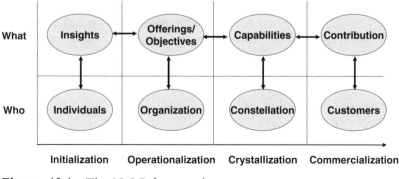

Figure 13.1   The IOCC framework

about true strategic innovation. Throughout the process who and what interact. Feedback cycles between the phases mean that capabilities are built step by step, based on the gradually clarifying offering vision. This means that the strategy gets refined and becomes more explicit all the time, as the focus shifts from ideas towards commercialization.

The shift in emphasis from strategy to strategizing also means that managers have to become better in putting new initiatives in place. When these initiatives are in the emergent phase it is valuable if participation is not just restricted to internal employees, but that the full potential of the extended enterprise can be used. Possible participants providing valuable insights are customers, suppliers, board members, consultants, and in certain cases, even competitors.

Managers applying the IOCC framework have to start from the issue of insights and individuals. Who will participate? Who should contribute to the creative process? Once the new offering vision and the corresponding organizational priorities are crafted, it may be that perfecting the strategy requires other individuals to take charge of finetuning the capabilities and securing customer delight. Firstly, the following responsibilities have to be considered: who initiates and who commercializes? A lot of confusion about strategy versus structure follows from not explicitly setting boundaries between these two roles, and not communicating their respective accountabilities properly.

The leader facilitating capability building also has to secure the efficiency of the organization. Different contexts have to be managed in parallel, and the orchestrator has to be able to shift his style depending on the particular requirements at hand. These various orchestrating contexts will be the subject of the concluding part of this book.

PART IV

THE LEADER AS ORCHESTRATOR

*I*n Part I we introduced the building blocks for orchestration: capabilities; learning; and orchestration. Part II looked in detail at the four learning contexts: information acquisition; problem solving; co-experiencing; and insight accumulation. Part III in turn provided examples of how to build operational capabilities in networks with respect to: core resources; offering concepts; customer interactions; and value constellations. The final part combines the insights derived thus far in order to see what is expected from the leader as an orchestrator.

One of the tasks in any high-performing profession is to make things as simple as possible, but not to oversimplify. Psychologists have introduced the word flow to describe the state of total concentration that high performing artists reach at peak performance.[1] The leader as orchestrator in many respects resembles such an artist. The challenge is to master the performance but with ease. Which are then the performances that the orchestrator has to meet? To answer that question the orchestrating context has to be profoundly understood. The previously presented cases can be used to illustrate how different situations can benefit from an orchestration approach.

The example of Nokia's integrated supply chain showed how a company can strengthen its core resources by efficient use of information acquisition as the primary learning mode. The objective was to continuously improve and finetune the details of the supply chain process. But other learning forms were required as well. After the fire in the semiconductor plant in Albuquerque problem-solving skills were needed, and in order to develop Club Nokia co-experiencing became a major part of the development efforts.

IDEO, being an offering design firm developing constantly new concepts, shows a high degree of problem-solving skills. Here learning is based on an ability to systematically take on new problems, and with limited prior experience, still be able to solve them. In addition the problem-solving approach is complemented by co-experiencing in order to make the interaction between IDEO and the customer as effective as possible.

The two examples regarding customer communities, Games Workshop and Harley-Davidson, showed the importance of co-experiencing when developing a customer community. Of course these communities were also asking for very attractive basic products, so strong generative capabilities to build the core resources are complementary capabilities.

Insight accumulation is crucial when building value constellations and aggregating resources. Like Meg Whitman stated, it is the community that brings eBay forward.

What these examples indicate is that each of the four operational capabilities seems to emphasize one of the four learning modes, even if other types of learning are needed as well. The pairing of operational capability with dominant learning mode would thus be as follows:

- Core resources – information transmission.
- Offering concepts – problem solving.
- Customer interactions – co-experiencing.
- Value constellations – insight accumulation.

It is important, however, to notice one thing: for most companies all four types of learning contexts and capability-building efforts are relevant. It is a mistake to think that the company should specialize in only one of the four areas, for example only focusing on its core and only learning through information acquisition.

Lately a lot of management literature has been very focused on special cases, such as the way Li & Fung has built a successful business based on a superior system to aggregate resources from tens of thousands of suppliers in Asia. Also the way the eBay auction platform enables resource aggregation to take place in a self-organized manner easily gets oversimplified.

Another popular area for management writers is to highlight the way problem solving can effectively be conducted in large networks by combining the existing dispersed knowledge through a self-organized process. This has been illustrated by the example of the recovery from the fire at the plant of the Aisin Seiki division of Toyota. This is, however, only one type of learning that Toyota is good at. When launching the Lexus model Toyota showed sophisticated skills in staging experiences for its customers. And now Toyota is trying to further strengthen its position by influencing the global car industry to become more interested in hybrids – cars that combine gasoline engines with electric motors to boost power and improve fuel efficiency. To do this management must create relationships with different stakeholders who have environmental concerns, but who don't want to sacrifice power or comfort. This means building a stronger capability in cultivating diverse communities.

As the case of Toyota shows, leaders have to orchestrate in diverse contexts. One of the consequences of rapid change and increased focus on learning, such as in the cell-phone industry, is that a business leader cannot always rely on a clear vision, as the future is so unpredictable. Instead the leader has to closely monitor and act upon the behavior of others within the industry – competitors, customers, suppliers, and other actors. But at the same time the leader has to evaluate how to leverage upon the unique capabilities the firm possesses and how these capabilities could be combined with the capabilities of others. The challenge is then, how to mobilize and nurture learning in networks.

For the orchestrator the task is to coordinate, conciliate and exercise control, make decisions about the future course, and institutionalize the character of the organization. Orchestration brings the individual responsibilities of the leader to the fore. Orchestration is both to conform and to challenge the existing. Orchestration can in this respect be compared to ice hockey. Split vision refers to the ability to see the puck on the stick without looking directly at it. The player's eyes are up 'reading' the play and what options are available. Indirectly the player sees the puck out of the bottom of the eyes. But split vision is not enough in business, as the game of business does not follow the same rules all the time. There is also a need to figure out when to challenge the rules, when new unthought-of opportunities emerge. If the ice hockey player needs split vision, the orchestrator needs triple split vision.

The final part of the book deals with how leaders practically can apply orchestration as a leadership approach. The starting point is the different learning contexts. For each learning context a certain type of leadership influence is needed. The four leadership types are conductor, architect, auctioneer, and promoter. Each is covered in a separate chapter.

In Chapter 14 the work of two conductors is scrutinized: Bramwell Tovey, music director and conductor of the Vancouver Symphony Orchestra, and Esa-Pekka Salonen, artistic director of the Los Angeles Philharmonic. These examples show that the conductor, to a high degree, facilitates information transmission. An application of orchestrating leadership as a conductor is found in the way Nokia acted in the aftermath of the fire in the Philips semiconductor plant in Albuquerque, spring 2000. Another leader applying the same principles is Bill Belichick, coach of three-time Super Bowl winners New England Patriots.

Chapter 15 looks into the way leading architects work, by the examples of Frank Gehry, the architect most known for the Guggenheim museum in Bilbao in Spain, and Eric Carlson, the architect who co-designed the flagship Louis Vuitton store on the Champs-Elysées that was reopened in October 2005. The meticulous work of an architect, solving individual problems one at a time, was also the approach taken by General Wesley K. Clark when overseeing the NATO forces in the Kosovo war.

Auctioneers have captivated audiences for centuries. In Chapter 16 leading auctioneers from Sotheby's and Christie's present their views on what makes auctioneering such a fascinating art. It is also argued that one of the best leaders to apply auctioneering skills in today's business world is Steve Jobs.

The topic of Chapter 17 is the mobilizing of large groups of people behind some important idea, or the work of a promoter. One of the most successful promoters has been Bob Geldof, and the characteristics behind his Live Aid and Live 8 concerts are compared to the work of another promoter, Linus Torvalds. A surprise promoter has been Captain America, less known perhaps, but a generator of what seems to be an eternal cult.

Finally, in Chapter 18 we summarize the overall character of the business orchestrator, the one with highly developed situational awareness, conciliating different interests within the value constellation and being responsible for its course. His or her work is first and foremost about managing action, but using information and learning extensively to establish the shared awareness needed to inspire and mobilize the other members of the value constellation.

Business orchestration emphasizes the notion of character. The word thriving is used to symbolize the values embodied by the orchestrator. Orchestrating leadership cannot be detached from the character of the individual carrying the leadership role. The orchestrators resemble top performing artists. Their lives are highly disciplined but also highly creative. Their work is often directly followed and evaluated by thousands of people, and perhaps by millions indirectly through the media. Below-par performance is a disaster.

Orchestrators carry out their work because they like it. They find both intellectual and emotional satisfaction from having the privilege to see how they can influence large groups of people with astonishing results. In this way business orchestration represents a fresh injection of new dynamism into corporate life, as it brings the creative human being back on the business stage.

CHAPTER 14

THE LEADER AS CONDUCTOR

An orchestrating leader has to live with a constant pressure for efficiency and sustained good performance. At the same time the leader has to nurture creativity, build trust, and inspire professionals. When doing this the orchestrator often has to conciliate between different stakeholders with alternative opinions. Being in charge of a symphony orchestra in many ways brings together all these demands into one single profession.

Henry Mintzberg followed Bramwell Tovey, at that time the artistic director of Winnipeg Symphony Orchestra, for a day to figure out how a conductor practices leadership. He wrote an article of what he saw.[1] The observations Mintzberg made will be reflected upon in the following.

CONDUCTING AN ORCHESTRA: INSTILLING DISCIPLINED CREATIVITY

Mintzberg sought to determine how the orchestra is controlled. Tovey indicated that he selected the program, determined how the pieces are played, chose the guest artists, staffed the orchestra, and managed some external relationships. Control through designing systems, creating structures, and making choices is very much built into the profession. Professional musicians know these things by training, and do not have to be controlled by the conductor to perform 'according to the rules'. The level of detail is so minute that everybody even knows and accepts how one should sit according to a strict and externally imposed pecking order, inherited from the tradition of classical music. The work in itself, though considered to be a very creative profession (who would argue a musician is not?), is highly standardized. The role of the individual is tightly coordinated and integrated with the roles of the other musicians in the orchestra. The professional is utterly adhered to the setting within the group, upon which he or she depends, when practicing the profession. Disciplined creativity describes this. The role of the leader is to make sure that the ongoing activities of the group are timed correctly and performed in the proper sequence to achieve results.

An apparent question when discussing the work of a conductor is what directing an orchestra actually means. According to Tovey this function has to be carried out with great sensitivity. Singling out individuals in rehearsals is forbidden in certain symphony orchestras, and even if it is not forbidden, the usual way of communicating to the musicians is by commenting on sections of the orchestra rather than on individuals.

The leadership of a conductor is focused on the presence. The conducting work is about listening with a trained ear and diagnosing how well the orchestra is doing. Based on what is heard the conductor has to decide whether to give feedback or not. If feedback is given, the way to give this is to inspire and not to demotivate. The OODA loop (observe, orient, decide, and act) will have to be completed in tenths of a second. The success of the conductor very much depends on how well he interprets the situation and is able to immediately give appropriate feedback in a way appreciated by the other person.

Conducting is very much about coaching, requiring high expertise in the subject matter. It also asks for delicately tuned communication skills adapted to the network in which the conductor works. A conductor who does not understand music will not be accepted by the orchestra. But a musical genius unable to communicate with the musicians won't succeed either. These two tasks cannot be split. Orchestration is about managing content and process simultaneously, with high integrity, and in good synch. The focus is much more on doing than on predesigned leading. Leading is covert. Rehearsals, for example, are about results – about pace, pattern, tempo, and about smoothing, harmonizing, perfecting. Mintzberg describes the preparation for a concert as a project, with the conductor as a hands-on project manager. Rehearsals are not about enhancing skills but about coordinating the skills that are present.

Orchestration entails subordination. A musician is always subordinated to some extent. Playing a symphony means that the musician is subordinated to the composer. Being part of an orchestra is just another kind of subordination. To the musician such subordination makes perfect sense, because only through some mechanisms of subordination can the whole emerge as more than just the sum of the parts. The orchestrator, be it the composer or the conductor, has precisely used the possibilities to subordinate different performances at different parts of the piece of music in order to create a unique esthetic experience. Applying the principles of subordination therefore becomes one of the major tasks of an orchestrator. How to skillfully practice subordination and timing is what distinguishes a celebrity conductor.

His interpretation of a well-known piece of Mozart, Haydn, or Beethoven is about how he subordinates different instruments at different moments of the performance, subtly improvising on the instructions originally provided by the composer. But even if the notion of subordination is important, how it is handled is extremely important.

The British conductor, Daniel Harding, whom Claudio Abbado once called 'my little genius,' is considered to be one of the more brilliant conductors of his generation. He has stated that musicians expect that the conductor gives them freedom. The conductor has to give them the feeling that they are free to do whatever they want. The conductor has to give people the feeling of being supported rather than being dictated to.

The internal relationships within the orchestra are also sensitive. Tovey said that he could not socialize with the musicians outside of work, as there were too many agendas. The relationship between the leader and the subordinates has to be based on mutual respect. If the players do not accept the conductor's authority or if the conductor does not acknowledge the musicians' expertise, the whole system breaks down. Leadership is about energizing and treating the musicians as respected members of a cohesive social system. The leadership arsenal is restricted: the systems and even the culture are built into the profession. What the leader can bring is expertise, and a way to inspire and motivate.

The role of a successful conductor is to apply the orchestration skills both internally when conducting and externally when shaping the context wherein the orchestra can perform. Entertaining sponsors to be able to form the boundary conditions within which the musicians can continue to rehearse and build up new overwhelming performances is in its own way another dimension of the orchestration philosophy.

A conductor works first and foremost around the core, the internal activities, to build up the performing capacity of the orchestra. The learning is about perfecting the performance, consolidating. But then there is the complementing task of renewing the program. Here the work is much more about involving the external world. What are the expectations of the audience? The sponsors? Are there interesting guest artists that could be available? In this role the challenge is to come up with new ideas and present a new repertoire that will thrill the audience and make the musicians enthusiastic. Due to these different requirements the music director has to fill many roles, being teacher, interpreter, cheerleader, and salesman.

Esa-Pekka Salonen, the music director of the Los Angeles Philharmonic, has spent a great deal of time on how to create interest in the orchestra in the context wherein it resides. He has had a determination to bring young people into the concert halls. This has forced him to break the bounds of the conventional concert, with whacky programs and unlikely collaborations.

Together with the orchestra's 'creative consultant,' maverick director Peter Sellars, he has presented a series of staged productions and instituted a 'Filmharmonic' project. Hollywood composers have been hired to write new works for the orchestra, prominent film directors engaged to shoot movies to accompany the music. And it is working: at each of his LA orchestral concerts, at least 500 students will be in the hall. By doing this Salonen is not just conducting in the music sense, but also he is very much applying the conducting skills to build a business, the business of the Los Angeles Philharmonic.

In the same way, when Bramwell Tovey moved to Vancouver to become the conductor and music director of the Vancouver Symphony Orchestra, he also emerged as a fierce advocate of arts education for children. He organized Kids Koncerts, aimed at children aged five to twelve, and started a program called Tiny Tots, interactive concerts teaching songs and actions to those under the age of five, who then tended to sing the songs for days afterwards.

Pertti Korhonen: a Business Conductor[2]

In the following the principles of orchestrating as a conductor will be used to analyze the way Nokia handled its relationship with Philips after the fire in the Albuquerque plant on March 17, 2000. How the underlying orchestration capability had been built up over time will also be described.

Of the five components that the damaged Philips plant in Albuquerque supplied to Nokia two were indispensable. One of those was made by various suppliers around the globe. But the other, semiconductors known as ASIC chips (for application-specific integrated circuits), which regulate the radio frequency that cell phones use, were made only by Philips and one of its subcontractors.

Nokia officials had learned the hard way that supply disruptions are more the rule than the exception in their business. Within hours of getting the bad news, Nokia's top supply chain managers assembled their team of supply engineers, chip designers, and top managers in China, Finland, and the US to attack the problem. Information traveled fast within Nokia, it reached the right locations and led to immediate actions.

Meanwhile, across the Gulf of Bothnia in Stockholm, top Ericsson officials still hadn't realized what they were up against. Like Nokia, Ericsson officials first heard of the fire three days after it occurred. But that communication was 'one technician talking to another,' according to Roland Klein, head of investor relations for the company. 'There were a few bits and pieces of information before that, but nothing formal.' When word came from Philips about how serious the problem really was, more time passed before middle managers at Ericsson fully briefed their bosses. Jan Wareby, who directly oversaw the cell-phone division as head of consumer products for the company, didn't find out about the problem until early April.

'It was hard to assess what was going on,' he said. 'We found out only slowly.'

By that time, Pertti Korhonen, Nokia's top troubleshooter, and Tapio Markki, chief component purchasing manager, were on a plane heading for Philips' headquarters in Amsterdam to meet with Philips' chief executive. They were joined by Jorma Ollila, who rerouted a return trip from the US to attend.

Nokia convinced Philips' chief executive, Cor Boonstra, and the head of the company's semiconductor division, Arthur van der Poel, to turn over every stone looking for a solution.

Korhonen and his team were racing to restore the chip supply line. To replace more than two million power amplifier chips, they asked one Japanese and one US supplier of the same chip to make millions more each. Largely because Nokia was such an important customer, both took the additional orders with only five days' lead time. Nokia also demanded details about capacity at other Philips plants.

This was one of the key things Korhonen insisted on. Together with the Philips staff he dug into the capacity of all Philips factories and insisted on rerouting the capacity. He asked them, told them, to re-plan. And he got results. The goal was simple: for a short period of time, Philips and Nokia operated as one company regarding these components.

Soon more than 10 million of the ASIC chips were replaced by a Philips factory in Eindhoven, the Netherlands. Another Philips plant was freed up for Nokia in Shanghai.

At Ericsson, on the other hand, officials were finding themselves increasingly behind the curve. In this situation Nokia, by being proactive, secured its portion of the restricted output and was able to meet its production targets despite the fire. Less skillful orchestrators suffered.

The way the conducting skills of Pertti Korhonen had been built up went back to the mid-1990s. When he became vice president of logistics for Nokia Mobile Phones in 1996, he had to find solutions to a big problem – fast. Profits for Nokia's cell-phone operations were falling due to rising inventories and falling component prices. With an annual growth rate of 50%, these losses could not be sustained much longer.

The competitive context was challenging. Nokia was competing in a business characterized by very rapid growth and turbulence. Product life cycles were short, and there was strong standardization- and technology-based competition. These tendencies emphasized the importance of right timing, as well as speed of bringing new innovations to the global marketplace. These two elements, right timing and speed, became the cornerstones of the supply chain strategy that Korhonen designed and implemented.

What he recognized was that the cell-phone market was starting to resemble the computer business with shortening product cycles due to rapidly changing technology. To handle this Nokia had to manage its logistics for plants and distribution centers on a regional basis, but follow global strategies and processes. The regional logistics managers started to meet about six times a year to discuss supply chain issues. These meetings were overseen by a team of global logistics managers from headquarters in Finland. The objective was to establish as good situational awareness as possible among the team, and to institutionalize a culture of continuous information sharing.

An office in Singapore oversaw logistics for the Far East, while a Dallas office managed the Americas. Logistics for Europe, Africa, and the Middle East was managed from Nokia's head office in Espoo, Finland. The sourcing strategy for each component that came into a Nokia plant was reviewed by the company's supply chain management team. This team determined if the components should be sourced from a global, regional, or local supplier.

In the aftermath of the Albuquerque fire Korhonen was merely applying the conducting skills in a situation of emergence, based on superb situational awareness. This was an ingrained part of the supply chain management capability he had built up for Nokia for more than five years.

ORCHESTRATING BASED ON POWER OR KNOWLEDGE?

When Korhonen was orchestrating he had a clearly defined role with a strong interest in mobilizing other actors into a joint value-creating activity. In doing this he had to relate to three sets of actors: (i) customers; (ii) possible co-producers, in this case Philips; and (iii) competitors. The question of the nature and use of power has to cover the two ends of the spectrum of orchestration: orchestration for efficiency and orchestration for creativity. In the aftermath of the fire, power had to be used, whereas knowledge was the main asset when trying to build the foundation of Club Nokia, as discussed in Chapter 4.

As the Albuquerque case shows, skillful orchestration can lead to considerable gains in the long term. In this respect the orchestrated network distributes power and gains asymmetrically. Those actors that gain less, in certain cases cannot withdraw from it. So did the forced collaboration between Nokia and Philips strengthen Nokia's position in the face of Philips, as one of the outcomes was the relative weakening of Ericsson.

A similar development can be identified in how the subcontracting field of Nokia has evolved after the burst of the Internet bubble at the beginning of the millennium. The subcontractors that had Nokia as their major customer had limited bargaining power when Nokia started to ask for price levels comparable to the ones offered by competitors from South-East Asia. Those companies that were the first to recognize the shift in competition agreed to be acquired by global players like Flextronics to get some financial compensation for the rapidly deteriorating market value of their core product and process capabilities. Some of those who were slower to adapt didn't survive.

Nokia, in turn, had no problems in institutionalizing similar subcontracting arrangements in Asia. Once the technology could be sourced with limited risks from countries with considerably lower costs than Finland, Nokia possessed the capabilities to set up and run the orchestrated network outside Finland. Because of the accumulation of a broader set of capabilities for Nokia (or the orchestrator), this meant that the bargaining power over the suppliers was very strong. During the final phase of sourcing domestically, the local suppliers were prepared to bow to almost any demands that Nokia was putting forward, because they were well aware of the Asian threat. Of course the inevitable end result was that labor intensive subcontracted production was gradually leaving Finland. However, at the same time Nokia's own production of complex and demanding products was increasing in Finland. Finland also remained a hub for introducing the latest technologies to the market.[3]

This raises the question of the roles and responsibilities in an orchestrated network. The orchestrator can select who to include in the value constellation. The member in turn, like a musician in an orchestra, is often inclined to specialize in a certain field, become a master in a particular instrument. Musical performance is skill based. Business performance has two components: quality and costs. For the member of a business network facing increased competition, simultaneous emphasis on both quality and cost efficiency is needed. For Nokia's subcontractors in Finland the challenge was that they could not compete with the cost levels achievable by their Asian competitors. Possible quality or innovation superiority was not enough to compensate for the shortfalls in cost competitiveness.

For Nokia this was, however, not completely unproblematic. Nokia had developed in-depth product development collaboration with several of these suppliers. Compensating the existing product generation with lower cost supplies from more nimble competitors reduced the access Nokia had to trustworthy developer partners. This became evident in 2003 when Nokia faced the situation of not having an appropriate product range to match the rapid change in demand for cell phones. Subsequently the orchestrator has to consider the balance between efficiency and creativity not only as an intra-organizational matter, but also from the perspective of the properties of the whole orchestrated network.

Nokia had been favoring efficiency over creativity. This implied that the network had been streamlined. The supply chain integration efforts had provided some flexibility in respect of product volumes and alterations, but only within specified modular product structures. To achieve efficiency, restrictions had therefore been put on how flexible the product architecture could be. This, combined with the fact that product management within Nokia was late in detecting the change in form factors affecting demand, caused Nokia to be late in catching up with the clamshell trend at the end of 2003.

Supply chain management is a process as weak as the weakest link. For Nokia, the threat of a major disruption due to component shortage, forced management to use power very firmly to minimize its own risks. Due to the restriction of available supply this was a crude necessity. As Philips was forced to team up with Nokia most of the suffering was put on Nokia's main competitor, Ericsson.

Another area where leaders are confronting with either win or lose is professional sport. The whole logic of making sports so popular for spectators is that it puts teams to compete, win, or be defeated. When trying to better understand how the conducting type of orchestration plays out in a highly competitive context, looking into sports provides some interesting comparisons. In this field one of the most successful coaches ever is Bill Belichick.

Bill Belichick: the Master of Game Management

Bill Belichick, born in 1952, started his NFL career in 1975. When he coached the New England Patriots for its third Super Bowl title in four years in February 2005 he had more years of NFL experience than any of the other head coaches.

After Belichick had settled into his first head-coaching job at Cleveland, critics insisted he had no 'people skills'. But over the years the players could recognize subtle changes that merged and matured and gave him the last dimension he needed to become one of the elite head coaches in a game so closely watched by America. He had learned to delegate responsibility. He was less controlling. And he had learned to talk to his players instead of down to them.[4]

Throughout his career Belichick has allowed himself to take the time to get it right. He is a workaholic, starting his working days at 5:30 in the morning, and staying in coaches' meetings until past midnight. The players see that and they work a little harder to keep up. His attention to detail has been widely recognized. He lives his own credo: preparation, attitude, and teamwork. He is considered a substance over style guy. His advice to those aiming at succeeding is to look at the short term and explore something you can put all your passion into. When everybody is committed to the same cause and purpose you can accomplish things as a team that nobody thought possible. He laid out his management philosophy in the pre-Super Bowl press conference in February 2005 as follows:

> I think game management is something you probably learn a little bit about in every single game. You prepare certain situational strategies, and plays to use in those situations, at the beginning of the season, and sometimes modify them a little bit as you go through the year – maybe as new situations occur, or as your personnel changes, or your groupings get modified

a little bit through the course of the season. But they're not always quite the way you draw them up. There are always some little wrinkles – field position, field conditions, the weather, time, timeouts, score, etc. So I think you're always learning on that. And it's something that as a coach, and as a quarterback, and as a coordinator and a play-caller, you've always got to stay on top of. You've always got to keep thinking about it. And the more you think about it, I think the quicker you can react when those situations do occur in the game. But it's tough. It's a lot easier when you can plan ahead. The toughest ones are the ones that change in a hurry . . .

As Belichick noticed, the toughest decisions are the ones that have to be made in a hurry. But at the same time, a good coach is the one outperforming his rivals exactly at that. When the fragments on which to base the decision are few and fine, then only the expert can recognize the pattern. Staying on top of it, having a situational awareness superior to the rest, is what distinguishes the pro from the amateur.

Like the job of a conductor, a large amount of the work of Belichick is devoted to communication, with the players and with the external stakeholders. In addition to the 20 to 30 minutes he spends each day conducting news conferences, he often spends an additional 10 to 15 minutes afterwards talking to reporters who have more in-depth questions. One of his management priorities is to make sure his message is properly conveyed.

With 70 players involved in the program, the need for communication is constant. But the means vary. There are meetings, but they vary depending on what he wants to say and what message he wants to get across.

Some meetings are five minutes and some are a half-hour. Some have bad language and a few probably don't. Sometimes there's video involved, sometimes there isn't. Sometimes it's all about the other team and in the meeting the Patriots are not even mentioned. Sometimes it's offense or kicking game or practice habits or attitude. There's no set formula, Belichick just uses his gut feeling regarding when and how to address the team.

The players admit that Belichick demands responsibility. That brings discipline. The players know that they need that discipline to do what they need to do and it's to the point where the players demand it from each other, too.

Belichick explains that discipline is not having short hair and walking on the sidewalk and all that. Discipline is, when the ball is snapped, doing one's job, playing within the team concept, and taking care of one's responsibility. That is what a disciplined team does.

But when it comes to getting his employees working together the right way, one thing is clear. Belichick is very particular about how to conduct his team.[5]

THE GAME PLAN

Tovey, Salonen, Korhonen, and Belichick all share the common feature that they have proven their skills in getting others to perform based on their vision of how things should be done. To achieve this they have to be able to communicate well, and to convince others to perform according to the game plan, or in respect of the conductors according to the score they have prepared. In this respect the conducting type of orchestration asks for high attention to detail. Only by mastering the details can the conductor get the respect from the subordinates, and only by explaining the details of the future state to be achieved can the conductor be properly understood. So the same way that Tovey and Salonen finetune the scores of music based on their own interpretation of the piece of music, Korhonen had to finetune the plan for how to restructure the supply chain of the ASIC chips subsequent to the fire. Conductors have the luxury of rehearsing the performance with their orchestra. Korhonen and Belichick have to adjust their game plans based on how the real-world events unfold.

Three things characterize the preparation of a good game plan:

- The orchestrator uses his or her instincts about what is relevant for the type of situation to be faced. Singling out what is relevant, and especially what is not relevant, is absolutely crucial to succeed in a complex orchestrating setup.
- Using available information the orchestrator undertakes a thorough evaluation of the participants and their expected behaviors.
- Based on what is relevant and what can be expected from the other participants the orchestrator decides what part of the game plan to pre-plan, and how much should be left for improvisation.

The more the orchestrator relies on improvisation, the more important it is to read the playing field appropriately. As leadership increasingly is about collaborating and making decisions as things evolve, there is in general a need to have a unifying inclusive game plan. Such a plan provides the network members with a shared view of how to integrate and synchronize efforts and actions that are taking place throughout the network. The more complex operations to undertake, the more there is a need for a plan that will guide the actions within the frame of the whole in order to reduce the risk of suboptimization.

The game plan is the orchestrator's recipe for how to create value in a specific situation. It represents a more fine-grained interpretation of the principles for value creation outlined in the business model (see Chapter 1) and is also less rigid. The game plan is first and foremost the cognitive framework used by the orchestrator in order to be able to master the task at hand. One beautifully described case of how this mental process can work can be found from contemporary notes regarding how Beethoven approached the work of composing:

> I carry my thoughts about with me for a long time, sometimes a very long time, before I set them down. At the same time memory is so faithful to me that I am sure not to forget a theme which I have once conceived, even after years have passed. I make many changes, reject and reattempt until I am satisfied. Then the working-out in breadth, length, height and depth begins in my head, and since I am conscious of what I want, the basic idea never leaves me. It rises, grows upward, and I hear and see the picture as a whole take shape and stand forth before me as though cased in a single piece, so that all that is left is the work of writing it down.[6]

Composers, conductors, and architects all by necessity have to put attention to details. They also have to be involved in a lot of hands-on work, taking direct and personal charge of what is getting done. What distinguishes an architect, however, is the need to be more attuned to how he can learn from those he serves in order to be able to fulfill their expectations. This will be the main topic of the next chapter.

CHAPTER 15

THE LEADER AS ARCHITECT

*L*eading an orchestra is not just about improving on its existing repertoire. The whole institution has also periodically to be upgraded. For Esa-Pekka Salonen this was a large portion of his job for a multitude of years when he collaborated with architect Frank Gehry to accomplish the new concert hall in Los Angeles. Even if their work resulted in a highly admired new concert hall in Los Angeles, Gehry had to go through some quite difficult moments before the project was concluded.

Frank Gehry and Esa-Pekka Salonen:
Orchestrating for a Concert Hall

The new home of the Los Angeles Philharmonic orchestra was designed by Frank Gehry, the architect most known for the world-famous Guggenheim Museum in Bilbao, Spain. He designed the new venue in tandem with Esa-Pekka Salonen. Salonen in many ways represented one of the most important customer voices for Gehry.

For Salonen it was important to establish intimacy between the audience and the performers, to create a closed, communal experience that would transport people, transform them even. So if the task was to create a platform for continuous experience provision, many problems had to be solved before the end result was accomplished. First of all, it was still a concert hall. The interior had to fulfill certain criteria and could not be as radical as the exterior. This in turn meant technical problems relating to the acoustics and the details of the auditorium such as the stage, how the orchestra was seated, how the risers were positioned etc.

There were also broader challenges relating to the ambition of Salonen to bring young people into the concert halls, meaning a need to break the bounds of the conventional concert. So when looking for the purpose of the building, it was important to consider what the Los Angeles Philharmonic represented in a broader sense. The identity of the orchestra had to be looked upon with an analytical eye. What was the role of the orchestra? What was it supposed to be doing? Who is going to be the audience in 20 years' time? The idea of a symphony orchestra as a kind of blueprint of the Berlin or Vienna Philharmonic moved to another part of the world, was not how Salonen perceived a symphony orchestra. It had to function in the context of its cultural environment.

As Salonen looked for the mission of the building, Gehry tried to transform this into a physical design. Gehry's work started with ink-on-paper scribbles. He then directed his apprentices in Santa Monica to build scores of models that interpreted and expanded on his sketches. When Gehry declared himself satisfied, other experts were called in to translate the final models and digital images into two-dimensional plans and working drawings, as well as complex electronic instructions that could be fed to the makers and assemblers of millions of parts.[1]

But when the final result arrived, it was undoubtedly the result of a team effort, and Gehry was very generous about the roles played between the two of them. He said that concert halls always have a conductor. Von Karajan will forever be associated with Berlin because he helped build it. This hall was to be Esa-Pekka's hall forever – everyone else will be a visitor.

Even though the process resulted in a happy Disney ending, it did not progress without its own drama. The true orchestrator behind the concert hall was neither of the two men, but Diane Disney Miller, the daughter of Walt Disney, that stepped in to secure the project when it reached a crisis in 1997.[2]

Intensely private and self-effacing, Miller, together with her sister Sharon Disney Lund and their mother Lillian Disney, had been behind the original donation based on which the whole project was initiated. But Lund died of cancer in 1993, and an ailing Lillian Disney, who died in December 1997 at age 98, was too ill to take responsibility for major decisions when the project ran into troubles. Miller suddenly became the owner by default of the wildly unorthodox design for the $274 million concert hall.

The Walt Disney Concert Hall had been set in motion by a 1987 gift of $50 million from Lillian Disney to do 'something grand' in the name of her late husband. The project had ground to a halt in the mid-1990s due to financial troubles, but it was enjoying a second wind. Gehry was riding high on critical acclaim for his Guggenheim Museum in Bilbao, Spain, and a group of LA's corporate and civic leaders, led by then Mayor Richard Riordan and billionaire businessman Eli Broad, began soliciting multimillion-dollar donations to meet the soaring cost estimates for the hall.

But even as the money rolled in, friction developed. Riordan and Broad threw their considerable weight behind a plan that would take the job of completing the working drawings for Gehry's unusual, all-curves design out of the hands of the architect's firm. Broad (who had fallen out with the architect when Gehry designed his Brentwood residence), Riordan, and other major donors feared that Gehry's firm was too inexperienced, even though it had executed the working drawings for the similarly curvy Bilbao museum.

Gehry responded by threatening to walk off the project. That's when Miller stepped in. The nature of the Disney family's gift made them, and not the Music Center, Gehry's client. She mandated that the money still left from Lillian Disney's original gift – at that point, about $20 million – be used to hire Gehry's firm to do the working drawings.

Her logic was simple. She trusted Frank, and there wasn't anyone else that she had confidence in. As Gehry had convinced her that he could do the drawings, she saw no reason to not let him continue with the job.

Gehry did not get to know Miller well until after she had chosen to support him. Once he asked her why she defended him so much during this hectic period of the project. Miller had then replied that when she was a kid, her father sometimes came home from the studio after getting beaten up by studio people and hearing stories about how they compromised his work. She didn't want that to happen in this case.

She became co-chairwoman of the Disney Hall committee and it was only after a year of commuting to Los Angeles from the Napa Valley winery or her apartment in San Francisco to attend meetings that she finally felt confident that Gehry's vision would be preserved. Then she stepped down happy to get out of being the center of controversy. Afterwards she confirmed that if Gehry's name had been taken off the project, so would Walt Disney's. She had often been thinking, in those dark times, if it had gone ahead and would have been done the other way, she would not have let her father's name be on it.

Miller credited her father for her love of music. They didn't have all that much music in the house, because not very many homes had good sound systems at that time. But through the movies she learnt to love music. In every movie, it seemed that Arthur Rubinstein or Jose Iturbi was playing something by Chopin or Rachmaninoff. So when Miller became seven, she was given a piano for her birthday present.

Diane Disney Miller was thrilled when the Walt Disney Concert Hall opened on October 23, 2003. She was personally present with 25 family members including all 13 grand-children.

The Walt Disney Concert Hall had to be closely integrated with the local culture. It was also an example of close collaboration between a conductor and an architect. This seemingly odd combination is actually not so strange. Beethoven also had an air for architecture. Even if he was rather bohemian in his private life, in respect of music he was extremely systematic and even pedantic. An overriding impression of Beethoven's works is their meticulous attention to detail, not merely in notes but in articulation and dynamics, despite the outward untidiness and often chaotic look of many of his autographs. His lifelong concern with accuracy was shown in his vehement letters to publishers and copyists. A close study of any of his large-scale works reveals the crucial relation between dynamics, harmony and tonality, on which the overall architectural strength depends.[3]

Seeing architecture as a means has also been the point for architect Eric Carlson. He has had to be much more attuned to the commercial impact of the building as he has been designing several of the stores of Louis Vuitton, the world's largest luxury brand. In October 2005 the flagship Louis Vuitton store, 1800 square meters on the Avenue des Champs-Elysées in Paris, designed by Carlson and colleague Peter Marino, was opened after a multi-million euro renovation project.

Eric Carlson: Creating a Physical Embodiment of Modern Luxury[4]

In the Champs-Elysées store the challenge was how to make a four-story shop appear as a cozy selection of intimate rooms and not as one gigantic shopping mall. The idea was that people would get the feeling of exploring different small shops within a harmonious environment. The design of the Champs-Elysées store is somewhat reminiscent of Frank Lloyd Wright's design of the Guggenheim Museum in New York. Customers can make their own way through the store from the ground floor up or by using a 20-meter long escalator directly to the top level and gradually wind their way down the store, which is designed around a central 20-meter high atrium. The design thus eliminates the idea of floors. By strolling around the consumer will discover little rooms, one after the other. The constraints of the building brought with them the concept of continuity, the idea of a promenade, punctuated with short cuts. But at the same time the store has to be able to handle a lot of traffic, up to 5000 shoppers per day.[5]

Intentionally the store has also been linked to its surroundings. The paving stones of the Champs-Elysées are replicated inside and the wide avenue is in focus through the plate glass windows. Within the store there are views to the exterior, the

Avenue George V and along the Champs-Elysées from Place de la Concorde to the Arc de Triomphe.

The role of the architecture is to nurture the heritage of Vuitton, to be a monument to modern luxury. The ambition has been to reach down to the roots of the firm, and put them at the heart of the building. The whole shop is designed to offer different sensations.[6] Keeping the soul of the brand and feeding its myths is the centrifugal force of modern luxury. Transforming this into a physical design is not only about integrating architecture and shopping, but about integrating the ethos of Louis Vuitton as well. So the paradox of having a big store but creating a feel of intimacy had to be resolved. The acclaiming response from the customers and the fashion press proved that this was possible.

By flying in 3000 guests to celebrate the opening the commercial benefits of the store were fully exploited. How exactly the presence of Sharon Stone and the originality of the design influenced the international press was for owners LVMH less important. The main thing was that once more a large amount of brand-strengthening publicity was achieved. *Women's Wear Daily* heralded the new store as a new must-visit attraction in the City of Lights, and a showcase that is bound to have a global impact on the world's biggest luxury brand.

For Louis Vuitton the positive response on the new design of the Champs-Elysées store was expected. For several years the company had been working on a strategy that had put architecture in the midst of its brand building. It had installed its own highly publicized team of architects to help extend its glossy image worldwide. This group of architects was led by Eric Carlson, who had been asked to create what Louis Vuitton expressed as 'commercial cathedrals'. The goal was to communicate the strong Louis Vuitton brand identity.

Carlson had convinced the Louis Vuitton management that retail architecture has a direct impact on image. Good shop

> design creates image concepts that strengthen customer affection and increase sales. But there has to be a balance between the global brand concept and the adaptation of the physical architecture into its own local surroundings. Finding this balance is the landmark of a skillful architect.

ARCHITECTURE SHAPING ITS ENVIRONMENT

An architect can be engaged to implement the wishes of the customer, but he can also be in the role of actually creating something beyond what the customer is able to express. In the context of orchestration it is especially the latter role of the architect that is of interest. In urban planning this means that if a new building is enough of a draw, it can revitalize a city or region as effectively as the most comprehensive master urban plan.

So was Frank Gehry named lead architect in 2005 on a massive project in each of America's two largest cities, Los Angeles and New York. These projects indicate that ambitious developers are not just open to work with architecture's boldest talents, but are desperate to avoid working without them. These 'starchitects' have become valuable marketing vehicles for the developers. This means that these architects of stardom have started to negotiate contracts like the star directors of Hollywood. For Gehry the breakthrough was of course Bilbao. The Guggenheim Museum in Bilbao symbolized a new age. An architect invaded a foreign country armed with flashy computer programs, abstract theories, and globally shaped esthetics, radically transforming the architectural landscape of the area.

The museum was also an astounding economic success. In its first two years, Guggenheim visitors added 433 million euros to the local economy, paying back the project's 132-million-euro investment more than threefold, according to an analysis by an accounting firm.

Because of Bilbao, Gehry changed the way we think about urban planning. The Guggenheim Museum had a unique and powerful role. It changed that city. It brought people to Bilbao. People praised the building. Suddenly every region wanted its own Bilbao. They wanted it because that piece of great architecture made the city a global attraction. They wanted a building that has a presence in the community. Such aspirational architecture had also previously existed in different surroundings, for example Alvar Aalto's Baker House – a dormitory at the Massachusetts Institute of Technology in Cambridge. The Baker House successfully embodied MIT's desire to build 'a physical atmosphere of order, peace, and beauty' to support the activities of 'the constructive mind'. But it was not in a similar way a tourist attraction as was the Guggenheim Museum.

If Alvar Aalto's design was groundbreaking, the Louis Vuitton Champs-Elysées shop is groundbreaking as well. For the first time, contemporary art became an integral part of Louis Vuitton, as works by a selection of cutting-edge artists are on permanent display in specific areas. The integration of art is an extension of Louis Vuitton's pioneering approach to perfect luxury retailing as an esthetic experience. The intention is to provide customers with sensual stimuli no other retailer can provide.

Traditionally architecture could shape the environment as standalone artifacts; today buildings increasingly have to integrate the activity of the surrounding environment to create attention and form people's opinions. Concert halls and shops are buildings that have this ability. Architects have recognized this and visitors and customers can benefit.

OPERATIONAL ARCHITECTURE

There are many areas where the principles of architecture are applicable outside the profession of designing buildings. One such area is when companies consider how to establish ways of combining different skills and capabilities to come up with new competitive products and services. Professors Henderson and Clark[7] used the notion of architectural innovation when explaining the failure of established firms when facing an innovation that changed a product's architecture but left the components, and the core design concepts that they embody, unchanged. Through in-depth studies of six companies, Henderson and Clark found that the role of communication channels, information filters, and problem-solving strategies were the major factors explaining why the established market leaders failed to implement the new architecture, even if they possessed the component technologies needed.

Organizations build information filters and communication channels that are aligned with the dominating ideas embodied in the present architecture. Because the individuals rely on their existing knowledge, they misunderstand and misinterpret signals about new products and processes. And even if they are able to understand the threat posed by the new architecture, the need to 'unlearn' the existing way of thinking and build and apply new architectural knowledge requires time and resources. The reluctance of some of the members of the steering committee of the Walt Disney Concert Hall was an example of such a difficulty in accepting new architectural thinking. Gehry introduced a network-centric approach to implement his designs. The capabilities used for the implementation were the shared capabilities of a vast network. However, the understanding of this approach was not easily communicated. To provide the missing link between Gehry and the steering committee Diane Disney Miller had to step in to chair the committee.

The Disney Hall case also reveals another thing about orchestrating in a complex setting: it varies over time, and the lead orchestrator can also be different at different moments. So did Salonen and Gehry jointly carry the role of orchestrator during the first phase of the project, when defining the overall functionality and esthetics of the concert hall. Subsequently Gehry was the lead orchestrator during the technical design phase. But as the dispute over the future of Gehry's involvement emerged, focus shifted from the operational to the political level, and Diane Disney Miller had to conciliate the different interests. Again when the building approached completion, Gehry and Salonen worked very much in tandem finalizing the architectural details to accommodate for optimal esthetic and acoustic results.

The operational architecture thus has to cover both the parts and their core underlying concepts. The underlying concepts in the case of the Walt Disney Concert Hall represented an evolving context. Thus the operational architecture had to enable a process of learning, both technically and in respect of leadership. The operational architecture thus includes not only the architecture for the products, but also for the services and the managerial processes necessary for the value-creating activities to be carried out efficiently and effectively.

The operational architecture also includes the means for how to acquire and assimilate new information needed to accomplish the undertaken task. This does not simply depend on the organization's direct interface with the external environment. It also depends on transfers of knowledge across and within subunits that may be quite removed from the original point of entry. How successfully this works depends on the structure of communication between the external environment and the organization, as well as among the subunits of the organization, and also on the character and distribution of expertise within the organization. In the case of the Walt Disney Concert Hall there were severe problems in this communication.

Based on the above observations the operational architecture can be defined:

*The **operational architecture** contains the tasks, roles, and responsibilities within in a value constellation defining, producing, and providing an offering to customers.*

In the case of the Walt Disney Concert hall the operational architecture was both emergent and dynamic, as the organization was a network consisting of a multitude of relationships. Within this network individuals were aware of each other's capabilities and knowledge to a varying extent, but collectively the understanding of each other's complementarities improved over time. But such a broad and active network also poses some risks. For example, Gehry's focus on the technical solution, and less successful communication with the steering committee, represented such a risk. So there is a trade-off between level of expertise (which is a prerequisite for efficient internal communication and rapid learning) and diversity of background (which is necessary to recognize the importance of new complementary information). A similar, but even more complex web of relationships had to be mastered by the Commander of the Allied Forces when fighting Slobodan Milosevic in Kosovo.

General Wesley K. Clark: Waging Modern Wars – Using Diplomacy Backed by Force[8]

General Wesley K. Clark, Supreme Allied Commander, Europe, was the American commander who oversaw the military efforts by NATO against Yugoslavia leading to the Serb withdrawal from Kosovo. He was responsible for the conduct of the military operations. Above him everything was political, or political-military. Below him was the military. He described himself as the waist of the hourglass, and the grains of sand were pouring past in both directions. To succeed in such an environment he many times had to set his own compass and follow it, as the external world was full of contradictions. When doing this he relied on a command pattern he had developed early on in his career. Be personally competent. Know and work the details; set high standards; provide lots of personal, up-front leadership and good planning; and work to bring out the best in the people you have.

When he began his position as NATO commander in July 1997 General Clark had to consider all his duties from four different perspectives: political, strategic, operational, and tactical. His task was to deal with a complex military-diplomatic situation. In such a case the assertion of power itself changes the options. In this respect it was not possible to apply the recommendation of Clausewitz: no one should start a war without being clear in his mind what he intends to achieve by that war and how he intends to conduct it. This operation could not be pre-planned at the outset, as the events unfolded in an evolving fashion, highly affected by the decisions made by General Clark himself.

When the crisis deepened it was decided to increase pressure on Serbia and its president Milosevic by starting precision air strikes in March 1999. As the air campaign proceeded General Clark had to constantly negotiate about how the operation should proceed. In doing this he had to consult the heads of state and military representatives of 19 sovereign countries, some of which had only recently joined NATO to immediately find themselves at war, the first one NATO had ever fought. In doing this his primary task was to maintain the Allied cohesion. He knew that he had to conduct the military operations in a way that held the Alliance together, despite the differing national perspectives that would be brought to bear. This meant reaching out to the Chiefs of Defense, and to the ambassadors, as well as the public opinions on both sides of the Atlantic. As the air campaign moved on he also faced the possibility that the Pope in his speech on Wednesday, before Easter, would argue for the strikes to cease. Through diplomatic efforts this could be avoided.

At the beginning of April the Serbs began organizing trainloads of Albanians from Pristina, and shipping them to be dumped at the border with Macedonia. This mass explosion of Kosovar Albanians was a serious strategic blunder by Milosevic and brought NATO much needed support and legitimacy in the public opinion. But simultaneously the participating countries were politically very risk averse, avoiding the escalation of the war into something that couldn't be controlled later on. Thus there was continuous disagreement about what to strike, and in what priority. This illustrated the dichotomy between political aims and military aims. General Clark had to operate in both fields. As Supreme Allied Commander he had more than purely military responsibilities. He was a close adviser to Secretary General Solana on the overall policy and strategy of NATO's effort in the Balkans and had frequent discussions with NATO ambassadors, ministers, and heads of state. He also retained the authority as Supreme Allied Commander to speak directly to the President of the United States.

The mission was completed on June 10, 1999 when the NATO representatives verified the Serb withdrawal from Kosovo and the suspension of bombing. Diplomacy had worked. NATO completed its mission without a single NATO soldier killed in combat. The Kosovo campaign was a limited war: limited means limited objectives. It was coercive diplomacy, the use of armed forces to impose the political will of the NATO nations on the Federal Republic of Yugoslavia, or more specifically, on Serbia. In this modern war, achieving decisive political aims did not require achieving decisive military results or winning 'big battles'. This was quite an achievement, because when the conflict began, the West lacked preparedness. But as the conflict escalated the NATO member states became more and more committed to the joint success, and could not afford to fail. Ironically the very controversy that the operation aroused helped to propel its success.

The experiences that General Clark presented in many ways show the application of the mindset of the architect to complex leadership contexts. It also exemplifies the difficulties of setting clear objectives up front when facing complex real-world problems. In traditional military thinking a military operation should have a clear objective, rely on unity of command to focus all efforts toward this aim. Plans and operations should be simple in conception, massing forces at the most critical points, relying on economy of force in the peripheral areas, and achieving surprise over the enemy. The operation in Kosovo violated almost every one of these principles.

The air campaign began with one objective – drive the Serbs back to negotiations – and quickly moved toward other aims, such as halting the ethnic cleansing, and then after the NATO summit, the five conditions endorsed by the G–8 foreign ministers – a cease-fire, the withdrawal of all Serb forces from Kosovo, the return of all refugees and displaced persons, the presence of a NATO-led international force, and subsequent participation in a political settlement. NATO was in a process of continuous adaptation, moving from an initial military effort driven by political dynamics toward a more effective military campaign.

But at the same time General Clark also had to very carefully engage all the NATO members in the joint operations. Giving nations an appropriate voice in the campaign was essential to maintaining Allied unity, making the target clearance process all important. However, it was also true that the less opportunity given for discretion by the nations, the better for military effectiveness, since almost every country could question or suggest alternatives. So there had to be the right balance between sharing information and requesting approvals.

As the air campaign was based on precision strikes there was a simultaneous need for 'precision acquisition and identification of targets'. Specific information was needed in real time. Neither specific information nor the estimated range of actions can be gathered from a distance. There have to be people on the ground to observe and listen. They can be supported with fabulously powerful communications and other technologies. But they will also require physical courage and a willingness to take physical risks.

In the end, the strategic adaptation was all the more powerful because it represented a unified Alliance, not a single nation. A price was paid in operational effectiveness by having to constrain the nature of the operation to fit within the political and legal concerns of NATO member nations, but the price brought significant strategic benefits and cohesiveness regarding the overall ambitions with the operation. The orchestrated approach proved to be highly successful.

Another example of how the leader has to delicately build up a successful team with rationed resources is American football. Bill Belichick has been seen to epitomize the post–modern, post-industrial collective enterprise, putting resources together in a minute way and identifying the best way to bring out top performance from his players. In the same way General Clark had to constantly consider how to perform within the constraints put on him by the NATO members afraid of committing to a military operation getting out of control. To understand and accept the operational architecture also means actively molding this architecture.

This chapter has identified the architect as one type of orchestrator. Orchestrating as an architect emphasizes problem solving and expertise. But it also asks for skills in engaging the external stakeholders. This engagement can be to involve the main constituents in the joint problem solving and creative undertaking. Gehry did this with Esa-Pekka Salonen and the Disney family. General Clark engaged heads of state to enable the Kosovo operation. But the other way is that the creation of the architect becomes the platform for engagement. So of course is a concert hall designed for experiences, and the successful football team is the locus of local pride and excitement. When the new shop of Louis Vuitton in Tokyo, designed by Eric Carlson, was opened in September 2003 the most fanatic Louis Vuitton admirers were standing in the line throughout the night to be the first ones to look around the new shop. That is dedication to shopping!

For an auctioneer engaging the public is the raison d'être of the whole profession. Getting others thrilled is therefore something an auctioneer has to excel at. The next chapter looks deeper into how good auctioneers do this.

CHAPTER 16

THE LEADER AS AUCTIONEER

A good conductor has his attention totally devoted to the musicians. The most important sense is listening. Some conductors do their jobs with their eyes closed, as Beethoven did when conducting. An auctioneer, however, has to watch the audience to identify the slightest indication of interest in a potential buyer and through his own behavior motivate the buyer to put forward a bid. A good auctioneer tries to maintain lots of excitement and the momentum that keeps at least two bidders active.

So how does a good auctioneer describe his work? According to Dermont Chichester, co-chairman of Christie's, a good auctioneer adds at least 10% to a sale. The auctioneer controls the room, enjoys a lively rapport with the audience, varies the pace, and, most importantly, keeps the audience awake. It is an essential sixth sense to know when a bidder still has a little more gas in the tank – the bidder who has stopped reluctantly – because with timing and judgment, the auctioneer can encourage him or her to go to one more bid.[1]

Harry Dalmeny of Sotheby's sees the auctioneer as part-actor, part-accountant, enthroned like a judge but treated like a beggar. It can be the most exalted pulpit or the loneliest pillory – and if you get it wrong, the variety of abuse is unparalleled in polite society. Get it right, and you appear to have orchestrated something magical, and will bask in all the glory – at least until the next lot comes along. The very best auctioneers can marry the art of theatre with their expertise to drive prices to unthinkable levels, while the very worst can lose control and forfeit the confidence of the room.[2]

Jussi Pylkkanen, deputy chairman of Christie's UK, lists three cardinal virtues for an auctioneer: pace, poise, and preparation. Pace governs atmosphere. Too quick and the audience is uncomfortable; too slow and the audience is lost. Poise is critical. However well or badly a sale is going, the auctioneer who falters is lost. The most experienced buyer may hesitate when an auctioneer's fluency is broken. Preparation means knowing your merchandise. For an auctioneer, knowledge is most certainly power.[3]

Pylkkanen adds two additional virtues, which, according to him, cannot be learnt. The really great auctioneers have tremendous panache and brilliant instinct. The first entertains and lulls the audience into the right mood; the second identifies an opportunity and extracts a final bid where none exists.

When Christopher Burge, honorary chairman of Christie's America and one of the world's best fine art auctioneers, climbs the rostrum in Christie's New York salesroom to sell Impressionist and modern art he has rehearsed the sale four or five times in his head. He has memorized where all the potential bidders are in the 1500-seat auction room, and he will have a shrewd idea of how aggressively they will pursue their quarry. His auction book will be black with annotations.[4]

To Burge auctioneering is an art. He has to hold the audience in thrall. What makes the auction such good theatre is the unpredictability, the mercurial mood of the room. And despite the increased sophistication of the business over the past two centuries, little has changed. The auctioneer's job was and is to get the best price for the vendor. When he climbs into the rostrum he has to know what to expect from the salesroom. He needs to know the history and solicitation background of the goods up for sale, the expectations of the vendors, the price limits, the results achieved by other recent auctions, and the strength of demand in different geographical markets represented in the room. He will synthesize all this into an overall sentiment, based on an intuitive compilation of hundreds of fragmented pieces of information.

Thus, as Christopher Burge takes the stage, he knows how to work the room, and to ensure the requisite publicity. A great auctioneer sustains the thrill and instinctively knows when to alter his pace and where to conjure that one last bid – even when the bidder himself thought he had finished. As Burge puts it: 'Sometimes when a bidder shakes his head, instinct tells you that if you pause, look down in a friendly way and ask: "Just one more?", even experienced buyers will find themselves saying yes.'

It is therefore no coincidence that the senior executives of auction houses often are auctioneers. They know and live the market, are on the pulse of the shifts in supply and demand, at the core of the business. A senior executive who is also an auctioneer is therefore a highly respected professional for both sellers and buyers. From the company perspective this means that the most critical information repository resides in the heads of the leading individuals of the organization.

Auctioneering and conducting an orchestra share the commonality that they are taking place in a setting where the role of the leader is predefined into the system. So in the same way as the musicians know what to expect from the conductor, the auction buyers know the role of the auctioneer. Even if the level of detail or the choreography is not so detailed in the way the auctioneer relates to the room, the work of the auctioneer is highly standardized. The auctioneer endlessly improvises the same basic scene, as each successive lot demands a fresh commitment, irrespective of the previous lot's fate. The greatest crime is to let the previous lot's triumph or disaster spill over and deflect you from concentrating fully on the next lot. But still good auctioneers do it differently from less successful ones. Again disciplined creativity could be used to describe the difference.

Conductors and auctioneers alike will succeed if they can create a particular spirit among those under their influence, the musicians or the auction buyers. But the way they do it differs. The conductor aims for a harmonized performance where the rehearsed musicians will reach unprecedented levels in their artistic achievement. The auctioneer in turn will create a momentum, which almost hypnotizes the audience and establishes confidence in a market that didn't exist or price levels not yet seen. Whereas the success of the conductor is how well he could mobilize the artists to perform against a predefined target, the auctioneer will be exceptional if he can push the limits of the market far beyond the expected levels. As the conductor looks for coherence, the auctioneer wants to find irregularities and rapidly exploit them to become new de facto standards. But both are immersed by the presence and intuitively complete their observe–orient–decide–act loops at breakneck speeds with process and content tightly interwoven in their considerations.

In a similar way that the musicians are subordinated to the conductor the auction buyers are subordinated to the auctioneer. As the conductor has to maintain the authority among the players, so the auctioneer has to do it in front of the buyers. But an auctioneer, contrary to the conductor, has to engage the customers, his role is to make the audience, the room, perform. The resources have been built up through the solicitation activities of the auction house. When the auctioneer enters the rostrum the objective is to get everybody involved in a joint experience that will establish acceptance for higher price levels of the goods for sale. This learning is very much in the sensing and experience-staging mode. Perception is everything. If the auctioneer can make the audience perceive that the price level is right, then it is right.

Both vendors and auction buyers are attracted to an auction house based on how successful its previous auctions have been. Auction buyers will go to auctions with interesting catalogs, and the more buyers, the higher the likelihood to get good prices. An auction house known to bring in high prices will have a strong position among the sellers.

The comparison of conducting and auctioneering reveals that on the micro-level orchestration of superficially similar types of events may be radically different in respect of the capabilities and the learning taking place. Conducting is more inward-focused and the learning is according to preset objectives, whereas auctioneering is outward-focused with open-ended learning emphasizing experience staging and sensing. Transforming this to the business arena means that the art of orchestration is all about the details, and acting based on the wrong assumptions may lead to catastrophic end results. So a conductor turning his back towards the musicians would be as bad as an auctioneer turning his back to the audience.

The conductor and the auctioneer as professions have existed for ages. Some implications for leadership in business can be raised from these vocations. The first one is that both types of orchestrating challenges can be found in a modern business organization. The race for efficiency improvements as a process reengineering effort can be described as trying to create an orchestra from the organization. If the process chart (as the music score) is well understood by all individuals, then the process will work very smoothly, and the need to supervise and lead and create additional systems and overhead costs will decrease.

A different situation arises when growth is looked for, and new product introductions are in the limelight. In such a case the question is about making the market. Here the challenge is very much the one faced by an auctioneer selling a piece of art, the market price of which is not clearly established. How to sense the possibilities, create a momentum and involve the audience in a dialogue that will generate gradual confidence in the new price level is the trick to pull off. The learning has to make use of weak signals, which are amplified and reflected back to the room to establish the new market. Such a logic could be identified when Steve Jobs masterminded the buildup of Apple's music business.

Steve Jobs: Using Auctioneering Skills to Reconfigure the Music Industry

Apple CEO Steve Jobs, in early 2001, became known in the music industry as Mr. 'Rip, mix, burn'. That was the title of an advertising campaign that Apple ran for its iTunes software. Music executives fumed that it was a clarion call to Apple customers to steal music by downloading it from the Internet. Then, in 2002, Apple's portable MP3 player, the iPod, went on sale and quickly became the hippest way to listen to music on the move.

When Steve Jobs, in April 2003, launched Apple's iTunes Music Store he was betting on simplicity – a concept not usually associated with music sites. Each song cost 99 cents, no strings were attached and no subscription required.

To pull it off, Apple had to get enough labels and artists to agree to this simple 99 cents-a-song approach: a stiff challenge. The key to do this was a copy protection scheme. This enabled Apple to offer songs from all five major music companies – something other digital music services had failed to do, even as the music industry continued to lose staggering dollars to digital piracy. The auctioneering skills of Steve Jobs are well illustrated by Andrew Lack, CEO of Sony Music Entertainment: 'I don't think it was more than a 15-second decision in my mind (to license music to Apple) once Steve started talking.'

When the iTunes Music Store had been under preparation Steve Jobs personally lobbied to get individual artists to sign up. According to Irving Azoff, the manager of the rock group, The Eagles, Steve Jobs called to ask if music by The Eagles could be included in the new online music service that Apple was launching. 'Please, please, please clear this,' he said, knowing The Eagles in the past had blocked the use of their songs on digital-music services. So like the auctioneer asking for one more bid, Jobs was appealing to the feelings of the artists to support his case. He even offered to personally demonstrate the service for Azoff and to make his case directly to Eagles singer Don Henley.[5]

Scheduling conflicts prevented the personal visits, but the entreaty worked, The Eagles and Warner Music struck a deal, allowing most of the band's music to be used by Apple's service. Azoff had previously turned down other music download services, but he liked the way iTunes Music Store worked, and Apple's product. Steve Jobs impressed Azoff, in the same way that he impressed other music-industry executives with his intricate knowledge of the new service. In some meetings, he sat at the computer himself to demonstrate. With his trademark confidence, he asserted Apple would transform the online music business, claiming that consumers would pay to download millions of songs in just a few months. He was right, or actually he proved to be too modest; the first million songs were sold in six days.

When the service was launched Steve Jobs was featured in 'exclusive' interviews with *Fortune* and the *Los Angeles Times* and appeared on CNBC and CNN. The Music Store was topline news in most newspapers. His message was straight-forward but visionary at the same time:

> We make computers. We make software. We make devices like the iPod. And now we're distributing music. We're trying to bring that all together into solutions for our customers. We all love music here, and the whole piracy thing was such a mess. We thought maybe we can clean it up with a really cool product. We're just focused on what we're doing, which is making the best music store in the world, and making the most popular and best MP3 player in the world, the iPod. (*Los Angeles Times*, April 29, 2003)

The successful launch of the iTunes Music Store cemented the fact that Steve Jobs had become a digital-entertainment impresario. Over the years, he had turned Apple into a pro-ducer of entertainment technology for digital photos, movies and music, culminating in the unveiling of the online music service. He exhibited a zeal for self-promotion and pleasing performers that made him at home in Hollywood's culture of schmooze. Perpetually clad in jeans and a black turtleneck, he wasn't shy about pitching himself as an artist-friendly alterna-tive to Silicon Valley's techies. At a two-hour breakfast with Icelandic singer Bjork at New York's Four Seasons Hotel in July 2001, he told her the motivation behind much of his work was to make tools for creative people.[6]

The track record of Steve Jobs, dating back to 1976 when at age 21 he founded Apple, reveals that he has the ability of foreseeing how to make technology inviting to consumers. He helped pioneer the distinctive Macintosh computers, with features that became standard: a screen divided into windows, pull-down menus, icons, and the mouse. In 1985, he started a high-end computer company, NeXT Software Inc., which he later sold to Apple for $430 million. In 1986, he purchased the computer division of Lucasfilm, renaming it Pixar, and made it into a big success in movie animation. Since releasing the movie *Toy Story* in 1995, the studio's first four feature-length films were all critical and financial successes. In this respect Steve Jobs shares those two characteristics that Pylkkanen expects from a good auctioneer: tremendous panache and brilliant instinct.

Through Pixar, Steve Jobs got a lengthy Hollywood tutorial in how to further strengthen his panache. When *Toy Story* unexpectedly took off, Pixar and Walt Disney had a five-film deal, sharing production costs and profits. But at the same time Steve Jobs also showed the attention to detail comparable to a conductor. He was intimately involved in all aspects of the negotiations. At one point, according to people familiar with the matter, he haggled with Disney over how the two companies' logos would appear in film credits and advertising.

What remains to be seen is whether Steve Jobs and Apple can sustain its magic formula to build an ever-expanding business. Another good salesman that has succeeded in doing so for more than 50 years is Ingvar Kamprad.

Ingvar Kamprad: Seducing Shoppers

When Ingvar Kamprad, a dyslexic son of a farmer, started his company in 1943 at just 17 years old he could not foresee that he would create a global cult brand. He gave the company the name Ikea (his initials and his own origin, the farm Elmtaryd outside the village of Agunnaryd).

Today Ikea operates more than 200 stores with 2005 sales of almost $18 billion, and Kamprad has been voted the most influential tastemaker in the world by British design magazine *Icon*. When new shops are opened they become big events in the neighborhood. For example, the opening of a new Atlanta store in June 2005 had more than 2000 Ikea fanatics in line by the store opening. The promised $4000 in gift certificates to the first person in line had attracted Roger Penguino to start queuing a week in advance.

Kamprad has been able to institutionalize his own values and salesmanship into the company. He has created a company that has a universal, egalitarian appeal that almost no other business can claim. His credo 'to contribute to a better every-day life for the majority of people' has fostered a culture of frugality in combination with design. There are numerous legends of Kamprad's obsession with penny-pinching. These stories tell about his habit of ripping out car rental coupons from in-flight magazines and hunting for cheap air tickets, or taking the subway rather than a taxi, to make use of his pensioners' discount.

What really has been making Ikea so successful is its ability to develop unique products that become global best sellers. In this respect the auctioneering philosophy is not one of getting the highest possible price for any single product, but to be able to sell large quantities of individual products. But the auction logic prevails, the need of the customer has to be properly understood, and then the resources needed to make the product have to be assembled. The strength of Ikea is to be able to constantly make its offering more attractive, by improving quality and reducing prices. The Klippan sofa is a good example.

In the 1970s Lars Engman, Ikea's design manager, wanted to create a sofa that was hard-wearing and child-friendly without compromising on design. It had to be soft around the edges yet sturdy enough to withstand years of wear and tear, and have machine-washable slipovers to make it easy to keep clean. In addition it had to meet the Ikea challenge of good looks at a low price. After endless testing of materials and fabrics, Klippan was born in 1980. More than two decades later the sofa with its clean lines, bright colors, simple legs, and compact size remains one of Ikea's best sellers with 1.5 million sold since 1998.[7]

Klippan was initially manufactured in Sweden, but soon production was outsourced to Poland. Today there are five suppliers for the frames in Europe, plus three in the United States and two in China, each of which is guaranteed a minimum volume. Thanks to continuous improvements of the product its price has been constantly reduced. For example, the frames that originally were made of solid wood are now made from a combination of particleboard, fiberboard, and polyurethane foam. This has made the frame both lighter and cheaper. Another major change from the original design is that it is now flat-packed, coming in four separate pieces.

Designing beautiful products that are inexpensive and functional and providing customers with superior value has become a winning formula. For example, Kamprad grasped early on that young couples who can't afford nannies need to distract their children when they are looking at sofabeds. Subsequently the Ikea stores come with play centers, snack bars, and restaurants specializing in Swedish meatballs. The paradox with Ikea is here well illustrated: it is highly customer oriented, but it offers limited customer service. It provides customers with value by preempting what the customer may ask for, and wires these value-adding elements into the self-service concept. The customer is seduced by the ingenuity of the concept. Ikea is an institutionalized auction house seducing customers to buy more than they originally intended, because they get the feeling that it is so cheap.

Three characteristics can be identified to distinguish a good auctioneer-based business model: sensing market needs; the ability to seduce customers; and a highly effective information system enabling smooth logistics. Both Apple and Ikea are very good at gathering weak signals about customer need. They are also good at creating buzz and engaging customers. On top of that both companies have developed sophisticated information systems that provide the backbone for the operations. For Apple the main part of the offering, the iTunes Music Store, is one big information system. In the case of Ikea managing the 1300 suppliers in 53 countries is a significant challenge. The information architecture consequently has an important role in the successful business model of both these companies.

INFORMATION ARCHITECTURE

Steve Jobs accomplished the design and implementation of a totally new value constellation for music delivery. Such an undertaking also means installing the appropriate means for how the different participants in the constellation communicate and share information. When there are diverse systems being brought together in an ad hoc manner, you risk losing visibility as to who is on the network and who is in control. This puts focus on information sharing. The challenge is how to share information across multiple user communities, and to be able to protect this information at appropriate levels, while simultaneously providing the situational awareness that is gained through sharing relevant information.

The role of the information architecture is to support better situational awareness within the network and at the same time to facilitate collective knowledge sharing. If the information architecture provides easy access to relevant information it also encourages unexpected positive self-organization to take place. In the case of Apple the development of podcasting is one such example. No one actually invented podcasting; it was just an application that emerged from the network.

If the information-sharing platform simplifies and encourages collective action, then such self-organized learning processes are intensified and the attractiveness of the network increases. These factors, to a great degree, explain why and how Linux has been such a strong movement, in spite of a limited amount of exercised leadership. The open sharing of information right from the start has had a profound community strengthening impact. The information-sharing platform has also provided the community with a transitional object for more effective learning.

Establishing a robust information architecture represents a co-evolution of technology, organizing, and concepts. Admiral Arthur K. Cebrowski, who from 2001–5 served as the director of the Office of Force Transformation in the US Department of Defense, suggested moving away from the concept of 'focused logistics' to what he called 'sense and respond logistics'. Emerging logistics concepts suggest that the widespread application of information technology can enable new supply chain concepts to achieve unprecedented levels of performance creating much more fluid and self-organizing operations.[8]

The information age also changes the meaning of power. Power comes from a different place, it is used in different ways, and it achieves different effects than it did before. Traditionally power came from mass. Now power tends to come from information, access, and speed. That said, Cebrowski suggests that in the military field we are now witnessing important, though nascent changes, emerging in the realm of sensors and how they will be used on future battlefields. We are seeing warfare dominated more by sensors than perhaps any other piece of equipment. The ability to sense the environment, to sense the enemy, and to be networked enough to transmit that critical data to all who require it, is the decisive factor for who will win future wars.

This was also highlighted by General Clark as he described the need for the 'precision information' required for precision air strikes. We are shifting from a weapons game to an intelligence game. The Special Operations personnel on the ground in Afghanistan were human sensors. That was their main mission.

The information architecture can subsequently be defined as follows:

The **information architecture** *consists of the descriptions, systems, data elements, interconnections, and user interfaces supporting access to and usability of information needed for value creation within a value constellation.*

However, information and technology have their limits. Military history has shown that overconfidence regarding the power and impact of new technologies can prove disastrous in real-world combat. Information superiority does not guarantee sound decisions or ultimate victory. Although increasingly critical, information is just one of many factors in the commander's success in combat. Timely and relevant information is of little value if the strategy is unsound and incoherent or the tactics and operations are poor.

Therefore leading proponents of a network-centric perspective, like Cebrowski, do not see it as primarily a technology issue. It is about the implications of the network itself, and how the role of the network is changing the perspective on how to use information and knowledge, how to create situational innovation. So it is about a new way of working – how to get people to share information, and how to change cultures.

Cebrowski has suggested that the Pentagon – and the nation at large – should continue to debate the pros and cons of the network-centric approach, while pursuing an aggressive program of experimentation and research. His concern is that somebody would attempt to pursue the 'one best way'. This would be a grave error. He doesn't believe in one best concept. There should not be one single architecture. There have to be alternatives, competing concepts. The network-centric concept should develop along several parallel paths – such as technological, cultural, and organizational. What is needed is tolerance for alternative ideas and continuous learning.

Information architecture is a key component of successful orchestration according to the auctioneering philosophy. But information is not the only relevant issue; the social context wherein the auctioneer acts is also relevant. When promoting a new idea on a global basis this becomes even more important. The next chapter will further explore this.

CHAPTER 17

THE LEADER AS PROMOTER

*I*n the same way that Linus Torvalds never planned for Linux to have a life outside his own computer, he also never planned to be the leader of a developers' community. It just happened by default. At some point a core group of five developers started generating most of the activity in the key areas of development. It made sense for them to serve as the filters and hold the responsibility for maintaining those areas.

The leadership philosophy of Torvalds was to let people do things because they wanted to do them, not because the leader wanted them to. Torvalds' credo was that good leaders should know when they are wrong, and should be capable of pulling themselves out. And the best leaders enable others to make decisions for them.

The Linux community is an intricate web of hundreds of thousands of participants relying on mailing lists and developers' conventions and corporate sponsorship in maybe 4000 projects that are taking place at any one time. At the top, arbitrating disputes over the operating system's kernel, is a leader whose instinct is, and has always been, not to lead.

Torvalds divested himself of things that didn't hold much interest for him, such as the user level as opposed to the deep-down, internal code. First somebody volunteered to maintain it. Then the process for maintaining all the subsystems became organic. People knew who had been active and who they could trust, and it just happened. No voting. No orders. This was possible because the people working on Linux participated because they loved programming. And they loved being part of a global collaborative effort, dedicated to building the best and most beautiful technology that was available to anyone who wanted it. It was that simple. And it was fun.

Additional motivation was provided to the most active programmers who got their names associated with their contributions in the form of the 'credit list' or 'history file' that was attached to each project. The most prolific contributors attracted the attention of employers who trolled the code, hoping to spot and hire top programmers. Linux programmers were also motivated, in large part, by the esteem they could gain in the eyes of their peers by making solid contributions. This was another significant motivating factor.

For Torvalds the personal motivation was the beauty of programming and technology. But he recognized that one increasingly important attraction of Linux was its antiestablishment sentiment. Bill Gates vs. Linus Torvalds. But for Torvalds this wasn't really the key issue. He saw it as something far more wide-reaching. For him Linux represented a more organic way of spreading technology, knowledge, wealth, and having fun than the world of commerce had ever known. But he never felt that he was in an idealistic camp. He saw open source as a way of making the world a better place. But more than that, he saw it as a way of having fun. And he considered idealistic people as interesting, but kind of boring and sometimes scary.

Linus Torvalds understood what was expected from him as a leader. He had to be trusted on two levels – both technically and politically. He had to be able to acknowledge the fact that a project may have been flawed from the start. Instead of hiding from such problems, he had to be able to convince everybody that the best thing to do is to go back and start over, which meant breaking stuff. This was not a message people wanted to hear. However, coming from someone who commanded respect, people accepted it. On top of that he recognized the importance of being perceived to stay neutral. Therefore he systematically avoided getting involved with any individual Linux company.

So unintendedly Linus Torvalds became the originator of a movement that in 10 years became institutionalized as one of the icons of the information age. Another unintended institutionalizer of a cult behavior was Captain America.

Captain America: the Epitome of Cool[1]

In the mid-1960s Harley-Davidson made a conscious move to provide its customers with motorcycles well adapted for long highway rides. The Duo Glide model was given electric start and became Electra Glide. The big Harley was no longer the performance king; instead it was a touring motorcycle, including optional accessories such as saddlebags and top box. In the late 1960s this represented anything but fashion. The more rebellious Harley owners didn't like it. What the true enthusiast did was to do the opposite. When the traditionalists added bags, boxes, case guards, fairings, lights, fringes, and so forth the rebels began taking things off.

At first the new fashion mimicked TT racers, adding raised suspension and exhaust and small tanks to their big twins; then they went beyond function, with high pipes, extended forks, and no front brake or fender. These creations were called choppers, and they were mostly for show. Peter Fonda and

Dennis Hopper put this movement eternally into the history of the late 1960 culture through the movie *Easy Rider*. The long-haired, hippie attitude towards an America in turmoil is portrayed in the form of a biker film.

Peter Fonda originally purchased four Harley-Davidson Panheads from an LA police department auction. The bikes were then customized by Fonda, customizer Tex Hall, and actor Dan Haggerty. The three did all the chopping, welding, fabricating, and painting to produce four bikes for the movie. They made two 'Billy Bikes' named for and ridden by the character played by Dennis Hopper and two of the more radically chopped Captain America machines ridden by Fonda. This 'Captain America' chopper became the epitome of cool. For subsequent generations of Americans, that motorcycle has symbolized freedom, hope, and independence – not to mention that it looked just plain wild! The Captain America chopper symbolizes the American dream for many people. One of them is Sam Lewis, VP of sales at an electronic company in San Diego.

In August 2001, while Sam was swapping bike tales with some friends, one of them said that he knew the man who had built the Captain America replica for the Otis Chandler Museum. That bike was later sold to the Guggenheim and put on display in their 'Art of the Motorcycle' exhibit. He had also built a second replica for the Harley-Davidson Museum. While sharing their deep awe of the Captain America chopper, one thing led to another and Sam ended up talking seriously with his buddy about asking the fabricator to build another replica.

Sam heard nothing until February 2002 when his friend called to say 'Jim' was willing to talk to him. The very next weekend, Sam drove 100-plus miles to San Bernardino to discuss the details with master metal man Jim Grasius, and the gentlemen came to terms by the following week. Sam got the bike in late July, just in time to put it on a trailer and have a friend tow it to Sturgis (South Dakota) for the big Harley rally.

Sam's new Captain was an exact duplicate of the quintessential chopper. Chrome adorned nearly every piece of the bike, including its rigid frame, rear fender, and the now classic upswept fishtail exhaust. Elsewhere there was a tall chrome sissy bar, chrome hubs, chrome oil tank, chrome foot pegs, chrome buttons on the black leather seat, chrome . . . well, just about everything. It also correctly sported four bullet taillights and two sets of risers – the first a section of straight bar that, in turn, had a set of dog-bone risers attached that lead up to the ape hangar handlebars. The tiny 'peanut' gas tank was adorned with several lustrous coats of candy apple red paint, with whites stars and stripes added next, followed by the field of blue. Naturally, Sam had a helmet to match.

Sam's replica was so stylish and accurate that it took First in the Glenco Antique Bike Show at Sturgis, and then it proceeded to take Best of Show. Later on the Captain won several more awards. In addition Sam loaned it to the San Diego Automotive Museum for their three-week motorcycle exhibit. He has also ridden it around the San Diego area, but mostly short rides, as it isn't very comfortable. The minimalist approach of the 60s-style rolling work of art lacks such comforts and safety items as a front fender, front brakes, turn signals, and has absolutely no rear suspension or seat springs. But being able to show the chopper to others is part of the fun. Many people react positively when they see it because of the memories it brings back.

When comparing the Linux and Harley-Davidson communities it is evident that both have a strong cult-like aspect. And both were initiated more or less by mistake. But once they took off, the role of the central figure (in the case of Harley-Davidson not a person, but an artifact) has been very important. This central figure has stimulated the thoughts and the dreams of those who have joined the community. Captain America is therefore also a transitional object, providing the community members with a means to emotionally and intellectually engage in something that they personally feel important. In that respect Torvalds and Captain America represent a set of values that unites and strengthens these communities. Captain America was the ultimate manifestation of a youth rebellion in the early 1970s, a period still very much driven by the industrial logic. Linux became a similar symbol for rebellion 20 years later.

If both Linus Torvalds and Captain America became promoters of an idea unconsciously, there are also promoters that have had the ambition to create something big up front. Baron Pierre de Coubertin was such a promoter, and the Olympic Games has proven to be able to adapt and evolve while still maintaining its legacy and values. Another promoter who wanted to achieve something important on a worldwide basis was Bob Geldof.

Bob Geldof: from Songwriter to Promoter of a Better World

It was in November 1984 that Geldof saw a BBC news report by Michael Buerk on the famine in Ethiopia and vowed to do something about it. He felt grossly inadequate in the face of this obscenity. He tried to think what he could do as a songwriter. So he called people he knew to find out if they felt the same way that he did. And he got a lot of support. More than 40 of the best known pop-music stars of that time, including Sting, Phil Collins, Boy George, U2, and Wham, teamed up under the name Band Aid.

He also called Midge Ure from the pop band Ultravox. Together they quickly co-wrote the song, 'Do They Know It's

Christmas?' He subsequently used a prior appointment with BBC Radio 1 DJ Richard Skinner to appear on his show. Instead of discussing his new album (the original reason for the booking), he used the airtime to talk about the upcoming charity single. In this way intense media interest in the subject was created even before the single was recorded.

When the record was released in December it sold more than 2.5 million copies in three weeks, becoming the best-selling record ever in England.

Singer Harry Belafonte, inspired by the Band Aid project, started the ball rolling with the USA (United Support of Artists) for Africa project late December. Pop music manager Ken Kragen was engaged to organize it. Kragen recruited Quincy Jones as producer.

On January 28, 1985 a studio full of American musical superstars got together in Los Angeles. They worked 12 hours straight, emerging with a song, 'We Are the World,' which was the all-American version of the British single, 'Do They Know It's Christmas?'

Jones and Kragen had planned the whole session – who would sing which solos, who would stand where. They had made the decisions musically. It was based on whose voice would sound better singing a certain line. Figuring out where everyone stood had been like piecing together a jigsaw puzzle. When the artists arrived at the studio, their names were taped on the floor. All they had to do was go to their spot. Jones and Kragen had not left anything to doubt.

Jones commented afterwards that he could not be democratic when he had that many stars working together. If you try to be democratic, you're in for chaos.

Once released in March 1985 'We Are the World' went to the No. 5 spot in two weeks, the second ever best-selling debuting single for Billboard, behind Michael Jackson's 'Thriller'. By mid-May the single had sold 7.5 million copies and the album 4.5 million copies. The anticipated net income from record sales alone to that point was more than $45 million.

According to Kragen the overwhelming success of USA for Africa was because it was the right cause at the right time. The song 'We Are the World' became the anthem for the times. On Good Friday more than 8000 radio stations all over the western hemisphere played 'We Are the World' simultaneously in a burst of compassion. Though Kragen had done plenty to instigate the success of the record, he had nothing to do with the radio chain reaction. The reason for the strong support was partly due to the fact that the climate was right because of an economic upturn, which took people a little out of the 'Oh, I better look out for me' attitude to the feeling that they could take a little bit of a deep breath and look outward. Another important reason was those dramatic pictures coming out of Africa. There was the BBC documentary that really touched people – hard to watch, but spectacularly moving.[2]

On July 13, 1985, two rock concerts in London and Philadelphia were staged to raise money for famine victims in Africa. The two 'Live Aid' concerts were broadcast worldwide on radio and television. Some called the Live Aid rock concerts 'an electronic Woodstock' with 16 satellites involved in the concerts' global broadcast. With a live 16–hour telecast beamed to 152 countries around the world from stages on either side of the Atlantic, the massive Live Aid benefit for Ethiopian famine relief was the biggest show ever staged at that time, bigger than the Super Bowl or the 1984 Olympics closing ceremonies.

What Bob Geldof initiated in November 1984 culminated in the Live Aid concerts. The weekend raised about $80 million for famine relief in Africa. The Band Aid record for Christmas had raised $33 million, and the USA for Africa records $47 million.

On July 2, 2005, Geldof repeated the Live Aid concept, but with a different objective: not to raise money directly, but to put pressure on the G8 meeting to be held in Scotland the following week. Thus the name of this event: Live8.

SOCIAL ARCHITECTURE

Geldof had a good understanding of how to mobilize the show business world for his project. To get the initiative off the ground a high-profile media setup was needed. Using his own celebrity he could direct the media interest towards Band Aid. In this way he influenced the social architecture, which helped him to get colleagues on board.

Bob Geldof illustrates an orchestrator strongly influencing the environment. As the network is a learning network the orchestrator from a social perspective can be compared to the teacher in an educational setting. In the same way that students are affected by the social architecture (the classroom, program, school, physical environment etc.) fostering and supporting their beliefs, members of any social system are affected by similar settings.

The orchestrator can influence the network in three ways. The orchestrator can apply the charismatic leader model – the way that Geldof did. Another approach is to apply the 'together we'll make it' philosophy. This has been largely the style used by Linus Torvalds. A third alternative is that the concept becomes institutionalized and reaches cult status. This is what happened with Captain America. In such a case the role of the individual as orchestrator diminishes. The shared practice around the common theme gets its own life. Self-organization takes place inspired by the idea, not necessarily by an individual. The communities of Harley-Davidson motorcycle owners or Games Workshop aficionados are examples of this.

The social architecture includes the culture, communication patterns, reward system, policies, procedures, and form of organizing. This architecture influences people's capacity and willingness to adapt to changes and their attraction to the network. The network may exist only temporarily, as when the Lagerfeld campaign was launched by H&M, or the network may exist with explicit longevity as the goal, as is the case with Linux (see Chapter 7).

A social architecture with a strong collective sense of accountability can produce superior performance in a turbulent environment by creating a web of committed self-organizing members. When the external environment is turbulent and things start happening fast and furious, a network of knowledgeable and committed individuals with the resources they need to succeed can collectively achieve higher levels of performance. Here Toyota-Aisin is a good example. The social architecture can be defined as follows:

The **social architecture** *means the resources embedded in social relations among people and organizations that provide a common language and trust, and facilitate collaboration among the individuals engaged in a value constellation.*

For an orchestrator aiming at radically changing behavior among large groups of people the social architecture aspect of the orchestrating endeavor becomes utterly important. If on the other hand the role of the orchestrator is to mobilize value-creating activities according to accepted rules and procedures, but in a more efficient or effective way than the competition, then the focus is more on the operational architecture. But irrespectively, in all situations of value creation, the social architecture affects the outcome. How much the orchestrator can, or should even try to, influence the social settings depends on the case.

THE ORCHESTRATION ARCHITECTURE

This fourth part of the book has made in-depth expositions of the four archetypes of orchestrators: conductors, architects, auctioneers, and promoters. In connection with each of these roles one orchestration architecture area of particular importance has been highlighted. For the conductor it was the game plan, for the architect the operational architecture, for the auctioneer the information architecture, and for the promoter the social architecture. Together these architectural components form a whole that can be called the orchestration architecture. How the different parts come together is depicted in Figure 17.1.

Orchestrated value creation is always a dynamic process. The interaction between the customer, the orchestrator, and the network members forms the operational architecture of the value-creating process. Depending on the degree of improvisation the role of the game plan varies. If the orchestrated performance is a repetition of something well practiced, then the game plan in itself can almost replace the need of the orchestrator. A well-rehearsed symphony orchestra can probably perform a piece of music without the conductor present, even if the experience would not be exactly the same. The other alternative is a very complex and long-lasting project, such as the construction of the Walt Disney Concert Hall or the Kosovo operation. Here the

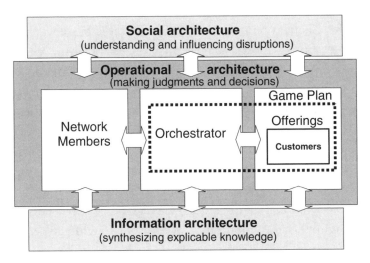

Figure 17.1   The orchestration architecture

operational architecture in itself has to be periodically redefined to enable a happy ending.

The role of the operational architecture is to secure dynamic decision making, allowing for continuous judgments as the undertaking proceeds. Because orchestration expects learning to take place, the operational architecture has to be adaptable to the improved understanding resulting from this open-ended approach.

The operational architecture is dependent on the cultural settings framing the collaboration between the network members. Here it is relevant to make a distinction between the Western and Eastern ways of thinking. The Western philosophy has had a long tradition of separating the subject who knows from the object that is known. This is in philosophy called the 'Cartesian split' between the subject (the knower) and the object (the known). The Eastern intellectual tradition doesn't have a similar deeply rooted split between subject and object.

Professors Nonaka and Takeuchi[3] have exemplified the Eastern way by describing the Japanese intellectual tradition. They present three distinctions of this tradition: oneness of humanity and nature, oneness of body and mind, and oneness of self and other. Professor Ming-Jer Chen,[4] a renowned expert in Chinese business practices, notes that unlike most Western societies, the Confucian state is composed not of 'individuals' per se but of their interconnections and interdependencies. This means that the Chinese in general prefer to do business with people they know, or with friends of friends. Consequently they devote a substantial amount of time and energy to establishing relationships with people they find respectable. From an orchestration perspective this means that the Western perspective usually puts more focus on the game plan and the operational architecture, whereas the Eastern perspective more highlights the importance of the social architecture.[5]

The social architecture tends to show differences along Western and Eastern lines in the areas of organizational focus, the role of the individual and attitudes about risk. The Western focus is on determining goals and arranging for task completion. The Eastern focus includes those same elements, but a significantly larger amount of energy is spent on determining how those goals and tasks fit into the broader scheme of the players involved. For example, who should be making which decisions, who should be the experts, who should set the goals etc.

The role of the individual is also different. Westerners admire rugged individualism. In a Darwinistic sense this results in highly skilled and experienced leaders emerging from those who are successful after having gone off on their own. In contrast, the Easterners tend to gravitate more strongly to their social networks, and place more emphasis on the credibility and social capital of those they would choose to work with instead of just evaluating pure skill and experience criteria.

The role of the individual in the Western and Eastern social architecture in turn influences the attitudes about risk markedly, manifested in how the risk tolerance can be detected.

Westerners as individuals tend to take on social risk relatively more freely, expressing very personal opinions and being more flamboyant with lifestyle choices than Eastern counterparts. The Westerner is more independent and has less to gain or lose individually from the social context. This provides greater lifestyle and expression freedoms, but on the flip side it means that risks in business and career undertakings are borne mainly by that individual.

Conversely, the Easterners, being more conservative in their social context, preserve their social capital and network, which enables them to assume more individual risks in their career. They rely more heavily on their extended network to resource their business to fuel faster growth or to have a safety net when their risky venture fails. When the Easterner succeeds, the network also benefits from this. But if the Easterner fails, there is support acting as a safety net, enabling the individual's recovery.

If the Western way of thinking emphasizes rational or logical thinking, based on analytic, dialectical, and analogical argumentation, the Eastern way of thinking may be called correlative thinking. This implies more spontaneity grounded in informal and ad hoc analogical procedures presupposing both association and differentiation. Subsequently the Eastern way of thinking shows more clustered ideas, multi-directional, intuitive, and holistic. In many ways the orchestration approach combines the Eastern and Western ways.

Orchestration starts with a holistic view of the whole issue, and then moves to details. At the same time, the users' preferences and interests are actively taken into account. This conforms to the Eastern approach. But the orchestration approach also emphasizes the need for efficiency, and introduces the information architecture as a complement to the social architecture. This clearly corresponds to the Western way of thinking. By systematically trying to make most of the knowledge explicit, the known is separated from the knower, and made more accessible to anyone interested in knowing.

The surrounding culture thus has considerable influence on the formation and design of the orchestration setup. Only when the cultural elements are considered will the orchestration approach successfully transfer from one culture to another. When trying to infer from individual cases into general conclusions it is always important to reflect upon the specificities of the case at hand. The Toyota-Aisin and Linux cases share two commonalities that do not often prevail in large organizations. The actions observed took place within networks that culturally were remarkably homogeneous. Toyota-Aisin is a national network with a long shared tradition in a common industry. Linux is a very technologically specialized community. Even if the Linux community is a global one, the theme around which it is organized makes everybody extremely knowledgeable about the subject matters that form the basis for the shared activities. So in this sense, both these communities, for different reasons, represent socially very coherent institutions. Unfortunately few commercial organizations can present such uniformity in respect of their culture.

Consider the specific case of a Western organization trying to adapt to the Chinese culture. The Western organization is more focused on getting things done, and are thus primarily task driven. The Chinese organization is more attuned to the social aspects around the task, the network and the interdependencies of the issue at hand. Due to this the Chinese culture is also more favorable to intensive communication between the different individuals to better understand how the issue fits into the larger context, even if this may generate some additional transaction costs. Based on the reflections of General Clark from the Kosovo crisis outlined in Chapter 15 one could say that the traditional war-fighting doctrine with clear objectives and executable plans is according to a Western mindset, whereas the way that the Kosovo operation played out more resembles the Chinese approach.

The Chinese attitude is also more towards keeping the group intact, harmonious, and democratic. Subsequently decision makers try to make the whole process go smoothly and to respect each other's 'face' (status). The orchestrator has in such a context to be sensitive when singling out individuals, be those suppliers, customers, or co-workers.

In general, orchestration most naturally fits into a collaborative culture, emphasizing community relationships over individual autonomy. In many respects the existing shareholder-centric business philosophy and the emphasis on 'competitive' strategy has discouraged business people from considering this perspective. Also incentive systems and management practices have glorified the effort of the single individual, highlighting individual accountability and responsiveness. This has put the attention on the individual as a standalone knowledge worker, and not as a member of a learning social community.

For an orchestrated setup to outperform the traditional 'competitive' market arrangements the key is how to create shared situational awareness, provide incentives for information sharing, and motivate individuals to feel a strong intellectual and emotional desire to achieve something extraordinary within the orchestrated setup. Still all this has to happen in the context of the market, which asks for the simultaneous emphasis on efficiency and creativity.

In any cultural setting the orchestrator has to be able to facilitate increased collective awareness of the ever-changing business context and willingness to take on new challenges in order to stay competitive. The main responsibilities of the leader are and will remain making insightful observations, providing a determined stance when the realities are unquestionable, setting up new priorities, and initiating new behavior. The operational, informational, and social challenges this imposes cannot be outsourced. The leader has to meet them, one way or another. The organization has to be provided with awareness and confidence. How the leader does it is a question of style and taste.

This book has shown that there are situations where the orchestrated approach has provided outstanding results. The next chapter will summarize what we can learn from individuals that have chosen orchestration as their leadership philosophy.

CHAPTER 18

THRIVING, AWARE, AND ENGAGING

When knowledge and orchestration become the basis for commercial success, the leader increasingly is dependent on trusted companions. The core team has to provide both the intellectual resources to expand and develop the business, and the organizational heart to carry the organization through any potential crisis.

In such a context the leader has to rely on the support of creative colleagues he cannot force into cooperation. Orchestrating a collaborative performance built on the present and shaping the future is what is expected. When the going gets tough the two things the leader is left with are his values and his knowledge. What he will be evaluated upon is whether he is credible, generates confidence, and exposes a character that is inviting to collaboration. In respect of the Linux community Linus Torvalds has expressed this quite eloquently:

Good maintainers are hard to find . . . I have got about ten–twenty people I really trust, and quite frankly, the way people work is hard-coded in our DNA. Nobody really trusts hundreds of people. The way to make these things scale out more is to increase the network of trust not by trying to push it on me, but by making it more of a network, not a star-topology around me. So we have to help existing maintainers, or maybe help grow new ones. That is the way to scalability.[1]

The leader has to constantly have an eye on the big picture, yet focus on what makes the difference in the present. For purposeful emergence to happen the proper architecture for orchestration has to be established. This boils down to three imperatives:

- Provide the proper balance between efficiency and creativity in the ongoing activities of the firm, i.e. work continuously on the evolving operational architecture.
- Build the infrastructure to monitor and digest the dynamics of the value-creating context, and the role of the firm therein, to increase efficiency and track changes, i.e. develop the appropriate information architecture.
- Stimulate the formation of productive internal and external personal interconnections to enable an abrupt change of course, if required due to rapid shifts in the environment, i.e. enable the suitable social architecture to form.

The three elements of the orchestration architecture form the managerial dimension of the orchestration agenda. Another part is the question of strategic focus. Here the orchestrator has to consider the different components of the competitive arsenal of the firm: the core resources, the offering concepts, the customer relationships, and the constellations wherein the firm acts. Which part needs the most emphasis at this particular time? What can be delegated to lower levels within the firm? In which areas is the strong involvement of external parties needed to secure success? By answering these questions the leader will be able to define the priorities and identify the type of leadership style most appropriate to carry out the high priority tasks. Will it be the meticulous work of a conductor, finetuning and perfecting the performance? Will it ask for in-depth problem solving and the formation of new revolutionary offering concepts, asking for the mentality of an architect? Or is the focus more on engaging customers and getting them to recognize the value of the resources already available, meaning that the leadership challenge is one facing the auctioneer? Or is the challenge more to mobilize external partners and promote an emergent vision that has not yet been fully understood and accepted?

The role of the orchestrator is thus to form the context for the organization to properly function in respect of the operational, informational, and social arrangement. Within this setup the leader subsequently has to carry out the orchestrating role, pondering between the need for conducting, architecting, auctioneering, or promoting. This context forms the orchestration framework. This is illustrated in Figure 18.1.

As Figure 18.1 indicates the orchestrator is responsible for both the managerial and the strategic setup. The managerial context is represented through the circles and the strategic context through the four quadrants. On both dimensions the orchestrator has to consider the issue of how to balance efficiency and creativity. How much to further improve existing strengths, and how much to look for new opportunities. What to emphasize depends on the business logic surrounding the leader. In the following we shall look into these considerations based on the experiences from two different companies: one being an industrial wholesaler, and the other providing electronics manufacturing services.

Both wholesaling and electronics manufacturing services (EMS) are businesses that by definition have a strong

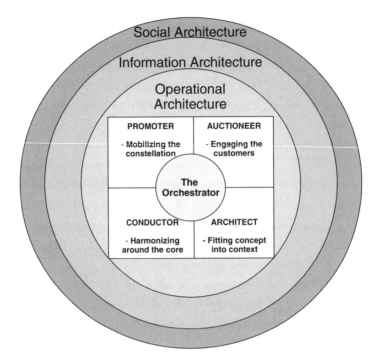

Figure 18.1 The orchestration framework

orchestrating dimension attached to their logic of value creation. But when looking deeper into them some profound differences become obvious.

The wholesaler is first and foremost an organization built up to handle complex relationships, both with suppliers and with customers. Indeed, its operational function is to offer logistic services, to make sure that goods will be delivered at the right time to the right place. But the logistics performance will not make the wholesaler radically different from the competition. What distinguishes a good wholesaler is the ability to find new supplies for a customer not yet aware of the possibilities, and to provide the suppliers with new customers. The strategic value added of the wholesaler comes from the interactions with the external world, and the skill to come up with new creative solutions together with both customers and suppliers. If the value added is reduced to pure logistics the wholesaler could gradually be replaced by a pure logistics company. However, if the wholesaler is unable to provide the optimal logistics solutions, then the company is out of business. Subsequently logistics is a hygiene factor in the business model, creative business solutions are what provide the differentiation. The ethos of the company is thus one of a creative customer servant.

The EMS company faces all the harsh realities described in connection with the aftermath of the Albuquerque fire in the Philips plant (see Chapter 9). The EMS company has to perfect its just-in-time capability, providing the customer with cost-efficient production capacity in a flexible way. The EMS company also has to have a high degree of creativity when it comes to how the internal processes are organized. But in the relationships with the customers the expectation is to deliver according to specifications. In this respect the ethos of an EMS provider is one of a global transaction engine.

Comparing these two types of companies, the creative customer servant and the global transaction engine, provides an illustration of the span of considerations an orchestrating leader faces when practicing the art of orchestration. Especially if the leader is entering the company afresh the question of where to begin is of great importance. If the objective is to move the corporate culture from an industrial mindset towards one of orchestration, there are interesting perspectives arising when comparing these two companies. In the following the authentic description of the first nine months for a new CEO of an industrial wholesaler is used to illustrate how the orchestration mindset can be introduced into an organization. Subsequently comparisons to the EMS company will be made.

Introducing the Orchestration Mindset in Practice

The new CEO had been able to follow the development of the wholesaling company as a board member for two years prior to his appointment. He was familiar with the industry, as he had served in other companies from that industry throughout his career.

Once he had been in office for about a week he decided to express his leadership approach openly to the whole organization by publishing his thoughts on the company intranet. He announced that he wanted to see an even stronger customer and market orientation, but also more transparency and team work. However, this was not to be seen as an end, but as a means for business growth and increased profitability. He wanted the company to be a winning team.

After discussions with a large number of people in the organization he presented his more concrete ideas about how to initiate a transformation process. Again he formalized this into a letter addressed to the whole personnel.

In the letter he invited people to participate in three workshops that aimed at gradually building up the new way of working. The first stage was defined to last for only two months, and the subsequent refining should enable the whole firm to be reorganized when the new CEO had been six months in his position. The 20 most senior professionals were selected to participate in the workshops, but others were invited to participate as well. The third workshop attracted 40 participants.

One of the tasks of the participants was to collect input from the rest of the organization; they also gathered information from customers and suppliers. This was one of the key objectives in the first part of the transformation process: to clearly focus on the outside world to generate a shared awareness about the competitive situation. Based on well-documented interviews with more than 50 customers and 20 suppliers, consensus started to emerge relating to the competitive challenges that the company had to address.

Throughout the process all information was made accessible to the whole organization through the corporate intranet. In this respect the CEO used the principles of blogging, i.e. making a constantly updated journal available through the intranet. But he didn't apply the narcissistic communication style normally attached to blogging. Instead the communication was purely based on facts. This fact-based conversation was seen to increase the collective awareness about the competitive situation. This in turn created consensus in respect of how to prioritize, to put the company among the top in the industry. The theme unifying these aspirations was defined as 'Desire for Partnership'.

The CEO had a natural tendency to establish an inclusive and progressive transformation process. He saw himself as an open, optimistic, enthusiastic, and sometimes impulsive and impatient person. He preferred to work in teams, and he liked to work with people. He therefore genuinely expected the members of the organization to come up with ideas and comments, in order to find ways of how the company could become a preferred partner of its customers, principals, and personnel. He saw this as something best achieved through a collective effort, and he willingly opened up the discussions regarding how to achieve this.

Taking this perspective the new CEO, by the first open letter to the personnel, initiated an unprecedented dialogue within the company, after only one week in office. It was a bold move, but it created a lot of spontaneous buy-in from the organization. He was able to make everybody aware of what he wanted to achieve. In one stroke he had presented himself, his interpretation of the situation, and the collective process through which he expected to bring the company towards new growth and improved profitability.

He also recognized the need to strengthen the degree of integration within the company. As a trading company it had been very successful by relying on strong internal entrepreneurship. The different teams had produced continuous growth, but it was still felt that there was more potential out there. To mobilize this additional potential the organization had to be engaged in more shared internal conversations.

When he reflected upon what he had learnt from the history of the company it seemed that the central elements for previous successes had been innovation and motivation. The competent and motivated personnel had successfully strived to delight customers and principals. And success had always been celebrated. He therefore outlined the basis for how the company could become a winner: it had to identify the best areas and opportunities for growth. To do this the shared responsibility was to assess where there were strong market positions and which principals provided the best platform for further expansion. But this could not be done without simultaneously considering where the biggest threats from competition were. Once this was done, the necessary decisions for the future could be made.

The positive atmosphere created around the 'Desire for Partnership' initiative enabled the CEO to further increase the level of ambition. He could indeed invite the whole organization to share the experience to create a new common future. The intermediary goals, growth, and increased profitability were clearly outlined; they represented the legitimacy for the shared effort. But they were only the technical foundation. The more fundamental ambition was to make a permanent shift in the organization to emphasize information sharing, active dialogue, and continuous emphasis on innovation and change.

By using the company intranet as the communication channel the CEO could effectively explain his aspirations and values and start to shape the ethos that he wanted to establish within the organization. The role of this transparent communication was to establish shared awareness and invite people to an open dialogue.

This first very simple form of posting information on the intranet was gradually expanded. The ideas of an orchestration platform were adopted. Senior executives responsible for both principals and customers started to actively use the common information repository as a tool to improve the dialogue they had with principals and customers.

Six months down the road as a new CEO the new organizational structure was announced. Of the original management team half had been changed, as not everybody felt comfortable with the new style. The inclusiveness of the orchestration approach made individual senior managers much more vulnerable to the rest of the organization. And the orchestration approach together with principals and customers provided the company with firsthand feedback on how well different people within the organization were handling their duties from the perspective of the outside world. This transparency created increased social pressure for outstanding performance throughout the organization.

Within six months the company was steadfastly on its way for a permanent change of the organizational culture from an industrial mindset favoring individual entrepreneurship and limited cross-functional action towards a much higher degree of integration and collective value creation. This didn't mean taking away individual accountability. One of the paradoxes was that shared understanding and the acceptance of the power of collective capabilities helped the organization to better agree on clearly defined individual accountabilities and responsibilities. But this was not forced upon the different departments and managers from above, but resulted from joint workshops, where the representatives from different functions together agreed upon the most appropriate ways to carry out different activities.

During the first six months the CEO was very closely involved in shaping the new interactive way of working. He selected those individuals that excelled during the workshops as new key managers. Rapidly it was seen how a new level of initiative taking and self-organization started to generate results. The new operational architecture had been collectively built, so there was no need for separate implementation. Instead of being sequentially designed and implemented the new way of working had been crafted; it had been gradually constructed, without any specific moment of time where the specification would have been cemented. The announcement of the new organizational structure was just manifesting that the crafting had reached a stage, where it was well enough documented to be communicated externally. But it didn't mean that the crafting as such ended by that. Increased ambitions were generated by both the management and the rest of the organization all of the time. In the same way that an orchestra can never settle with its existing repertoire the organization also has to constantly work on its own next success stories.

Once the new organization had been put in place, the following three months were spent, to a high degree, focusing on how the orchestration mindset was understood and applied by the senior managers. Many of these managers were new in their positions, and others had to adapt to a radical change in the expectations. Just meeting the fiscal number was no longer enough; the managers were expected to show the same inclusive and nurturing leadership as had been the atmosphere surrounding the series of workshops, through which the 'Desire for Partnership' ethos had been defined and propagated. Not all managers were able to make this shift, and some of them left. Others having substantial difficulties posed a serious problem to the CEO: whether to rapidly shift them out, or whether to try to support and coach them to be able to learn and adapt. These decisions were the most difficult ones to make.

The transformation process of the wholesaler provided good results during the first nine months. Sales and margins developed favorably. The feedback from inside the organization was overwhelmingly positive. Suppliers and customers also welcomed the initiative. The next challenge was of course how to maintain the momentum, and secure that the new way of working would become permanently established. In this area the plans for the second year were focusing on the support systems. The incentive systems were completely overhauled. Planning and reporting were redesigned in order to correspond to the more holistic perspective introduced instead of the previous more departmentalized philosophy. A roadmap for a substantially upgraded IT architecture was developed and the first crucial improvements were implemented with high priority.

The ethos of the wholesaler as a creative servant shaped the design of the transformation process. The first actions were forcing the whole organization to engage in an active dialogue with the outside world. The CEO himself interviewed a number of customers and principals to learn how the company performed in the eyes of its constituents.

A key success factor in this transformation process was the use of workshops as a means to foster shared awareness. By airing the comments from customers and suppliers in the workshops participants greatly improved their situational understanding. The workshops also strengthened the ties between the employees thus building the social architecture. From this perspective the workshops retrospectively proved to be very effective transitional spaces.

The learning in the workshops was, however, almost an unnoticed byproduct of the transformation process, because each participant was primarily focusing on his or her own area of expertise, interviewing own customers or suppliers and presenting the results to colleagues. By using the workshops as a means to familiarize all participants with the experiences of others, the learning from these workshops significantly improved the agility of the organization. Each individual was now better equipped to understand his or her role in the broader context, and was also more aware of what could be expected from colleagues. In this respect the workshops provided increased organizational cohesion.

In the case of the EMS company the point of departure was completely different. This company had been growing rapidly in pace with the growth of its most important customers in the field of telecommunications equipment. In pace with the customers' expansion it had expanded internationally, and built new plants. The number of customers was quite limited, and a large part of material supply for the manufacturing was provided by the customers. In this respect the social architecture of the company was considerably less important compared to the wholesaler. But the need to simultaneously drive efficiencies and build new capabilities was a theme shared by both companies. Both companies also shared the feature of having a strong entrepreneurial spirit, which historically had given managers a high degree of independence and authority to locally optimize their business to achieve agreed upon financial targets. As was explained above, one of the key objectives of the transformation process of the wholesaler was to increase the collective awareness of the competitive situation. For the EMS company increased collective awareness was also needed. In this case the question was, however, more about leveraging internal experiences to improve the production process, providing both cost efficiency and flexibility, in order to be able to adapt to the quick market changes.

The EMS company chose to use the information systems as a transitional object. Because of the rapid changes in the marketplace, both in respect of technology and fashion-driven customer preferences, the EMS company faced constant pressure to be able to generate fast and accurate cost estimates for new products. Due to the complexity of the supply chain, the product costing practices had been locally adjusted to reflect the idiosyncrasies of respective plants. As long as the products were less complex and better specified by the customers, and the batch runs were longer, the organization had coped well with its entrepreneurial model. Now facing shorter product life cycles, increasing amounts of requests for quotes (RFQs), and more complex production configurations a new approach was needed. It was a necessity to improve the internal exchange of best practices, and to facilitate common procedures for accounting and costing. Therefore the costing application was chosen as the platform to be used to increase the level of integration within the company.

Within the EMS company the orchestration effort was built up more slowly compared to the wholesaler. The effort started as a pilot project in one of the plants, and was then successively improved and tested in a few other plants. Once there was enough buy-in from both the financial and the manufacturing experts it was decided to give the green light to a group-wide rollout.

The costing platform was rather complex. It was therefore very important to combine the technical preparations with cross-functional and cross-regional exchange of ideas and best practices. In addition it had to be remembered that the costing platform was not only seen as an internal matter. It was also envisaged that once the new process was firmly in place, the information platform could be expanded and used jointly with the most important customers. In this respect there had to be preparations for the possible exploitation of additional benefits that could result as byproducts of the costing platform.

CHARACTERIZING AN ORCHESTRATOR

The two transformation processes described above are examples of practical orchestration taking place outside media attention and on a very practical level. In addition to this we can also witness how the work of the most successful orchestrators is profoundly changing the world around us. Linus Torvalds, Steve Jobs, Frank Gehry, Wesley Clark, and Bob Geldof have all made contributions to mankind that will be remembered by generations to follow. What is interesting to notice is that these orchestrators seem to share some basic characteristics with the more mundane orchestration performed by companies like the wholesaler and the EMS company.

Three qualities stand out as traits of successful orchestrators. Firstly, their aspirations are very high. Secondly, they are personally heavily involved in the substance matters that form the basis for their activity. Thirdly, they have the skill to engage other people to come along. All successful orchestrators tend to share these qualities. The orchestrator thus seems to be a thriving character, with high situational awareness, and trusted lieutenants.

A thriving character

Steve Jobs had surgery for cancer in 2004. The week after he underwent surgery he sent out an email to all Apple employees, and he returned to the helm of Apple only a month after the surgery. Linus Torvalds described his somewhat depressing state as a nerd only having the fun of joining the other students once a week. He was totally immersed by his computer hobby, and socially feeling rather insecure. What Jobs and Torvalds seem to share is a great commitment to the job they are doing. It also appears that one of the important things that this job provides is an opportunity to constantly learn new things. By being persistent they have been able to bring their own learning to such heights that the results have generated major innovations. They are creative geniuses able to adapt to the broader context. The successful orchestrator applies his or her creative talent in collective efforts partly defined from the outside. Such a character will here be called thriving.

A thriving individual puts less attention on what he or she 'is' or 'has,' and instead emphasizes doing, thinking, and feeling. Thriving is thus more process than goal and more an evolving philosophy of life than a step-by-step program. Those who thrive are 'consciousness creators'. They are characterized by high mental alertness, emotional responsivity, and spiritual engagement. They seem to seldom worry. If they do, it is in the form of presenting themselves with options and looking for strategies, not just making a mental list of potential disasters. They are rational optimists and have high aspirations. They find ways to flourish both despite of, and because of, circumstances or conditions:

> Thriving is a kind of mental, emotional, and spiritual alchemy through which we are able to turn life's most bitter pills into an elixir that helps us not only overcome but also transcend our agony. It allows us to come to see the world with a renewed confidence, enduring faith, and unrelenting joy that makes us feel almost invincible.[2]

If we relate to the newly appointed CEO of the industrial wholesaler he has an impact on both the substance and the processes of the network of suppliers and customers, where he is engaged. He not only influences the culture through managerial activities, but also his character affects what types of like-minded individuals are attracted to him and the network. In this respect the orchestrator is highly influencing both the factual and the emotional characteristics of the network. An example of how the network culture is shaped is the way Linus Torvalds proclaimed that his ambition is to let people do things because they want to do them, not because the leader wants. So for him good leadership is not to lead!

But stating that the ambition is not to lead doesn't mean that the orchestrator will abdicate. On the contrary, the other portrayal of Torvalds is as a 'benevolent dictator'. In those issues that really matter he firmly directs the Linux community according to his own vision. This ability to be hands off and yet at the same time to be very firm in other issues has to be based on strong self-confidence. This need for confidence was also voiced by General Clark, when he described the choices he had to make during the Kosovo crisis.

Such a confidence implies an in-depth understanding of one's own ability and simultaneous interest in further strengthening this ability through active interaction with others. For a business orchestrator a key challenge is to enable the extended enterprise to meet different challenges and respond successfully based on its collective capabilities. But this is not enough. Confidence also means the preparedness to admit one's own restrictions and an openness to continuous learning, to respond to new needs emerging from changing competitive conditions.

The confidence of highly successful orchestrators seems to correlate with an interest in areas outside their core expertise. Individuals like Steve Jobs, Linus Torvalds, Pierre Omidyar, creator of eBay, and Sergey Brin and Larry Page of Google emphasize the importance of having fun in addition to accomplishing something important in their work lives. The thriving character is based on, and creates, positive drivers in life. Confident thrivers have the ability to spread their confidence among the people with whom they interact.

Establishing shared situational awareness

Awareness and confidence are quite infrequent notions in the management literature. Instead there is plenty of writing about attention and empowerment. Why? The big difference is that attention and empowerment start from the actions of the leader, the one who directs attention and empowers others. From a leadership perspective it is a production-centered approach. Awareness and confidence mean taking a customer-oriented perspective. The role of the leader here is to truly make the other person aware and confident. Suddenly the leader has to become much more attuned to the feelings and the impressions of others. As the leader invites individuals into a collective process, he takes the responsibility to deliver results, which have to be measured through the real impact on the people influenced by the leader.

The leader as an orchestrator has to balance two parallel processes that go on simultaneously: the creative process, generating new ideas through experimentation and open-ended processes; and the efficiency process scrutinizing the smallest details of the operations to reduce costs and improve agility. To achieve this, the leader has to be aware that these two tasks require different settings to be successfully conducted.

A truly creative process by definition ends up with something beyond expectations. Thus there has to be freedom to explore and wander unexpected paths when moving forward. But management can seldom give the organization full reign to conduct something without any form of commitment in respect of timetables and outcomes. There has to be some broad aspirations stated as the objective of the initiative. The newly appointed CEO of the industrial wholesaler invited the personnel to an open inclusive process, but he announced that he expected the new organization to be in place within six months.

Cognitively a group operating in the creative mode experiments by making new linkages between existing objects; for example, finding new dimensions based on which to segment the market, new structures to make a modular product, or new roles and responsibilities to rejuvenate a stale organization. The outcome depends on how well the individuals can communicate and interact to form a truly creative team. To achieve outstanding results the individuals have to emotionally commit to the process, and individually and collectively get a strong inner drive to perform something unique. Therefore the social context is crucial. A functioning chemistry between the leading individuals forming the core creative group is of utmost importance. This is why the wholesaler CEO put a lot of attention on how the workshops, the transitional spaces, of the 'Desire for Partnership' initiative were staged. Providing the right mix of challenges and results kept the participants curious and committed.

Orchestration in the efficiency mode is more disciplined. The objective is explicitly stated. Reduce the purchasing costs by 5% during the next budgeting period, or make sure that the network needed to put together the outsourced production of a 45-foot yacht is up and running in 12 months. Typically for an efficiency-driven process is that both the end state and the time available are given. The objective is to perform the given task as efficiently as possible within the given frame. The approach here is one of providing the conditions for a well-functioning process. Access to existing knowledge is important, and making the right connection between important knowledge holders is one of the main tasks to be carried out. Efficiency improvement also asks for creativity, but in a more incremental form. The development of the shared costing platform for the EMS company required a substantial amount of creativity, but primarily in the form of providing solutions to constantly appearing smaller problems encountered during the process.

The two above examples represent the ends of a continuum. Often organizations face tasks which simultaneously are expected to perform according to the efficiency norms and with some indisputably new creative outcomes as a byproduct. For the newly appointed CEO the initial phase was very much focusing on the creative elements, challenging the existing way of working, and finding out new unexploited venues for growth. In pace with increased feedback from customers and suppliers it became gradually clearer where the key priority areas were. This also singled out the key efficiency improving measures. In this respect an orchestrated process normally oscillates between emphasis on creativity and efficiency, depending on the pace of learning and the influence of the competitive environment.

The efficiency and creativity modes of operating should be conducted in different moods and settings. Often senior executives have to participate in initiatives of both sorts. The requirement is that the creative sessions are clearly separated from the ones focusing on efficiency – time wise and preferably also space wise. Having a management team meeting where the morning is devoted to tough budget discussions and the afternoon a highly creative blue-sky session just doesn't work. For an individual to be in a truly creative state of mind it is necessary to get some distance from the immediate pressure of efficient performance to obtain a more relaxed spirit.

Awareness also means that the orchestrator is aware of which are the best people to engage for different topics. The leader has to carefully choose the individuals that have the most to contribute. Normally an individual has a natural preference for either creativity or efficiency, and assigning responsibilities accordingly is a way to improve motivation and diligence in the organization. Making the selection of the right people has to be based on the confidence of the orchestrator to openly invite the individuals to a shared journey, during which it may also be necessary to admit that some of the initial decisions proved to be wrong.

It has been stated that often great decisions begin with really great people and a simple statement: I don't know. This means that it's a stream of decisions over time, brilliantly executed, that accounts for great outcomes. To generate such a stream of decisions there has to be a strong internal drive based on the core values and the aspirations shared by and guiding those great people. The orchestrator is in charge of this.

When Steve Jobs started his efforts to build a new software platform his emphasis was on building capabilities. When iTunes was launched his focus shifted to strong promotion of the new offering, iPod. In parallel he worked hard on getting the value constellation in place to enable the iTunes Music Store to come together. All three elements were tightly knit together. What distinguishes true leaders from less successful ones is that they seem to intuitively grasp in which order to make their moves, and retrospectively everything looks so natural and easy. But this seeming ease is often based on meticulous work over long periods of time. This deep understanding of the substance matters is what makes successful orchestrators able to put in place the needed activities in the right sequence.

Based on his insights the leader then has to provide the direction for the whole constellation. Here the challenge is how to establish shared situational awareness. But just being aware is not enough. In addition the orchestrator has to be able to mobilize the resources needed to exploit identified new opportunities to create value. This asks for the third quality of a good orchestrator, the ability to engage others.

Engaging others

Successful orchestrators recognize the importance of being inspirational leaders in front of their troops, as well as in the society at large under their influence. And influence is what they primarily do. They cannot dictate and they cannot command. But if their influence is strong enough, the efforts of the network as a whole may have an impact, which often would not have been achievable with more conventional means.

Daniel Harding, the conductor, expressed this when asked about his role as guest conductor of the London Symphony Orchestra. This orchestra fiercely guards its independence. The musicians won't have anybody tell them what to do, even the principal music director. They're absolutely in charge of their own destiny, they play with whom they want to play with and they dictate their own part. That's a very nice thing for a conductor to work with, because it means that you know if you're there they want you to be there.

Emotionally appealing leaders are better in engaging others. Unfortunately many executives have an underdeveloped capacity for understanding and dealing with emotions. All but the best are reluctant to ask themselves why they act the way they do; as a result, most fail to understand both their own behavior and that of others. They are sensitive to numbers and figures but treat people as anonymous entities. In an attempt to 'box in' behavior, they create heavily structured organizations devoid of creativity, play, and humor. The leadership ethos of an orchestrator is in stark contract to this. As the examples indicate, the orchestrator is deeply committed to business results, but he is also committed to the means by which to mobilize the necessary emotional and intellectual contribution of the knowledgable members of the network. To be able to do this the leader has to make his values explicit. These values become an important part of the emergent social architecture.

To engage others in a voluntary network the leader cannot base his leadership style on traditional control and command. Instead the orchestrator has to present his own aspirations and an attractive vision for how the collaboration may produce an exciting and rewarding future for all parties involved. But as the subordinates have to make strict business decisions regarding their involvement, the orchestrator also has to have an evidence-based business case, where the knowledge and the facts support the compelling vision.

The pieces of the orchestration framework are now in place. We ended very much as we began: with the aspirations of the orchestrator. This is probably the single most distinctive element of orchestration as a leadership style: it cannot be depersonified. The orchestrator has to stand for something, put forward his or her own values and beliefs to be judged by others. This means increased transparency and also more attention to longevity. In 10 years Linux became a global factor in the information systems world. During all these years Linus Torvalds very much stuck to his view on what he expected from Linux. For Apple it also took years to put together all the necessary parts to form the systemic value constellation enabling the remarkable success of digital music. Having the persistence to move along based on strong inner vision was openly questioned by the outside world. When the first Apple store opened in May 2001 the following comment appeared on *Business Week* online:

> While Apple execs won't comment on their plans, the idea seems clear: Well-trained Apple salespeople in posh Apple stores can convince would-be buyers of the Mac's unique advantages, including its well-regarded iMovie software for making home videos and its iTunes program for burning custom CDs.
>
> The way Steve Jobs sees it, the stores look to be a sure thing. But even if they attain a measure of success, few outsiders think new stores, no matter how well-conceived, will get Apple back on the hot-growth path. Jobs' focus on selling just a few consumer Macs has helped boost profits, but it is keeping Apple from exploring potential new markets. And his perfectionist attention to aesthetics has resulted in beautiful but pricey products with limited appeal outside the faithful: Apple's market share is a measly 2.8%. 'Apple's problem is it still believes the way to grow is serving caviar in a world that seems pretty content with cheese and crackers,' gripes former Chief Financial Officer Joseph Graziano.

The article finished: 'Maybe it's time Steve Jobs stopped thinking quite so differently.' Well, Steve Jobs didn't think so. He was persistent on getting the iPod to the market, sitting with his closest design colleagues night after night, working out the user interface for the iPod. The rest is history.

The increased importance of knowledge and learning has some paradoxical consequences. One is that due to the limit of the knowledge one person has, the leader can do much less alone. But at the same time there is growing importance for leaders that can engage others in productive collective actions. Another paradox is that constantly meeting quarterly financial targets, based on proper cost efficiency, cannot be achieved in the longer term without simultaneous focus on the building of new capabilities and offerings. Because of this there is a huge need for leaders that can balance efficiency and creativity in the context of the extended enterprise.

When the contribution of the leader is based on his or her unique competence combined with the ability to inspire and motivate a team, then the replacement becomes difficult. From a corporate governance perspective this poses a challenge. Boards have to thoroughly understand the whole set of capabilities that are orchestrated by the existing leader to figure out what will be needed by the new one. The undertaking is to find a future leader that can bring new dynamics into the network, and hopefully create a differently orchestrated value constellation that would be equally or more successful, but undoubtedly different.

A successful leader is shaped by the environment, but simultaneously the leader also shapes the environment. The leader has more interactions with a larger part of the environment than the other network members, and thus the leader also has a greater impact on how the environment may evolve. But the difficulty is that leading a particular organization with its particular idiosyncrasies is like practicing a team sport where you are the only competitor. That is why the art of orchestration in business is such a demanding but simultaneously, when well performed, rewarding task.

Good leaders have always been in demand; today this is even more so. These leaders are competing vigorously, looking for efficiency and agility, notoriously searching for new ideas, creating new options, and nurturing processes that contribute to innovativeness. They embody and radiate disciplined creativity. They master the art of thriving, offer situational awareness, and engage others to perform marvelously. They are true orchestrators.

EPILOGUE

When I read *Management for Growth* (actually the original Swedish version, *Skapande företagsledning*[1]) for the first time in 1977 I was very intrigued by two notions: the Business Idea and the Business Leader as Statesman. Both these concepts have strongly influenced my view on management and leadership, and have had a significant impact on the ideas developed in this book. This epilogue will therefore try to put these two notions into the perspective of the business world 30 years after they were originally introduced, and then conclude with some overall reflections on the main emphasis of orchestration in business.

THE BUSINESS IDEA

In the mid-1970s companies like Volvo, Saab, SKF, Electrolux, Stora, and Tetra Pak were making Sweden one of the most competitive nations in the world. In this context Normann and his colleagues had access to leading knowledge in respect of management and leadership. Through the formation of the Scandinavian Institute for Administrative Research they were able to combine education, research, and consulting in a new and creative way. This resulted in a multitude of research papers and books. Normann himself called this process 'clinical research'. His interest was in understanding the actor operating in a system that he wants to change. Normann was thus concerned with business change and learning processes.

Normann consequently took the perspective of the business leader when observing the world. He therefore suggested that any business is looking to dominate a territory. The system for dominance, which he called the business idea,[2] involved:

- the description of the niche in the environment dominated by the company, in other words the company's territory;
- the products or the 'system' that were supplied to the territory; and
- the resources and internal conditions in the company by means of which dominance was acquired.

The business idea thus consisted of three elements: the resources, the products, and the market niche. Now 30 years later we have to add the network dimension. Another significant change is the replacement of the word 'product' with 'offering'. Normann, as the author of *Service Management*, was a pioneer in describing how the service perspective was changing the competitive landscape.[3] These ideas were convincingly presented in a *Harvard Business Review* article[4] in 1993. Normann and Ramírez stated that the goal was not to create value for customers but to mobilize customers to create their own value from the company's various offerings. The *Harvard Business Review* article and the subsequent book[5] confirmed that the concept of the business idea could be well adapted to the change in business context. Normann updated the three factors forming the business idea as follows:[6]

- The external environment, its 'needs' and values and what it is valuing – what is crucial to the larger system in which the organization works and which it can provide.
- The offering of the company.
- Internal factors such as organization structure, resources, organized knowledge and capabilities, equipment, systems, leadership, values.

The business idea is still a valid concept, but as many of the examples of this book tell, the concept of a permanent dominance of a market niche has become less frequent, even if companies like Ikea have successfully maintained their business ideas for decades. But, as the examples of Apple and Levi's show, business ideas have become more elusive. This was also recognized by Normann, as he introduced the notions of offerings, value constellations, and reconfiguration to provide more flexible tools to deal with a more dynamic business context. He also emphasized the need of leaders to engage in high-level conceptual thinking:

> The fundamental process of leadership is that of interpreting a (continuously evolving) context, formulating our notions of our own identity and the emerging new contextual logic into a set of 'dominating ideas,' which are both descriptive and normative, and then translate these dominating ideas into various realms of action.[7]

This recognition of the importance of the dominating ideas also connects to the other notion from Normann's early writings, the leader as statesman.

THE BUSINESS LEADER AS STATESMAN

Normann referred to Selznick when he introduced the role of leader as statesman:

> . . . The default of leadership shows itself in an acute form when organizational achievement or survival is confounded with

institutional success . . . The executive becomes a statesman as he makes the transition from administrative management to institutional leadership.[8]

According to Normann the main characteristic of a leader as statesman is to get other people to learn and to see that the learning proceeds freely in various parts of the organization. This implies that the leader's most fundamental task is to see that the company has a satisfactorily functioning internal political system. Normann summarized the qualities of a leader as statesman in four points:[9]

- An acute sensitivity to internal political processes and tensions.
- A thorough understanding of the basic structure (particularly any structural changes) of the social systems to which the company and the particular industry belong.
- A language (or theory) to make possible the interpretation of the dynamics of the internal and external situation into management practice.
- The means to influence the organizational structure – in particular the power system, conflict-resolving mechanisms, cognitive system, and control system – so as to change the company's growth culture.

These notions include the social perspective, the information domain (language and interpretation in Normann's language), and the operational structure. The major difference from a leadership perspective today is that the resources have to be mobilized, and thus nurturing skills have become relatively more important than the sensitivity to internal political processes and tensions.

The issue of leadership, however, remains in the background in the writings about value constellations, and Normann and Ramírez used the notions of 'world of business' and 'world of management' when introducing their book on strategy.[10] In this respect the attempt of this book has been to bring back the perspective of the leader 'operating in a system that he wants to change'. This suggests that the third world to be added is the 'world of people'.

ORCHESTRATION AND THE WORLD OF PEOPLE

Today resources can be globally mobilized at significantly less cost than 30 years ago, and competition can catch up more rapidly. New entrants such as eBay and Google form totally new markets, and see their stock market evaluation reach unprecedented levels. But at the same time many companies are able to maintain the positions they had, even if they are severely challenged by new entrants. The Merrill Lynch case presented in Chapter 4 is just one example. Why is this possible?

One explanation seems to be that in a world overwhelmed with information and technology, people increasingly rely on other people, individuals they know and trust. By doing this they behave rationally and minimize risks. For a leader this poses quite a challenge. On the one hand there are examples of successes based on adapting a new perspective and aggressively exploiting the possibilities offered by digital convergence. On the other hand there are also examples where a more cautious approach has paid off. So what to do?

From the examples seen in this book it looks like the key element for success is the ability of the orchestrator to engage other actors in a value constellation. Merrill Lynch never lost touch with its formidable customer base. Once it could use the Internet to further strengthen the customer relationships, additional value-creating opportunities were unveiled, and business improved. Steve Jobs, thanks to his personal skills, could engage the music moguls, even if Apple had no previous experience in the industry.

Lesson number one is that orchestrating a new value constellation will ask for leadership to engage the necessary network members to come on board. Thanks to new information and communication technologies, such opportunities have greatly increased over the last 10 years. But at the same time, deciding with whom to interact also influences the future of the leader. To become one of the best one has to interact with the most demanding environments. Normann has suggested that we must continuously interact with, and question, the borderlines. We must ensure that the intellectual realm we deal with is much larger than the operational realm.[11]

The second finding from the examples is that successful orchestration asks for persistence. Steve Jobs worked for years to put all the elements of the iTunes Music Store in place. But once the pieces are in place, the development is often exponential and not linear. This has been the case with Apple, eBay, Amazon, Google etc.

A third observation is that companies that have emerged as successful orchestrators have leaders, who themselves are comfortable in the orchestrator role. They are thriving, aware, and capable of engaging others.

As there is 'little c' and 'big C' creativity there is also 'little o' and 'big O' orchestration. A lot of this book has been about 'big O' orchestration, using well-known companies and household names to familiarize the readers with the concept of business orchestration. But as the wholesale case in Chapter 18 showed, the orchestration principles can also be applied in much more mundane settings. So if 'big O' orchestration refers to those creating completely new genres of music, 'little o' orchestration refers to those coming up with successful new hits. Most leaders are in the position of considering the possibilities of applying the ideas of orchestration in the 'little o' format. But some words of caution may be needed.

Orchestration is not just a tool; it is a character, irrespective if applied in the 'little o' or 'big O' context. If a leader tries to 'mimic' the orchestration mindset, he runs a big risk of making the whole organization and the surrounding network highly cynical, if and when it becomes evident that the orchestration attempt was not for real.

One industrial company worked for several years to increase its internal integration, starting from forming global sourcing teams, and using these as prototypes for an orchestrated way of working. Management changes and intensified competitive pressure forced the main proponents of this perspective to change course, and take a much more traditional control and command perspective. The result severely hit morale, and several people that had been in favor of the more emergent and inclusive process left the company.

Mobilizing a totally new value constellation is extremely difficult. The success of Amazon, eBay, and Google hides the fact that thousands of attempts have failed. The reason for this is the previously mentioned paradox of the increasing importance of relationships in parallel with the many more opportunities available. So to build an orchestrated network the starting point has to be figuring out how to crack the challenge of the social architecture. If the operational advantages are extraordinary, as those provided by Amazon, eBay, and Google, then the social architecture will automatically unfold. But otherwise the social architecture has to be established first.

The importance of the social architecture also provides a new model for start-ups: experienced executives that rely on their valuable networks and relationships. This is what Exel, the sports equipment company, had to face. Exel was the first manufacturer in the world to start to manufacture composite cross-country ski poles in 1973. Until then ski poles were made of wood, bamboo, or metal. What really created a boom was the widespread use of poles to make walking physically more effective, the so-called

'Nordic walking'. Exel developed purpose-designed poles for walking, concentrating on details such as durable and light composite shafts, ergonomically designed grips, and interchangeable grip systems. But the challenge was that for a regular walker not much of this was easily comprehended. Exel had primarily targeted competitive skiers and alpinists, reachable through specialized stores and attuned to product features. The mass market of recreational walkers in turn was much more a distribution-driven fashion business, asking for access to major retailers.

Two seasoned sports veterans, one having worked for a number of sports companies including Nike, and the other a retired executive with Wilson Sports, decided in 2004 to put up a new venture in ski and walking poles. The company didn't have any own manufacturing. All production was outsourced to three manufacturers in China. The website was managed from Estonia. With 20 people the company was able to operate a business selling skiing and walking poles to more than 20 countries in its first year. Making this rapid market entry was highly dependent on the personal relationships that the two founders had. The trust embedded in these relationships enabled them to convince both retailers and manufacturers to join the orchestrated value constellation.

The new venture highlights the importance of the social context of orchestration, which probably still is not well enough understood. Similar to Harley-Davidson, Games Workshop, Mondragon etc. these executives didn't start from technology, but directed their attention on establishing the appropriate social architecture. How this is done in practice is something we still need to have better insights into.

Richard Normann provides some hints, when he reflects upon how leadership must take into account the emergent nature of change and development. He suggests that what is needed is immediate concept-based action. Combining action orientation – thriving – with a high conceptualization capability – awareness

– forms the basis upon which the leader engages others. What this requires from the leader is beautifully described by Normann:

> Leaders must ensure that they are not in total control – neither with regard to process nor outcomes – while never appearing to be lost.[12]

NOTES

INTRODUCTION

1. Mintzberg *et al.*, 1998.
2. Rhenman, 1973.
3. Normann, 1977, 1985, 2001; lately capabilities and competences have become an area of research in itself and I have had the privilege to work with a number of academics active in this field. On this occasion I want to extend my gratitude to professors Aimé Heene and Ron Sanchez, with whom many of the capability-related concepts have been discussed over the years.
4. Ramírez and Wallin, 2000.

PART I: CONDITIONS FOR PRIME MOVERSHIP

1. Durry, 1996.
2. www.sukellus.fi/archieves.
3. Normann, 2001.

CHAPTER 1: VALUE-CREATING CAPABILITIES

1. Zetterberg, 1992.
2. Wallin, 2000.
3. Ramírez and Wallin, 2000, p. 78.
4. Vygotsky, 1978.
5. Wallin, 2000.
6. Ramírez, 1999.
7. Normann and Ramírez, 1994.
8. Helfat and Peteraf, 2003 – among many capability definitions, this one by Helfat and Peteraf has achieved widespread popularity, and is therefore used here. However, my thinking about capabilities and competences has been strongly influenced by professors Ron Sanchez and Aimé Heene, who since the early 1990s have nurtured a community of researchers regarding competence-based management. Sanchez, Heene, and Thomas (1996) define *capabilities* as *repeatable patterns of action in the use of assets to create, produce, and/or offer products to a market* and *competence* as *an ability to sustain the coordinated deployment of assets in a way that helps a firm achieve its goals.* When the transistor was developed, superior capabilities in the manufacture and refinement of the vacuum tube could not save the vacuum tube market. The vacuum tube firms maintained their capabilities but lost their competitive advantage, as the dynamic environment underwent a competence-destroying change (Bogner and Thomas, 1994). Capabilities can thus be maintained even if the competence is lost.
9. van der Heijden, 1996.

CHAPTER 2: FOCUS ON LEARNING

1. Dapena, 1988.
2. Forman, Saint John, 2000.
3. Kobayashi, 1986.
4. Cunningham, 1994.
5. Yoffie, 1996.
6. De Laat, 1999.

7. Hamel and Prahalad, 1994.
8. Torvalds and Diamond, 2001, p. 111.
9. de Geus, 1988.
10. Penuel and Roschelle, 1999.
11. Simon, 1991.
12. Polanyi, 1969; Nonaka and Takeuchi, 1995.
13. Szulanski, 1996.
14. Orr, 1991, 1993.
15. Drucker, 1959.
16. Jalongo, 2003.
17. Florida, 2002, 2004.
18. Unsworth, 2001.
19. Barbási, 2002.
20. Watts, 2003.

CHAPTER 3: ORCHESTRATING LEADERSHIP

1. Nishiguchi and Beaudet, 1998.
2. Watts, 2003.
3. Cebrowski and Garstka, 1998.
4. Keller, 1990.
5. Lorenzoni and Baden-Fuller, 1995.
6. Van der Heijden, 1993.
7. Moore, 1998.
8. Pitt and Clarke, 1999.
9. Taplin, 1996.
10. Magretta, 1998.
11. Baker, 2002.
12. Scott and Hughes, 2003.
13. Boyd, 1986.

PART II: LEARNING CONTEXTS

1. Porter, 1980, 1985.
2. Mahoney and Panadian, 1992.
3. Wernerfelt, 1984.

4. Barney, 1986, 1991.
5. de Geus, 1988.
6. Guilford, 1959; Torrance, 1963.
7. Amabile, 1983.
8. Amabile, Hadley, and Kramer, 2002.
9. Pine and Gilmore, 1999.

CHAPTER 4: INFORMATION ACQUISITION

1. Hamm, 1999.
2. Spiro, 1999.
3. The notion of 'Luddite' goes back to Ned Ludd, who lived in England in the early nineteenth century, and who is believed to have destroyed two large stocking frames that produced inexpensive stockings undercutting those produced by skilled knitters. Since then 'Luddite' has become synonymous with somebody who opposes the advance of technology.
4. Leonard-Barton, 1992.
5. Davis, 2004.
6. Kantrow, 2001.
7. Kim and Mauborgne, 1998.
8. Fitchard, 2004.
9. Rajaniemi, 2003.

CHAPTER 5: PROBLEM SOLVING

1. Haas and Hansen, 2005.
2. Ball, 2000; Finn, 2002; Edmondson, 2002.
3. Palmisano, Hemp, and Stewart, 2004.
4. Kirkpatrick, 2004.
5. Agrawal and Cockburn, 2003.

CHAPTER 6: CO-EXPERIENCING

1. *Women's Wear Daily*. Truly fast fashion: H&M's Lagerfeld line sells out in hours. November 15, 2004.
2. *The Economist*. April 2, 2005. Motoring online.

3. Schlender, 2005.
4. Schlender, 2001.
5. Kamoche and Pina e Cunha, 2001.
6. Weick, 1989.
7. Eisenberg, 1990.

CHAPTER 7: INSIGHT ACCUMULATION

1. Torvalds and Diamond, 2001.
2. Tanenbaum and Woodhull, 1987.
3. Kim and Mauborgne, 2003.
4. Willoughby, 2005.
5. Wallin, 1997.

CHAPTER 8: TRANSITIONAL OBJECTS

1. Baskerville and Stage, 1997; Schrage, 2000.
2. Mehra, Bishop, and Bazzell, 2000.
3. Wastell, 1999.
4. de Geus, 1988.
5. Giovacchini, 2001.
6. Wastell, 1999.
7. Winnicott, 1953.
8. LaMothe, 2000.
9. Buskirk and McGrath, 1999.
10. Wastell, 1999.
11. Ms. Mingfang Lai made valuable research around transitional objects while working for Synocus Group, which is acknowledged here.
12. Normann, 2001.
13. The notion of knowledge stocks and flows was originally introduced by Dierickx and Cool, 1989.
14. Wesensten, Belenky, and Balkin, 2005.
15. Scott and Hughes, 2003.
16. Biddle, 1996.
17. Biddle, 1996.
18. Stacey, 1993.
19. Torvalds and Diamond, 2001.

20. McEvily and Marcus, 2005.
21. Murray, 1997.

CHAPTER 9: CORE RESOURCES

1. Latour, 2001.
2. Reicheld, 1996.
3. Gillis, 1997.
4. Ward, 2003.
5. King and Bounds, 1997.
6. Beatty, 2003.

CHAPTER 10: OFFERING CONCEPTS

1. This section is to a large extent based on 'How the Swans were born' by Pekka Koskenkylä, in addition oral communication with Nautor management during 2005 has enriched the material.
2. Christensen, 1997.
3. Nussbaum, 2004.
4. Brown, 2005.
5. Holmes, 2004.
6. Enbysk, 2002.
7. Back, 2002.
8. Lester, Piore, and Malek, 1998.

CHAPTER 11: CUSTOMER INTERACTIONS

1. Maslow, 1968.
2. Torvalds and Diamond, 2001, p. 111.
3. McManus, 1993.
4. Patterson, 2004.
5. Marsh, 2004.
6. Girdler and Hackett, 2004.

7. Wallin, 2000.

8. McConnell and Huba, 2003.

CHAPTER 12: VALUE CONSTELLATIONS

1. Mondragon Corporacion Cooperativa, 2001.

2. Hof, 2003.

3. Waldmeir, 2004.

4. Lashinsky, 2003.

5. Atkins, 2000.

6. Porter, 1997.

7. Dyer and Hatch, 2004.

CHAPTER 13: THE IOCC FRAMEWORK

1. Boyd, 1986.

2. Sullivan, 1995.

3. Reiff, 1996.

4. Lehnert, 1997.

5. Collins, 2001.

PART IV: THE LEADER AS ORCHESTRATOR

1. Csikszentmihalyi, 1990.

CHAPTER 14: THE LEADER AS CONDUCTOR

1. Mintzberg, 1999.

2. Latour, 2001.

3. I am thankful to Pertti Korhonen for this clarification in February 2006.

4. Izenberg, 2004.

5. Curran, 2005.
6. Sonneck, 1926.

CHAPTER 15: THE LEADER AS ARCHITECT

1. Littlejohn, 2003.
2. Haithman, 2003.
3. Matthews, 1987.
4. This case description has been further elaborated based on communication with Eric Carlson during autumn 2005.
5. Socha, 2005.
6. Menkes, 2005.
7. Henderson and Clark, 1990.
8. Clark, 2001.

CHAPTER 16: THE LEADER AS AUCTIONEER

1. Chichester, 2004.
2. Dalmeny, 2004.
3. Pylkkanen, 2004.
4. Moore, 2003.
5. Leonard, 2003
6. Tam, Orwall, and Mathews, 2003.
7. Capell, 2005.
8. Cebrowski, 2002.

CHAPTER 17: THE LEADER AS PROMOTER

1. Wallace, 2005.
2. McDougal, 1985.
3. Nonaka and Takeuchi, 1995.
4. Chen, 2001.
5. I am thankful to insightful comments from Cathy Peng regarding the comparison between Western and Eastern ways of thinking.

CHAPTER 18: THRIVING, AWARE, AND ENGAGING

1. Source: http://www.ussg.iu.edu/hypermail/linux/kerner/0201.3/1070.html.
2. Pearsall, 2003.

EPILOGUE

1. Normann, 1975.
2. Normann, 1977, pp. 37–8.
3. Normann, 1984.
4. Normann and Ramírez, 1993.
5. Normann and Ramírez, 1994.
6. Normann, 2001, p. 149.
7. Normann, 2001, p. 3.
8. Selznick, 1957, p. 27, p. 154.
9. Normann, 1977, p. 182.
10. Normann and Ramírez, 1994, p. 3.
11. Normann, 2001, p. 261.
12. Normann, 2001, p. 275.

REFERENCES

Agrawal, A. and Cockburn, I. 2003. The anchor tenant hypothesis: Exploring the role for large, local, R&D-intensive firms in regional innovation systems. *International Journal of Industrial Organization*, **21**: 1227–53.

Amabile, T.M. 1983. *The Social Psychology of Creativity.* Springer-Verlag.

Amabile, T.M., Hadley, C.N., and Kramer, S.J. 2002. Creativity under the gun. *Harvard Business Review*, **80**(8): 52–61.

Atkins, C. 2000. Intelligence transformation: Beyond paradigm shifts, changes in ethos. *Military Intelligence Professional Bulletin*, **26**(4): 23–5.

Back, B.J. 2002. Nike gets aggressive about soccer. *The Business Journal of Portland*, May 20.

Baker, J.E. 2002. When lawyers advise presidents in wartime. *Naval War College Review*, **55**(1): 11–25.

Ball, D. 2000. Ferragamo sails for sales. *The Wall Street Journal Europe*, September 14.

Barbási, A. 2002. *Linked: The New Science of Networks.* Perseus Press.

Barney, J.B. 1986. Strategic factor markets: Expectations, luck and business strategy. *Management Science*, **32**(10): 1231–41.

Barney, J.B. 1991. Firm resources and sustained competitive advantage. *Journal of Management*, **17**: 99–120.

Baskerville, R.L. and Stage, J. 1996. Controlling prototype development through risk analysis. *MIS Quarterly*, **20**(4): 481–504.

Beatty, S. 2003. Levi to restate 2001, 2003 results. *The Wall Street Journal*, October 10.

Biddle, S. 1996. Victory misunderstood: What the Gulf War tells us about the future of conflict. *International Security*, **21**: 139–41.

Bogner, W.C. and Thomas, H. 1994. Core competence and competitive advantage: A model and illustrative evidence from the pharmaceutical industry, in G. Hamel and A. Heene (eds.), *Competence-Based Competition*. John Wiley & Sons, Ltd.

Boyd, J. 1986. Patterns of conflict. Downloaded from the Internet in November 2005 (http://www.d-n-i.net/boyd/pdf/poc.pdf).

Brown, T. 2005. Strategy by design. Fast company. Downloaded from the Internet in November 2005 (http://pf.fastcompany.com/magazine/95/design-strategy.html).

Buskirk, W.V. and McGrath, D. 1999. Organizational cultures as holding environments: A psychodynamic look at organizational symbolism. *Human Relations*, **52**(6): 805–32.

Capell, K. 2005. Ikea – How the Swedish retailer became a global cult brand. *Business Week*, November 14.

Cebrowski, A.K. 2002. An interview with the director. Downloaded from the Internet in November 2005 (http://www.oft.osd.mil/library/library_files/trends_164_transformation_trends_28_october_issue.pdf).

Cebrowski, A.K. and Garstka, J.J. 1998. Network-centric warfare: Its origin and future. *United States Naval Institute Proceedings*, January 1998.

Chen, M.-J. 2001. *Inside Chinese Business*. Harvard Business School Press.

Chichester, D. 2004. Keep the audience awake. *Financial Times*, September 25.

Christensen, C. 1997. *The Innovator's Dilemma*. Harvard Business School Press.

Clark, W.K. 2001. *Waging Modern War*. Public Affairs.

Cohen, A. 2002. *The Perfect Store*. Little, Brown.

Collins, J. 2001. *Good to Great*. Random House.

Csikszentmihalyi, M. 1996. *Creativity: Flow and the Psychology of Discovery and Invention.* Harper Collins.

Cunningham, C.A. 1994. Microsoft's Gates conjures future computing. (Bill Gates presents keynote address at Comdex/Fall 1994.) *Electronic News,* November 21.

Curran, T.E. 2005. Belichick: Football coach as CEO. *Providence Journal,* January 25.

Dalmeny, H. 2004. An actor's lot. *Financial Times,* September 25.

Dapena, J. 1988. Biomechanical analysis of the Fosbury Flop. *Track Technique,* **104**: 3307–17, 3333; **105**: 3343–50.

Davis, A. 2004. Pressure mounts for Morgan Stanley. *The Wall Street Journal Europe,* October 8.

de Geus, A.P. 1988. Planning as learning. *Harvard Business Review,* **66**(2): 70–4.

De Laat, P.B. 1999. Systemic innovation and the virtues of going virtual: The case of the digital video disc. *Technology Analysis & Strategic Management,* **11**(2): 159.

Dierickx, I. and Cool, K. 1989. Asset stock accumulation and sustainability of competitive advantage. *Management Science,* **35**, 1504–11.

Drucker, P.F. 1959. *The Landmarks of Tomorrow.* Transaction Publishers.

Durry, J. 1996. Pierre de Coubertin – The visionary. Downloaded from the Internet in November 2005 (http://www.coubertin.ch/pdf/MEP%20Angl.%20Cou%202%20+%208p.%20+%206%20.pdf).

Dyer, J.H. and Hatch, N.W. 2004. Using supplier networks to learn faster. *Sloan Management Review,* **45**(3): 57–63.

Edmondson, G. 2002. Running before the wind. *Business Week,* September 30.

Eisenberg, E.M. 1990. Jamming: Transcendence through organizing. *Communication Research,* **17**: 139–64.

Enbysk, L. 2002. Nike is on a kick: Puts focus on innovation to improve its products. *Boston Globe,* June 17.

Finn, H. 2002. Moschino coast. *Financial Times,* June 6.

Fitchard, K. 2004. Nokia clears content bottleneck. *Telephony,* **244**(21):6.

Florida, R. 2002. *The Rise of the Creative Class.* Basic Books.

Florida, R. 2004. America's looming creativity crisis. *Harvard Business Review,* **82**(10): 122–36.

Forman, Saint John 2000. Creating convergence. *Scientific American*, November 1: 50–6.

Gillis, C. 1997. Mobile-phone giant overhauls its logistics. *American Shipper*, **39**(7): 38.

Giovacchini, P.L. 2001. Dangerous transitions and the traumatized adolescent. *American Journal of Psychoanalysis*, **61**(1): 7–22.

Girdler, A. and Hackett. J. 2004. *Harley-Davidson*. MBI Publishing.

Guilford, J.P. 1959. Traits of creativity, in H.H. Anderson (ed.), *Creativity, and its Cultivation*. Harper, pp. 142–61.

Haas, M.R. and Hansen, M.T. 2005. When using knowledge can hurt performance. *Strategic Management Journal*, **26**(1): 1–24.

Haithman, D. 2003. Disney's grand design spans the generations. *Financial Times*, October 20.

Hamel, G. and Prahalad, C.K. 1994. *Competing for the Future*. Harvard Business School Press.

Hamm, S. 1999. How to survive the cyber-revolution – Clayton Christensen on adapting your game plan. *Business Week*, April 5.

Helfat, C.E. and Peteraf, M.A. 2003. The dynamic resource-based view: Capability lifecycles. *Strategic Management Journal*, Special Issue, **24**(10): 997–1010.

Henderson, R.M. and Clark, K.B. 1990. Architectural innovation: The reconfiguration of existing product technologies and the failure of established firms. *Administrative Science Quarterly*, **35**: 9–30.

Hof, R.D. 2003. The eBay economy. *Business Week*, August 25.

Holmes, S. 2004. The new Nike. *Business Week*, September 20.

Izenberg, J. 2004. Belichick style is what it is. *The Star-Ledger*, January 30.

Jalongo, M.R. 2003. The child's right to creative thought and expression. *Childhood Education*, **79**(4): 218–28.

Kamoche, K. and Pina e Cunha, M. 2001. Minimal structures: From jazz improvisation to product innovation. *Organization Studies*, **22**(5): 733–64.

Kantrow, B. 2001. Club Nokia may pit handset maker against interests of mobile operators. *The Wall Street Journal Europe*, May 23.

Keller, J.J. 1990. AT&T jumps into highly competitive network applications software market. *The Wall Street Journal*, March 28.

Kim, W.C. and Mauborgne, R. 1998. Procedural justice, strategic decision making, and the knowledge economy. *Strategic Management Journal*, **19**(4): 323–38.

Kim, W.C. and Mauborgne, R. 2003. Tipping point leadership. *Harvard Business Review*, **81**(4): 60–9.

King, R.T. and Bounds, W. 1997. Clothing: Its shares shrinking, Levi Strauss lays off 6,395. *The Wall Street Journal*, November 4.

Kirkpatrick, D. 2004. Inside Sam's $100 billion growth machine. *Fortune*, June 14.

Kobayashi, K. 1986. *Computers and Communications: A Vision of C&C*. MIT Press.

Koskenkylä, P. 2005. How the Swans were born. Downloaded from the Internet, November 2005 (http://www.classicswan.org/swansbyss.htm).

LaMothe, R. 2000. The birth of reality: Psychoanalytic developmental considerations. *American Journal of Psychotherapy*, **54**(3): 355–71.

Lashinsky, A. 2003. Meg and the machine. *Fortune*, September 1.

Latour, A. 2001. Trial by fire tested mettle of rivals Ericsson and Nokia – Crisis bared one's weakness, other's strength. *The Wall Street Journal Europe*, January 29.

Lehnert, M. 1997. The end of the 'Attila the Hun defense'. *Marine Corps Gazette*, **81**(12): 61–3.

Leonard, D. 2003. Songs in the key of Steve. *Fortune*, May 12.

Leonard-Barton, D. 1992. Core capabilities and core rigidities: A paradox in managing new product development. *Strategic Management Journal*, **13**(1): 111–25.

Lester, R.K., Piore, M.J., and Malek, K.M. 1998. Interpretative management: What general managers can learn from design. *Harvard Business Review*, **76**(2): 86–96.

Littlejohn, D. 2003. A fantasyland for the Philharmonic. *The Wall Street Journal*, November 12.

Lorenzoni, G. and Baden-Fuller, C. 1995. Creating a strategic center to manage a web of partners. *California Management Review*, **37**(3): 146–63.

Magretta, J. 1998. Fast, global, and entrepreneurial: Supply chain management, Hong Kong style. *Harvard Business Review*, **76**(5): 102–14.

Mahoney, J.T. and Pandian, J.R. 1992. The resource-based view within the conversation of strategic management. *Strategic Management Journal*, **13**: 363–80.

Marsh, P. 2004. A warrior in the real world of fantasy. *Financial Times*, March 4.

Maslow, A.H. 1968. *Toward a Psychology of Being.* Van Nostrand.

Matthews, D. 1987. *Beethoven.* J.M. Dent & Sons.

McConnell, B. and Huba, J. 2003. Creating customer communities: A surgical approach. *Marketing Professionals*, March 11.

McDougal, D. 1985. USA for Africa – A star is born. *Los Angeles Times*, June 9.

McEvily, B. and Marcus, A. 2005. Embedded ties and the acquisition of competitive capabilities. *Strategic Management Journal*, **26**(11): 1033–55.

McManus, K. 1993. Nonviolent war games. *The Washington Post*, January 29.

Mehra, B., Bishop, P., and Bazzell, I. 2000. The role of use scenarios in developing a community health information system. *American Society for Information Science Bulletin*, **26**(4): 10.

Menkes, S. 2005. Louis Vuitton has landed. *International Herald Tribune*, October 11.

Mintzberg, H. 1999. Covert leadership. *Harvard Business Review*, **76**(6): 140–7.

Mintzberg, H., Ahlstrand, B., and Lampel. J. 1998. *Strategy Safari.* Prentice Hall.

Mondragon Corporacion Cooperativa. 2001. The history of an experience. Downloaded from the Internet, November 2005 (http://www.mcc.es/ing/quienessomos/historiaMCC_ing.pdf).

Moore, B.J. 1998. Situated cognition versus traditional cognitive theories of learning. *Education*, September.

Moore, S. 2003. The art of selling – 200 years on. *Financial Times*, November 1.

Murray, W. 1997. Clausewitz out, computer in. *The National Interest*, June 22, 57–64.

Nishiguchi, T. and Beaudet, A. 1998. The Toyota Group and the Aisin fire. *Sloan Management Review*, **40**(1): 49–59.

Nonaka, I. and Takeuchi, H. 1995. *The Knowledge-Creating Company.* Oxford University Press.

Normann, R. 1975. *Skapande företagsledning.* Aldus.

Normann, R. 1977. *Management for Growth.* John Wiley & Sons, Ltd.

Normann, R. 1984. *Service Management.* John Wiley & Sons, Ltd.

Normann, R. 1985. Developing capabilities for organizational learning, in J.M. Pennings (ed.), *Organizational Strategy and Change: New*

Views on Formulating and Implementing Strategic Decisions. Jossey-Bass.

Normann, R. 2001. *Reframing Business. When the Map Changes the Landscape.* John Wiley & Sons, Ltd.

Normann, R. and Ramírez, R. 1993. From value chain to value constellation. *Harvard Business Review,* **71**(4): 65–77.

Normann, R. and Ramírez, R. 1994. *Designing Interactive Strategy.* John Wiley & Sons, Ltd.

Nussbaum, B. 2004. The power of design: IDEO redefined good design by creating experiences, not just products. *Business Week,* May 17.

Orr, J.E. 1991. Sharing knowledge, celebrating identify: War stories and community memory among service technicians. In D.S. Middleton and D. Edwards (eds.), *Collective Remembering: Memory in Society.* Sage, pp. 169–89.

Orr, J.E. 1993. Ethnography and organizational learning: In pursuit of learning at work, in S. Bagnara, C. Zucchermaglio, and S. Stucky (eds.), *Organizational Learning and Technological Change.* Springer Verlag.

Palmisano, S., Hemp, P., and Stewart, T.A. 2004. Leading change when business is good. *Harvard Business Review,* **82**(12): 60–70.

Patterson, K. 2004. Grow up? You're kidding – Meet the kidults – A generation that never ages. *The Sunday Mail,* May 30.

Pearsall, P. 2003. *The Beethoven Factor.* Hampton Roads Publishing Company, Inc.

Penuel, B. and Roschelle, J. 1999. *Designing Learning: Cognitive Science Principles for the Innovative Organization.* SRI International.

Pine II, B.J. and Gilmore, J.H. 1999. *The Experience Economy.* Harvard Business School Press.

Pitt, M. and Clarke, K. 1999. Competing on competence: A knowledge perspective on the management of strategic innovation. *Technology Analysis & Strategic Management,* **11**(3): 301–16.

Polanyi, M. 1969. *Knowing and Being.* Routledge & Kegan Paul.

Porter, A.M. 1997. In some companies quality culture is tangible. *Purchasing,* **122**(1): 51.

Porter, M.E. 1980. *Competitive Strategy.* Free Press.

Porter, M.E. 1985. *Competitive Advantage.* Free Press.

Pylkkanen, J. 2004. How to be an auctioneer. *Financial Times,* May 29.

Rajaniemi, M. 2003. Nokia mobile phones' development of business logistics and customer support, in T. Reponen (ed.), *Information Technology-Enabled Global Customer Service*. Idea Group Publishing.

Ramírez, R. 1999. Value co-production: Intellectual origins and implications for practice and research. *Strategic Management Journal*, **20**(1): 49–65.

Ramírez, R. and Wallin, J. 2000. *Prime Movers*. John Wiley & Sons, Ltd.

Reicheld, F.F. 1996. *The Loyalty Effect*. Harvard Business School Press.

Reiff, D. 1996. Whose internationalism, whose isolationism? *World Policy Journal*, **13**(2): 1–12.

Rhenman, E. 1973. *Organization Theory for Long Range Planning*. John Wiley & Sons, Ltd.

Sanchez, R., Heene, A., and Thomas, H. (eds.) 1996. *Dynamics of Competence-Based Competition*. Elsevier.

Schlender, B. 2001. Apple's 21st-century Walkman. *Fortune*, November 12.

Schlender, B. 2005. How big can Apple get? *Fortune*, February 21.

Schrage, M. 2000. *Serious Play*. Harvard Business School Press.

Scott, W.B. and Hughes, D. 2003. Nascent net-centric war gains Pentagon toehold. *Aviation Week & Space Technology*, January 27.

Selznick, P. 1957. *Leadership in Administration*. Harper & Row.

Simon, H.A. 1991. Bounded rationality and organizational learning. *Organization Science*, **2**(1): 125–34.

Socha, M. 2005. King Louis. *Women's Wear Daily*, October 10.

Sonneck, O.G. 1926. *Beethoven: Impressions by his Contemporaries*. Dover Publications.

Spiro, L.N. 1999. Merrill's E-battle. *Business Week*, November 15.

Stacey, R.D. 1993. *Strategic Management and Organizational Dynamics*. Pitman Publishing.

Sullivan, G. 1995. Leading strategic change in America's Army: The way forward. *Planning Review*, **23**(5): 16.

Szulanski, G. 1996. Exploring stickiness: Impediments to the transfer of best practice within the firm. *Strategic Management Journal*, **17**(winter special issue): 27–43.

Tam, P.-W., Orwall, B., and Mathews, A.W. 2003. Going beyond Apple's core. *The Asian Wall Street Journal*, April 28.

Tanenbaum, A.S. and Woodhull, R.S. 1987. *Operating Systems: Design and Implementation.* Prentice Hall.

Taplin, I.M. 1996. Rethinking flexibility: The case of the apparel industry. *Review of social economy,* **54**(2): 191–220.

Torrance, E.P. 1963. *Creativity: What Research Says to the Teacher.* Association of Classroom Teachers of the National Education Association.

Torvalds, L. and Diamond, D. 2001. *Just for Fun: The Story of an Accidental Revolutionary.* Texere Publishing.

Unsworth, K. 2001. Unpacking creativity. *Academy of Management Review,* **26**(2): 289–97.

van der Heijden, K. 1993. Comments to Normann, R., and Ramírez, R. (1993) in 'Strategy and the art of reinventing value'. *Harvard Business Review,* **71**(5): 40–1.

van der Heijden, K. 1996. *Scenarios: The Art of Strategic Conversation.* John Wiley & Sons, Ltd.

Vygotsky, L.S. 1978. *Mind in Society: The Development of Higher Psychological Processes.* Harvard University Press.

Waldmeir, P. 2004. Seek and ye shall find. *Financial Times,* September 4.

Wallace, R. 2005. Uneasy rider, *Vette Magazine,* accessed from the Internet, November 2005 (http://www.vetteweb.com/features/vet_0312_uneasy/index.html).

Wallin, J. 1997. Customers as the originators of change in competence building: A case study, in A. Heene and R. Sanchez (eds.), *Competence-based Strategic Management.* John Wiley & Sons, Ltd.

Wallin, J. 2000. Customer orientation and competence building. Doctoral dissertation. Helsinki University of Technology.

Ward, A. 2003. Reign of the chaos maker. *Financial Times,* March 13.

Wastell, D. 1999. Learning dysfunctions in information systems development: Overcoming the social defenses with transitional objects. *MIS Quarterly,* **23**(4): 581–600.

Watts, D. 2003. *Six Degrees – The Science of a Connected Age.* William Heinemann.

Weick, K.E. 1989. Organized improvisation: 20 years of organizing. *Communication Studies,* **40**: 241–8.

Wernerfelt, B. 1984. A resource-based theory of the firm. *Strategic Management Journal,* **5**(2): 171–80.

Wesensten, N.J., Belenky, G., and Balkin, T.J. 2005. Cognitive readiness in network-centric operations. *Parameters,* April 1, 94.

Willoughby, C. 2005. Top cop in tough city. *The Gold Coast Bulletin*, March 18.

Winnicott, D.W. 1953. Transitional object and transitional phenomena. *International Journal of Psychoanalysis*, **34**: 89–97.

Yoffie, D.B. 1996. Competing in the age of digital convergence. *California Management Review*, **38**(4): 31–53.

Zetterberg, H. 1992. The study of values. Paper presented at the 87th Annual Meeting of the American Sociological Association, Pittsburgh, Pennsylvania, August 20–4.

INDEX

Aalto, Alvar 289
ABB Finland 150–2, 153–4
activity 14–15, 41
Alessi 67
alliance networks 35–6
Amazon 44–5, 67, 68, 69–70, 74,
    210–11, 228
Apple
  auctioneering skills 304–7, 310
  co-experiencing 74, 87, 131–5,
    136
  core resources 188, 189
  orchestrator's characteristics 350,
    352
architects, orchestrators as 76–7, 263,
    281–97, 324–5, 333, 334
architectural innovation 290
Arizmendiarrieta, José Mariá 231, 232
aspirations 12, 13, 15, 45, 351–2
AT&T 63
attention 347
auction houses 20–4, 29, 107–9, 263,
    299–301
auctioneers, orchestrators as 77–8,
    263, 299–313, 324–5, 333,
    334
awareness 344, 346–50, 362–3

Baltic Yachts 120–1
beauty 13
Beethoven, Ludwig van 280, 285
Belichick, Bill 263, 275, 276–8, 279,
    296
Bezos, Jeff 69
Bilbao, Guggenheim Museum 288–9
BMW 130
Boyd, John 248–9
Bratton, Bill 88, 147, 148–9, 152
Brown, Tim 199
building capabilities *see* capability
    building
Burge, Christopher 78, 300–1
business ideas 355–7
business leaders *see* leaders
business models
  definition 12
  industrial vs knowledge-based 46–7

Canon 223–5
capabilities
  definition 20
  digital convergence and 43–7
  distinctive 26
  leadership 26, 27, 45–6
  see also orchestrators

operational 24–30
  building *see* capability building
  dominant learning modes 260–1
  orchestrating leaders' role 71–3,
    261–2
  see also orchestrators
  orchestration 29, 45–7
capability building 169–72
  core resources 170, 173–89
  customer interactions 207–25
  IOCC framework 171, 247–58
  offering concepts 191–206
  orchestrating leaders' role 71–3
  see also orchestrators
  value constellations 227–46
Captain America 263, 317–20, 323
Carlson, Eric 263, 286–8, 297
Cebrowski, Arthur K. 311, 312–13
celebrities 122–3, 135
change
  capability building 171–2
  experience provision 136–9
  to orchestration mindset 335, 336–
    42
Charles Schwab 90, 92, 93, 94
Chinese business practices 326, 329
Christies 263, 299–301
civic virtue 13
Clark, Wesley 72, 263, 292–6, 312,
    344
co-dwelling 3
co-experiencing 51–2, 74, 86, 87,
    125–40
  building value constellations 245
  operational capability 260, 261
  transitional objects 163–4
  see also auctioneers, orchestrators as;
    customer communities
Cold War, US Army after 250–4, 255
collaborative culture 329, 331–2
Comme des Garcons 129–30
commercialization, IOCC
        framework 254, 255, 256,
        257
communication 267, 277–8, 291–2
  for orchestration mindset 336–9

communication technology *see*
    information and
    communication technology
communities 207
  customer 41–3, 44–5, 207–11
    history 211–17, 225
    see also co-experiencing;
        communities, nurturing
  ethos 240–3
  evolution 238–9
  learning in 39–43, 44–5
  nurturing 45–6, 66, 67, 68, 69–71,
    100–1, 207–25
  offerings 43, 44
  open source *see* Linux; open source
    communities
  resource aggregation 66, 67, 68–9,
    70–1, 210–11, 227–46
competition
  digital convergence 36–9
  in a knowledge society 2, 4
  value-creating logic 33–4
composers 134–6
computer technology *see* information
    and communication
    technology
conductors, orchestrators as 75–6,
    262–3, 265–80
  architects and 285, 324–5, 333–4
  auctioneers compared 299, 302–4
confidence 346–7
constructivism 49–50
contracts 244
Co-operative Wholesale Society
    (CWS) 213
cooperatives 171, 211–13, 228, 229–
    33, 236
core competence 38–9
core resources 170, 173–89
  learning mode 260, 261
  solidification 66–7, 68, 70–1
correlative thinking 328
costs, value creation 17–18
creative class 53–4
creative customer servant ethos 335,
    341

creative work 53–7
creativity 4, 5, 53
  balance with efficiency 202–6,
      242–3, 273–5, 332, 333,
      347–9, 353
  instilling disciplined 266–73, 302
  learning contexts 84–6, 142
  offering design 199, 202–6
  orchestrators' characteristics 347–8
crystallization, IOCC
      framework 252–4, 255, 256,
      257
cult behavior 317–20
culture
  experience provision 136
  group decision making 112
  in a knowledge society 4, 46–7
  orchestration architecture 326–30
  orchestration mindset 336–42
  orchestrators' characteristics 345–6
  role models 241–2
  values and 14
customer communities 207–8
  learning in 41–3, 44–5
  value co-creation 45–6, 66, 67, 68,
      69–71, 100–1
  see also co-experiencing; customer
      interactions
customer interactions 207–25
  learning mode 260, 261
customer ownership 182–7
customer preference tracking 192,
      197–9, 203
customer relationships 18–19
  see also customer communities
customer segmentation, learning-
      based 150–4

de Coubertin, Baron Pierre 1–2, 4,
      320
de Geus, Arie 47–8, 83
decision making
  group 111–12
  OODA loop 248–50
design of offerings see offerings,
      design

digital convergence
  capabilities 43–7
  cell phone market 179–83, 184,
      187–9
  learning 34–9, 44–5
  offerings 43–7
diplomacy, coercive 292–6
disciplined creativity 266–73, 302
discovery 14–15
distinctive capabilities 26
Drucker, Peter 53, 54

Eastern traditions 326–9
eBay
  ethos 171, 233–4, 237–8, 242–3
  evolution 239
  information transmission 100–1
  orchestrating leadership 74, 75
  resource aggregation 42, 71, 142,
      210–11, 228, 233–8, 261
  Wal-Mart compared 239, 242–3
eco-genesis 3
efficiency–creativity balance 202–6,
      242–3, 273–5, 332, 333,
      347–9, 353
electronics manufacturing services
      (EMS) 333–4, 335, 342–3
empowerment 347
engaging people 344, 350–1, 359–60
  see also communities, nurturing
enthusiasts
  leaders as promoters 317–20
  value co-creation 213–23
environment-shaping
      architecture 288–9
Ericsson 174–5, 176, 179, 270–1, 273
ethos
  creative customer servant 335,
      341
  global transaction engine 335
  resource communities 171, 233–4,
      237–8, 240–3
  US Army 252–3
E-Trade 94
exchange value 19
Exel 361–2

experience provision *see* co-experiencing
expertise 15, 84–5
extended enterprises 37, 38–9, 43–4
  Nokia's strategy 273–5

facilitators 126
fear, freedom from 208–9
Ferragamo, Leonardo 114, 122–3
Finnish economy 150–2
Florida, Richard 53–4
Fosbury Flop 31–3

game management 263, 275, 276–8, 296
game plans 278–80, 325, 326
Games Workshop 170, 213, 214–19, 221–3, 245–6, 260
Gates, Bill 34–5, 240
Gehry, Frank 76–7, 263, 281–5, 288–9, 290–2, 296, 344
Geldof, Bob 263, 320–3, 344
Gerstner, Lou 117
global competition 36–7, 38
global transaction engine ethos 335
globalization 184–6
golfing metaphor 79
governance, orchestrator–member 244
group decision making 111–12
Guggenheim Museum (Bilbao) 288–9

H&M 43–4, 51, 87, 127–9, 130, 134–5
Harding, Daniel 268, 350–1
Harley-Davidson
  customer interactions 75, 170, 213–14, 219–23, 260
  leaders as promoters 317–20, 323
hobbyists 213, 214–19, 221–3

IBM 74–5, 87, 117–19, 120, 121, 147
IDEO 192, 197–9, 260
Ikea 67, 82–3, 308–10
improvisation 137
individualism 327, 329

industrial organization strategy 82, 83–4
industrial society
  business model 46–7
  cooperatives 232
  creativity–efficiency balance 206
  customer segmentation 152, 153
  digital convergence 35, 39, 44, 46
  IOCC framework 250
  Robinson case 7–9, 27
  strategy in shift from 83–4
  values 41
industrial wholesaling 333–5, 336–42
industry mapping 187–9
influencing people 350–1
information acquisition *see* information transmission
information architecture 310–13, 325, 328, 332
  orchestration framework 333, 334
information and communication technology 2–3
  co-experiencing 130, 131–4
  customer communities 42–3, 44–5, 100–1, 218, 233–8, 239
  customer ownership 182–7
  digital convergence 34–9
    capabilities 43–7
    cell phone market 179–83, 184, 187–9
    offerings 43–7
  information transmission 86, 89–107, 159–61
  insight accumulation 142–7
  knowledge work 55
  network-centric warfare 63
  open source communities *see* Linux; open source communities
  orchestration 63–4
  orchestration strategies 68
  Steve Jobs's record in 307
  supply chain management 175–80, 181–3, 270–5
  transitional objects 159–61
information transmission 49, 50, 51, 52, 72–3, 86, 89–110, 113

building value constellations 245
operational capability 260, 261
transitional objects 159–61
see also conductors, orchestrators as
initial cost 17
initialization–operationalization–
crystallization–
commercialization (IOCC)
framework 171, 247–58
insight accumulation 52, 75, 86, 87–
8, 141–54
building value constellations 245
operational capability 261
transitional objects 164–6
see also promoters, orchestrators as
inspiring people 350–1
integration costs 18
intellectual traditions 326–9
interface costs 18
International Olympic Committee
(IOC) 250
Internet 2–3
customer communities 42–3, 44–5,
100–1, 218, 233–8, 239
digital convergence 35, 36–7
Merrill Lynch strategy 86, 90–7,
106–7
Nokia strategy 86, 98–107, 273–5
orchestration strategies 68
IOCC framework 171, 247–58
commercialization 254, 255, 256,
257
crystallization 252–4, 255, 256, 257
IDEO process and 197–8
initialization 250–1, 255, 256, 257
operationalization 251–2, 255, 256,
257

J.C. Penney 184–5
Jobs, Steve 131–3, 134–5, 136, 263,
304–7
orchestrator characteristics 344,
346, 350, 352, 359–60

Kaiser Permanente 198–9
Kamprad, Ingvar 307–9

Karl Lagerfeld collection 43–4, 51, 87,
127–9, 130, 134–5
knowledge
information architecture 310–11,
328
as a liability 113
orchestrating based on 273–8
orchestrators' characteristics 353
organizational learning 50
social construction 49
as a value 13
knowledge society 2–5
cooperatives 232
creativity–efficiency balance 206,
353
customer segmentation 153–4
IOCC framework 250
learning in communities 40–3, 44–
5
need for safety 208–9
orchestration capabilities 45–7
strategy in shift too 83–4
knowledge work 53, 54–5
see also creative work
Korhonen, Pertti 270–3, 278–9
Koskenkylä, Pekka 191–6, 203
Kosovo, NATO mission in 292–6
Kovac, Carol 118–19

Lagerfeld collection 43–4, 51, 87,
127–9, 130, 134–5
leaders 29, 259–64
as architects 76–7, 263, 281–97,
324–5, 333, 334
as auctioneers 77–8, 263, 299–313,
324–5, 333, 334
as conductors *see* conductors
overall character 263–4, 331–54,
362–3
as promoters 78–9, 263, 315–30,
333, 334
as statesmen 355, 357–9
world of people 359–63
leadership 4–5
community nurturing 223–5
conceptual thinking 357

efficiency–creativity balance 202–6,
    273–5, 332, 333, 347–9, 353
industry mapping 187–9
network-centric operations 249–50
orchestrating 70–80, 259–64
    experience provision 136–9
    information transmission 106–10
    insight accumulation 150–4
    problem solving 112, 121–3
    see also leaders
value constellation building 243–6
leadership capabilities 26, 27, 45–6
see also leaders
learning 4, 31–57
    in communities 39–43, 44–5
    constructivist view 49–50
    contexts see learning contexts
    creative work 53–7
    digital convergence 34–9, 44–5
    leaders as orchestrators 260–2
    leadership for 70–80
    need for 47–53
    organizational 50–3
        see also learning contexts
    situated 49
    value creation 14–15, 44–5
learning advantages 18
learning-based customer
        segmentation 150–4
learning contexts 47–53, 81–8
    building value constellations 245
    co-experiencing 51–2, 74, 86, 87,
        125–40, 163–4, 245
        see also auctioneers, orchestrators
        as
    cooperatives 232
    information transmission 49, 50, 51,
        52, 72–3, 86, 89–110, 113,
        159–61, 245
        see also conductors, orchestrators
        as
    insight accumulation 52, 75, 86,
        87–8, 141–54, 164–6, 245
        see also promoters, orchestrators
        as
    leadership types 262

architects 263, 281–97, 324–5,
    333, 334
auctioneers 263, 299–313, 324–5,
    333, 334
conductors 262–3, 265–80, 285,
    299, 302–4, 324–5, 333, 334
promoters 263, 315–30, 333, 334
operational capabilities 260–1
problem solving 51, 52, 73–5, 86–7,
    111–23, 161–3, 245
    see also architects, orchestrators as
transitional objects 155–68
learning journeys 125–7
Levi Strauss & Co 184, 184–6, 191,
    202–3, 208
Li & Fung 67, 68–9, 71, 185, 261
life-cycle costs 18
Linux 39
    building value constellations 244,
        245
    culture 328–9
    IOCC framework and 247–9
    learning in communities 40, 87,
        142–7
    orchestration strategies 71
    orchestrator as auctioneer 311
    orchestrator as promoter 78–9, 315–
        17, 319–20
Live Aid 320–3
Los Angeles Philharmonic 75–7, 262–
    3, 269
    concert hall 76–7, 281–5, 290–2
Louis Vuitton store (Paris) 286–8,
    289, 297
luxury, embodiment of 286–8

McCartney, Stella 135
Maersk Data 119
Marineau, Philip 185–6, 203
market capitalism 2
Maslow's hierarchy of needs 208–9
massclusivity concept 127–9
Mayo Clinic 118–19
Merrill Lynch 73, 74, 86, 90–7, 106–
    7, 359
Microsoft 68, 70, 134, 187, 240, 241

military operations *see* US armed
    forces; warfare
Miller, Diane Disney 283–5, 290–1
Mondragon Corporacion Cooperative
    (MCC) 171, 228, 229–33,
    236
Motorola 133, 187

NATO mission, Kosovo 292–6
Nautor 87, 113–17, 120–1, 122–3,
    170, 191–6, 203–4
NEC 34
net satisfaction contribution
    (NSC) 17, 18
network-centric operations 63, 72–3,
    248–50, 253–4, 290, 312–13
networks
    the business idea and 356
    digital convergence 35–6, 45
    eBay and Mondragon
        compared 236
    open problem solving 56
    orchestration *see* orchestration
New England Patriots 263, 276–8
New York Police Department 147,
    148–9, 152
Nike 67, 68, 69, 192, 200–2
Nokia 74
    community nurturing 98–101, 208,
        223
    core solidification 174, 175–83, 184,
        188, 260
    information transmission 86, 98–
        107
    the iPod and 134, 136–7
    leaders as orchestrators 260, 270–5
    offering design 203
Normann, Richard 3, 355–9, 362–3

observe–orient–decide–act (OODA)
    loop 73, 248–9
offering concepts 170, 191–206, 261
    see also offerings, design
offerings
    the business idea and 356
    definition 10–11

design 66, 67, 68, 69, 70–1
    see also offering concepts
industry classifications 189
value creation 15–16, 20
    auction house example 20–4, 29
    digital convergence 43–7
    operational capabilities 25, 27–8,
        29
offshoring 39
    see also extended enterprises
Ollila, Jorma 86, 99, 176–7, 271
Olympic Games 1–2, 4, 250, 320
Omidyar, Pierre 142, 233, 234, 235,
    237
OODA loop 73, 248–50
open problems 55–6
open source communities 39–41, 42–
    3, 209
    Linux *see* Linux
operational architecture 289–97, 325–
    6, 332
    orchestration framework 333, 334
    wholesaler example 340
operational capabilities 24–30
    building *see* capability building
    dominant learning modes 260–2
    orchestrating leaders' role 71–3,
        261–2
    see also orchestrators
operationalization, IOCC
    framework 251–2, 255, 256,
    257
operations–strategy distinction 81–2
orchestration 59–80
    definition 65
    IOCC framework 171, 247–58
    leadership 70–80, 259–64
        experience provision 136–9
        information transmission 106–10
        insight accumulation 150–4
        problem solving 112, 121–3
        see also orchestrators
    pitfalls 360–1
    strategies for 65–71
        community nurturing 66, 67, 68,
            69–71

core solidification 66–7, 68, 70–1
offering design 66, 67, 68, 69, 70–1
resource aggregation 66, 67, 68–9, 70–1
see also capability building
supply chain example 175–80
orchestration agenda 332–3
orchestration architecture 324–30, 332–3
see also game plans; information architecture; operational architecture; social architecture
orchestration capabilities 29, 45–7
orchestration framework 333
orchestration mindset, introduction 335, 336–42
orchestration platforms 106–10
orchestrators 29, 259–64
as architects 76–7, 263, 281–97, 324–5, 333, 334
as auctioneers 77–8, 263, 299–313, 324–5, 333, 334
as conductors *see* conductors
overall character 263–4, 331–54, 362–3
as promoters 78–9, 263, 315–30, 333, 334
world of people 359–63
organizational learning 50–3
see also learning contexts
organizing–strategizing sequence 255, 257–8
outsourcing 39
see also extended enterprises

Palmisano, Sam 117, 118, 147
Paris, Louis Vuitton store 286–8, 289, 297
people, world of 359–63
people content, value creation 22, 23
persistence 360
pervasive computing 37, 43
Philips 173–5, 179, 270–1, 273
philosophical traditions 326–9

physical content, value creation 21, 23
Pixar 307
power
information architecture 311–12
orchestrating based on 273–8
orchestrator characteristics 347
orchestrator–member 244
prime movership 1–5
capability building 169–70
learning 31–57
orchestrating leadership 59–80
value creation 7–30
problem solving 51, 52, 73–5, 86–7, 111–23
building value constellations 245
operational capability 260, 261
transitional objects 161–3
see also architects, orchestrators as
product/market thinking 16–17
professional communities 39–41, 209–10
see also Linux; open source communities
promoters, orchestrators as 78–9, 263, 315–30, 333, 334
prototypes 199
purposeful emergence 1–2, 332

quality of life 13

Rajaniemi, Markku 104
regional competitiveness 176
regional problem solving 120–2
relationship content, value creation 22, 23
relationships, customer life-cycle 18–19
relative risk position 18
research communities 176
resource aggregation 66, 67, 68–9, 70–1, 210–11, 227–46
resource-based strategy 82–4
risk tolerance 327
Rochdale Equitable Pioneers Society 212–13
Rubinstein, Jon 132

safety, need for 208–9
Salonen, Esa-Pekka 75–6, 262–3, 269,
        278, 281–3, 290–1, 296
Samsung 179–83, 203
Sarin, Arun 182–3
Scaramuccia, Luciano 114, 120, 122
Schwab 90, 92, 93, 94
Sears 184–5
self-synchronization 249–50
service content, value creation 21–2,
        23–4
Shouldice Hospital (Ontario) 225
situated learning 49
situational awareness 344, 346–50
skill differentials 160–1
Skoll, Jeff 235, 237
social architecture 323–4, 325, 326–7,
        332, 361–3
    orchestration framework 333, 334
social constructivism 49–50
social risk 327
socialization, technology-
        supported 39, 40, 41–2,
        209–10, 218, 219, 235,
        237–8
Sony 133, 134
Sotheby's 263, 300
Sparkman & Stephens 193, 194,
        196
start-ups 361–2
statesmen, business leaders as 355,
        357–9
Steffens, John 91
Stenbit, John 72
Stephens, Rod 193, 194
strategic focus 332–3
strategies, creation 7–12
    see also value creation
strategizing–organizing sequence 255,
        257–8
strategy–operations distinction 81–3
subcontracting 39, 273–5
    see also extended enterprises
subordination 267–8
supply chain management 175–80,
        181–3, 270–5

survival, as a cardinal value 13
systems integration 63–4

Taj Mahal 228
technology
    information and communication see
        information and
        communication technology
    military 159–61, 253–4, 311–12
television watching 42–3
terrorism 253, 254, 255
terrorists 242
Thomson Financial 95–6
thriving 344–6, 360, 362–3
Torvalds, Linus 39
    building value constellations 244,
        245
    collaborative culture 331–2
    customer interactions 209
    learning in communities 40, 142–7
    orchestrator characteristics 344,
        345–6
    as promoter 78–9, 263, 315–17, 323
Tovey, Bramwell 262–3, 265, 266,
        268, 269, 278
Toyota 59–63, 169–70, 179–80, 247–8
    culture 328–9
    IOCC framework 255, 256
    leaders as orchestrators 261
transitional objects 155–68
    EMS company example 343
    prototypes as 199
    wholesaler example 341
transitional spaces 155, 156
trust 44–5, 238, 244–5, 331–2
tsunami catastrophe (2004) 2–3

urban planning 288–9
US armed forces 63, 72–3, 83,
        159–61, 242
    IOCC framework 250–4, 255,
        256

value constellations
    engaging people in 359–60
    learning mode 261

mobilizing 361
orchestration 45–6
orchestration platform 107
reinforcement (resource
    aggregation) 66, 67, 68–9,
    70–1, 210–11, 227–46
value creation 16–17, 25, 27–8,
    45–6
value creation 7–30
    definition 15–16
    digital convergence 43–7
    learning in communities 39–43,
       44–5
    Mondragon model 232–3
    orchestration as way to 29, 45–7,
       65
values 13–14, 45
    definition 10
    eBay community 233–4, 237, 238
    embodied 217–23
    industrial society 41
    knowledge society 41
    orchestrators' characteristics 351,
       352
Vancouver Symphony Orchestra
    262–3, 269
virtual communities 37, 39

open source *see* Linux; open source
    communities
    see also Amazon; eBay
virtual personalities 235, 236
Vodafone 182–4
Vygotsky, Lev 14

Wal-Mart 185–6, 239, 242–3
Walt Disney Concert Hall 283–5,
    290–2
warfare
    information architecture 311–12
    NATO mission in Kosovo 292–6
    network-centric 63, 72–3, 248–9,
       253–4, 312–13
    transitional objects and 159–61
wealth creation 13
Western traditions 326–9
Whitman, Meg 142, 211, 234
wholesaling firm 333–5, 336–42
work environments 245–6
world of people 359–63

Yahoo 74

Zander, Ed 133
Zetterberg, H. 13

Index compiled by Liz Granger

PURCHASED WITH
PERKINS FUNDS
2009

3 M

PURCHASED WITH
PERKINS FUNDS
2009

FLORIDA COMMUNITY COLLEGE AT JACKSONVILLE LIBRARY

3 3801 01232171 9